Britain's Wasting Acres
Land use in a changing society

BRITAIN'S WASTING ACRES

Land use in a changing society

Graham Moss

The Architectural Press, London

To François, Anna-Louise and children
everywhere who will inherit Britain's wasting
acres: our excuses will be meaningless and
our apologies will go unspoken

Frontispiece
Land is Britain's most precious and irreplaceable natural
resource. (Photograph: Aerofilms Ltd.)

First published in 1981 by The Architectural Press
Limited, London

© Graham Moss 1981

ISBN: 0 85139 078 1 ✓

Set in 10/11½ Plantin by Alacrity Phototypesetters,
Banwell Castle, Weston-super-Mare, and printed by
W. & J. Mackay Limited, Chatham, Kent

Contents

Preface

As the activities of society have changed over the centuries and population numbers have risen, the uses of Britain's land have become increasingly complex and wasteful. The nature of this wastefulness has become progressively evident since the last War in the multiple forms of underused, idle and dormant, derelict or despoiled land which are equally characteristic of town and country. These are the most common descriptions of wasteland, and they recur frequently in this book and in other publications dealing with land. It is perhaps helpful, therefore, to attempt a simple definition of each:

underused — land that does not realise its full capability, or is not put to its fullest or most appropriate use, including buffer land between incompatible uses that may be affected by or be at risk from industrial pollution, other forms of environmental damage or change, special access rights, planning or legal restrictions

idle and dormant — land that is undamaged and does not require much treatment to make it useable, including vacant land used either temporarily or occasionally

derelict — land damaged by industrial development, disused or decaying buildings in cities, towns and villages and incapable of beneficial use without treatment

despoiled — land so damaged by mineral workings and other major industrial, mineral or extractive activities, flooding and natural erosion, that it requires substantial reclamation treatment before it can be used.

There is an additional category that contains areas of underused, idle, dormant and derelict land which is referred to throughout the text:

operational — land traditionally held in active use by public and private industries and statutory authorities, but containing, more recently, areas of vacant or derelict land that may have become surplus to requirements over the years, or is being held available for future use or disposal by sale. Continued reference to such land as 'operational' is an obstacle to calculating the true extent of Britain's wasteland.

Although there is no shortage of official and unofficial information about land use, it is held in various degrees of detail and accuracy by a host of bodies using a variety of definitions of land use, type and condition. Rarely is this information comprehensive, comparable or coordinated. However, this existing information is sufficient to indicate a trend towards increasing areas of underused, idle, derelict and despoiled land that appears to have arisen from a combination of change, conflict, planning, ownership, economics and carelessness.

Statistics quoted in this book have been drawn from a number of official and unofficial sources that are all open, in some way, to criticism — but I have not come across a single set of land use statistics which has not carried disclaimers or been scorned by other statisticians. This is perhaps not surprising coming from a nation that still cannot agree over the exact area of its total land surface. This confusion and disagreement over facts and figures is a minefield into which I have chosen not to stray too far.

When I set out to write this book, I was sceptical of the value of national statistics collected and held within a clearly defined system, but my experience since then has convinced me of the need for an official national land use classification, based on a comprehensive set of definitions that are not open to interpretation, and an official national land use survey that is accurate, up-to-date and readily accessible for charting land use changes and providing an early warning system of likely problems and areas at risk. Unless and until we are in possession of this information officially, then land use statistics will remain a minefield and the extent and location of Britain's wasting acres will remain uncertain.

Despite the attempts of Government to encourage metrication, a high proportion of available land use statistics is presented in imperial units. The use of metric therefore would have been not only incompatible with the main title of the book, but would have been a further complication in the presentation and understanding of statistics. For these reasons I have chosen to retain the imperial form.

I would like to acknowledge the help and encouragement given by many people during the preparation of this book. In particular I owe a debt of inspiration to the much-loved ecological pioneer Sir Frank Fraser Darling, whose death coincided with the completion of the manuscript; environmentalists everywhere have lost a much-respected champion. My thanks to Marek Meyer for devoting summer evenings and weekends to collecting information on the impact of technology upon land; to Nick Connor for his agricultural contributions and proof-reading; to John Burrows for allowing me to quote from his work on derelict land in inner-city areas; to Timothy Cantell for his observations on urban wasteland; to Mike Boddington for stimulating discussions and exchange of correspondence on land use surveys and classifications; to Reay Clarke for allowing me to quote from his appealing Churchill Scholarship paper on the uplands; to Alice Coleman, Director of the Second Land Utilization Survey for allowing me to reproduce her land classification diagrams; to John Barrick, the Royal Town Planning Institute's patient and helpful librarian; and to Leslie Fairweather, the Editor of *The Architects' Journal*, without whose encouragement this book would not have been written. I am extremely grateful for the help given in my 1979 survey of local authorities by Robert Bird, the Under-Secretary of the Association of Metropolitan Authorities; by George Matthews, former Under-Secretary of the Association of County Councils; by James Ritchie of the Convention of Scottish Local Authorities; and by all those local authorities and other public and private organisations that spared time to respond to my questionaire and who spent valuable time in discussing the problems of wasteland.

Finally, I would like to thank my wife, Liliane, whose patience and encouragement through many lonely hours made this book possible, and to François and Anna-Louise, who reluctantly gave up for two years their family weekends and holidays — my apologies.

Graham Moss
Richmond, 1980

PART 1

CREATION AND DESTRUCTION

'And God said, Let the waters under the heaven be gathered together unto one place, and let the dry land appear; and it was so.

And God called the dry land Earth; and the gathering together of the waters called he Seas; and God saw that it was good.

And God said, Let the Earth bring forth grass, the herb yielding seed, and the fruit tree yielding fruit after his kind, whose seed is in itself, upon the Earth: and it was so.

And the Earth brought forth grass and herb yielding seed after his kind, and the tree yielding fruit, whose seed was in itself, after his kind: and God saw that it was good.'

Gen. 1: 9-12

(Photograph: Loch Carron, Scotland by Graham Moss)

CHAPTER 1

Introduction

Land is a living entity: it is the foundation of all life and it is finite. For these reasons its sanctity should be absolute — we should not waste a single acre. But we do. We have continued to act as though we inhabit a vast virgin continent instead of a small overcrowded island. Successive generations have used and discarded land in their continuing quests for survival. As populations have risen, so too has the destruction and waste of land. The accumulation of this waste has accelerated since the last war. Underused, vacant derelict buildings and land and despoiled industrial landscapes have spread across the face of Britain. Rarely has anyone taken responsibility for clearing away the debris of past survivals or preparing their own redundant land for future generations. Urban wasteland has grown apace, while extensive areas of farmland have been turned over to new development. Thousands of old buildings still with an active life left in their structures have been demolished to make way for often mediocre 20th-century environments, that have necessarily but often wastefully depleted our mineral stocks of building materials, energy supplies and other non-renewable natural resources, whilst laying waste further acres of food-producing land. Rarely have we taken our environmental responsibilities seriously and the array of redundant debris and misused land discarded by successive generations is ever-increasingly apparent.

This book estimates that by the end of the 1970s the effects of past survivals and contemporary technology and activities could have created as many as 1.3 million acres of idle, derelict and despoiled land throughout town and country, and 1.2 million acres of buffer land affected by or at risk from industrial pollution or hazards, environmental damage or affected in some way by special access rights, planning or other legal restrictions. These areas total 4.5 per cent of Britain's land surface that is lying either idle, underused, derelict or despoiled or potentially idle, underused, derelict or despoiled and is equivalent to twice the area of the county of Northumberland. Wasteland in our cities, towns and villages is increasing and by the end of the 1970s was estimated to be sufficient to house 5 million families and is more than the total area of land required to build Britain's 34 post-war new towns. In addition, during the same period, land was being taken from farming, in England, Wales and Scotland at a rate equivalent in area to the loss of the whole county of Gloucestershire every five years.[1]

Society is gradually accepting that this cavalier attitude towards land cannot continue. Land is Britain's most precious and irreplaceable natural resource, providing food from its soil, water from its springs and streams, shelter within its hills and valleys, building materials and energy from its wealth of minerals, and a

Dereliction created by past societies dates from the earliest standing stones. (Photograph: Architectural Press Ltd.)

3

Medieval ridge and furrow field patterns have left their imprint upon 20th-century landscapes often hindering the operation of modern agricultural machinery and farm efficiency. (Photograph: Aerofilms Ltd.)

scenery and landscape that is as varied and beautiful as anywhere in the world. Abounding in a richness of alternatives that surpass any other natural resource, it is the very prosperity of all society: at once city of noise and bustle or hamlet of solitude and peace; incisive and determined motorway or meandering and gentle country lane; mining village or market town; rubbish tip or working coal mine; field of corn ebbing and flowing in the wind or deserted wilderness of rocks and upland sheep; expansive forest or delicate birch grove. Over the centuries it has been adapted by successive generations to meet their changing needs. From forest clearing, Saxon village, enclosure landscape and industrial town, to sprawling suburb, declining city, new town and modern agricultural landscape: land charts the restless course of a changing and growing society.

The evolution of Britain's land and mineral wealth was largely complete about 6,000 years ago. As the climate grew warm and moist, the starkness of pine forests gave way to a mellow richness of broad-leaved trees. Oaks spread themselves lazily across the lowlands, birch groves huddled together in chattering clusters on thinner

4

Celtic lynchets, medieval hamlets and enclosure field patterns blend with contemporary housing, open grazing and arable farming. (Photograph: Aerofilms Ltd.)

As people have left the land, a surplus of buildings has added to the stock of dereliction in the countryside. (Photograph: Architectural Press Ltd.)

5

The legacy of a once flourishing industrial society. (Photograph: HMSO)

and poorer soils, and crack willows and alders pushed themselves up through the wetlands and marshy valley bottoms, drooping their foliage low over lakes and water courses. The wilderness was dressing itself in an array of plants and trees, flowers and foliage, shapes and colours that were to become Britain's rich and beautiful landscape of infinitely varying forms and textures: the chalk hills of the North and South Downs with their greenish-grazed slopes and intimate communities of small summer flowers; the pastures of the Midlands, neatly hedged throughout the centuries; the bare commons of the South, burnt and grazed, covered with gorse and bramble and surrounded by legions of oak, elm and beech and secretive woods, shy animals and plants. In contrast, the bare and strange dunelands of the coasts or the windswept and marshy plains of the fens, reclaimed over the centuries from the seas, were to become as rich in soil and food as they were in their dearth of hedgerows and their exposure to the vagaries of weather.

Early man was congregating on higher, more easily deforested and lighter land in coastal areas, and upon sandy heaths and lowland moors, where the sparse tree cover

was easily removed. Everywhere, a spring of life heralded the beginnings of civilisation. Upon the surface an increasingly rich and fertile soil sustained the growth of living matter: an abundance of wood provided shelter and warmth, whilst animals and plants provided food. Below the surface lay an undiscovered wealth of raw materials and energy supplies. As forests were cleared and man settled the land his inventiveness gradually tamed and dominated nature. When food supplies were exhausted he moved on to other locations, leaving the soil to regenerate under forest and the wreckages of his survivals to the healing of time. The conflicts between his activities above and below the surface of the land became progressively difficult to reconcile through the ages and land became progressively less able to sustain rising numbers of people, who by the 18th century were clustering into towns in the wake of newly introduced technologies. The industrial revolution had begun creating cities of grimy back-to-back houses and dimly lit factories. Tall chimneys belched smoke and fumes amid grey undulating roof tops; industrial waste poured into rivers and water courses. Roads and railways, factories and houses grew upon land where once forests, animals and crops had given life, food, shelter and work to an earlier less crowded and more sedentary society.

Man's close relationship with land and nature, which had flourished since his evolution, was being betrayed out of necessity to accommodate a rapidly expanding population and a progressive society. Every mine, every road, every building and every toxic pullutant has somewhere erased land's agricultural potential generated over centuries, while depleting the biological and mineral wealth, formed over millions of years. Wild life no longer attends the activities of man; those species not destroyed by the new technologies have fled to less disturbed landscapes.

The hand of man has everywhere become increasingly active and a mixed inheritance of natural beauty and man-made ugliness has produced the stark contrasts that characterise late 20th-century Britain. Celtic and Roman field patterns and vestiges of their crumbling buildings coexist with modern silage towers and tuberculine-tested cattle. Ridges and furrows left by Anglo-Saxon farmers interrupt the movement of modern farm machinery, while their compact hamlets, farmsteads and villages — the very roots of rural society — bring congestion to a more or less fluent network of motorways and roads carrying high-speed traffic. Traditional field enclosures of hedges, ditches and rubble walls, harbouring a rich variety of wildlife, have been removed to prepare the landscape for large agricultural machinery and modern farming techniques which produce more food from less land. Vast acres of rapidly decaying towns, with their back-to-back remnants and narrow streets, jostle side-by-side with new housing estates and tower blocks, windy shopping centres and elevated roads. Land lies increasingly derelict in the dockland areas of our cities, with the unemployed awaiting jobs and vacant buildings awaiting re-use, and yet massive industries and new towns have been introduced into the countryside, biting deeply into good agricultural land.

The need for land to provide shelter, industry, leisure, communications and other forms of urban use have in the past rarely been measured against increasing demands for food, timber and textiles, and the conservation of landscapes. Society has always used and discarded land in the process of life, but now it has to learn to re-use it. We cannot continue to live at the expense of posterity. This book traces the impact upon land of a relentlessly demanding society: the causes and effects of 20th-century social, economic and technological changes upon land; the increasing conflicts that these changes have brought; and the expedients used in managing these conflicts — whilst attempting to create an acceptable living environment.

The book is divided into three parts. Part 1 'Creation and Destruction' traces the demands of a creative and expanding society upon land and the emergence of land as a major commodity and investment. The wartime spirit of care and protection of land disappeared as waste and destruction was wrought by a prosperous post-war society that awakened in the 1970s to the ugliness and waste that had emerged. Part 2 'The Growing Crisis' looks at those main issues that have brought wastage of land and natural resources and have created extensive areas of redundant and derelict land. The effects upon land of mineral extraction, conflicting land uses, urban growth, inner-city decline and the technological imperative are all discussed in detail. Part 3 'A Time for Caring' is a celebration of the awareness and concern for the environment that is spreading through Britain. The environmental movement, the emergence of environmental education and the need for greater knowledge of land are all bringing a national ethic of responsibility towards land and its use. The book ends with an appeal for this ethic to be encouraged more widely by the introduction

(Photograph: Architectural Press Ltd.)

of an official national land use survey, formal environmental courses in all schools and greater publicity of environmental achievements by extractive industries, developers, local authorities, community groups and individuals. With the speed at which life is now changing, the closing decades of this century may be our last chance to correct past mistakes and prepare the landscape for future generations.

Notes

1. Statistics prepared by the Ministry of Agriculture, Fisheries and Food in England and and the Department of Agriculture in Scotland for the period 1970-5 indicated that almost 130,000 acres of farmland were being lost annually to other uses (see Table 12 on pp.144-5). The area of the county of Gloucestershire is 652,747 acres.

CHAPTER 2

Land under Siege

'I confess I am not charmed with the ideal of life held out by those who think that the normal state of human beings is that of struggling to get on; and the trampling, crushing, elbowing, and treading on each other's heels which forms the existing type of social life, are the most desirable lot of human kind . . . Nor is there much satisfaction in contemplating a world with nothing left to the spontaneous activity of nature . . . If the earth must lose that great portion of its pleasantness which it owes to things that the unlimited increase of wealth and population would extirpate from it, for the mere purpose of enabling it to support a larger population, I sincerely hope, for the sake of posterity, that they will be content to be stationary, long before necessity compels them to it.'

John Stuart Mill, 1857

The universal problem

As the world population has grown since the ascent of man, forests have been cleared, wilderness areas tamed, deserts cultivated, rivers redirected or obstructed, wetlands and marshes reclaimed and fertile lowlands built over. Amid these changing landscapes of the world has emerged a patchwork of scattered farmsteads and villages, towns and cities as man has made his continuing bid for survival. Since the last century, new technologies and exploding population figures have brought conflict with the ecological uses of land and a selfish mastery over nature. The very activities of man are also in conflict with each other, bringing the mis-use and abuse of land. Everywhere the hand of man is evident as he has used and discarded land through successive generations leaving behind a trail of wasting or derelict land-scapes and buildings.

The greatest challenge facing the world today lies in settling a rapidly expanding population of 4 thousand million people — increasing in size by almost the equivalent of North America every 3 years — upon the habitable areas of the earth,* while providing the basic essentials for survival. Where once the world took a thousand years to accumulate a thousand million people, today it takes barely 20 years. Indeed between 1970 and the end of the century the world population is expected to have doubled. Such a speed of growth appears to be too rapid to enable the basic needs of life to be provided to so many people in so short a space of time.[1]† Ian McHarg's optimistic and compelling book *Design with Nature*, about man's

---

* The world population was increasing during the 1970s by approximately 70 million people each year. The population of the United States of America (North America) was 200 million people.

† Notes appear at the end of each chapter.

(Photograph: Tom Smith)

11

possible relationship with land and nature, would have us believe for all the world, that we use those precious gifts of life, land and hidden minerals so sparingly that there will always be shelter, food and comfort in plenty for all:

'The world is a glorious bounty. There is more food than can be eaten, if we would limit our numbers to those who can be cherished . . . Canvas and pigments lie in wait, stone, wood and metal are ready for sculpture, random noise is latent for symphonies, sites are gravid for cities, institutions lie in the wings ready to solve our most intractable problems . . .'[2]

But of this we cannot be sure, even with this glorious bounty of land and natural resources from which to produce food, building materials and energy, it is already proving increasingly difficult to provide for our present numbers. In areas where the Industrial Revolution brought a massive growth in population and concentrations of people, governments and local administrations today are rarely able to cope. Similarly in more recently developing countries, equally rapid population growth and industrial development is defying planning and often bringing extreme human misery.

Two-thirds of the world's population is surviving on an inadequate diet and living in remote and poorly served rural areas; on the rubbish-strewn edges of existing urban communities; or upon derelict inner-city land. Everywhere, communities caught up in a rapid rural exodus are living rough in industrial slums, or are staking their claims to a peripheral lifestyle, for example, in the rooftop squatter settlements or the water shanties of Hong Kong. Elsewhere in South America, India, China and to a lesser degree in more developed countries like Greece and Turkey, urban immigrants are contributing to suburban sprawl, as they settle upon the often unplanned, poorly served and insanitary fringes of large conurbations. Their random shanty settlements become overcrowded; food supplies and essential services are frequently insufficient; inadequate existing water supplies and drainage are soon polluted; and existing roads and communications become congested and almost impassable. The remaining third of the world's population are the descendants of a more gradual urban development. Living in predominantly developed regions of the world and absorbing the greater proportion of food and easily habitable land, they consume eight times more energy per capita than the remaining two-thirds.

The official United Nations forecast suggests that by the end of the century 60 per cent of the world will be living in urban areas and for the first time urban inhabitants will out-number their counterparts in rural areas. As increasing numbers of people, currently living a dispersed rural existence, begin to demand greater concentrations, better living standards and economies of scale, the careful use of land and natural resources is becoming a prerequisite of continued survival. The late Dr. Schumacher[3] warned against the dangers of allowing endless concentrations of industry and people in ever-expanding urban conurbations and their effects upon remaining under-developed areas. He argued that continuous growth of populations and economic activity in the Western world would lead to concentrations that are too large, too inhuman and too complex to administer without the greatest difficulty.

Local administrations have, until now, been able to cope with changes wrought by the drift of people into towns. There is however, growing evidence that whilst administrations within countries like Denmark, Sweden, Britain and France have exerted increasing controls over the way in which people have settled and used land

The countryside is expected to provide more food, timber and recreational space from diminishing stocks of land. (Photograph: John Topham Picture Library)

(particularly during the last 30 years or so) there are large urban areas in America and Northern Europe which have become too large to maintain successfully. These areas, with their early industrial origins, have often been over-reliant upon a single traditional industry, which has changed rapidly or grown redundant. Technological advances have been revolutionising traditional industrial needs, and are allowing a greater dispersal of people and industry away from existing urban conurbations. The result, particularly marked in cities like New York, London, Paris and Glasgow is unemployment and depopulation. This trend is characterised by declining urban environments where vacant and derelict industrial landscapes, empty and decaying buildings and growing pockets of poverty and deprivation abound.

Increasing populations bring demands for energy and building materials. In turn these demands bring even more rapid depletion of valuable fossil fuel deposits and of other minerals developed naturally over millions of years and located, by an accident of evolution, throughout particular areas of the world. All too frequently, land and natural resources are being used to support the often false demands of an existing economic machine rather than the actual needs of people. As a result, resources everywhere are being squandered. A recent United Nations conference on human settlements gave some indication of the needless consumption of irreplaceable resources:

'It has been estimated that, on average, a citizen in the world's wealthiest country – the United States – carries 11 tons of steel around with him in cars and household equipment, and produces each

year 1 ton of waste of all sorts . . . Is it conceivable that the next century may begin with 7,000 million people commanding say, at least half the energy use, food and metal consumption and output of effluents reached today in the United States?'[4]

In 1920 the average household waste thrown away in the daily pursuit of living was 2.7 lb of solid waste per person. It is estimated that this figure will have reached 8.0 lb by 1980. If all the wastes from mines and factories were also included, then each member of the world's population would be responsible for discarding 50 lb of waste onto the land, into the atmosphere or into the waters each day. These household and industrial wastes originate in one way or another from the earth, or from the produce of soils covering land. Rather than recycling this waste or discarding it in such a way that it would be invisible, it is more often than not splattered across the surface in a series of pit heaps and rubbish dumps, or discharged as liquid and gaseous waste and other forms of pollution that defile water, land and air. In America, 12 million acres of land (equivalent to twice the area of Wales) have been permanently sterilised by surface damage, subsidence, waste heaps and obsolete industry. But America is not unique; although only one-third of humanity has entered the technological age, considerable evidence is emerging more generally of man's damaging and uneasy relationship with land and nature:

'Rivers have caught fire and burnt their bridges. Lakes and inland seas – the Baltic, the Mediterranean – are under threat from untreated wastes many of which can feed bacteria and algae; these in turn exhaust the water's oxygen and threaten other forms of marine life. The burning of fossil fuels is increasing, with unforeseeable consequences for the earth's climates and atmosphere. Dust and particles in the atmosphere may also alter the earth's temperature in unpredictable ways. Even the vast oceans covering 70 per cent of the globe and providing an apparently inexhaustible reserve of moisture, an endless dump for wastes and a perpetual source of freshening winds and currents, are far more vulnerable to man's polluting activities than had been assumed. Run off into them too many poisons, insecticides and fertilisers, void too many oil bilges, choke too many of the estuarine waters where the fish spawn and multiply and even the oceans may cease to serve man's purpose as effortlessly and reliably as he now seems to suppose.'[5]

Surviving on our small land
Amid this turbulent activity of survival, our own island bounty may be so used up and polluted as to jeopardise the survival of future generations. Although only a small part of the world's surface, Britain* covers 56 million acres upon which an almost equivalent number of people have to reap at the very least their shelter, food, recreation and happiness. Traditionally, more than 2 acres of land to each person was thought necessary to meet the daily rounds of survival. However, at an average density of 1 person to each acre of land surface, Britain's open space is diminishing; and at often well over 100 persons for each congested urban acre, our neighbour is rarely far distant. The great majority of us are obliged therefore to live in less than 'ideal' conditions, in harmony with one another and making the best use of each acre.

While our Domesday ancestors inherited a land that in Oliver Goldsmith's opinion 'gave what life required, and gave no more',[6] where fertile land and forest

---

* 'Britain' refers to England, Wales and Scotland and their islands covering 56,221 acres. 'UK' refers to England, Wales, Scotland and Northern Ireland covering 59,552 acres.

were plentiful, and where people came together more by choice than by design, today it is the reverse. Fertile land and forest are no longer plentiful and people come together more by design than choice. By comparison with the Middle Ages, when there were more than 50 acres to each inhabitant, 20th-century Britain may, with some justification, be described as over-populated. Spaciousness has gradually given way to closeness and an often unsatisfactory use of land. It is argued that while one family may live in a mansion set in a half a million acres of tended parkland or barren wilderness, another family shares one acre of land with 99 other families, possessing often less than a balcony and a shared play area as their open-air estate, and a graffiti-covered lift and a scruffy staircase as their stately entrance.

Crammed together in a mixture of inadequate early industrial conditions and frequently inhuman modern living environments, over four-fifths of us — 45 million people — are heaped together in towns and cities covering approximately 4.5 million acres of Britain's surface. It is argued that we are dependent upon the grace and goodwill of the remaining population and their 52 million acres to provide us with some of our food, little of our timber and increasingly more of our recreational and leisure space. And yet could we have it otherwise? If we were to continue to spread ourselves across the countryside in a wasteful spaciousness we could affect food production and harm the landscape and the very values of openness that we seek to conserve for our leisure moments. As yet we cannot even spill over onto the 20 million acres of sea-bed around Britain's coast, above which rapidly declining fish stocks have served as a centuries-old source of food, and below which an untold wealth is making Britain an oil-rich state, for the time being at least.

'Landed' society, traditionally the planners of our countryside, has so far kept Britain's most important food-producing land intact. Yet, if we believe John McEwan's life-long study of Scotland's landowners, then they have fared equally as badly as our city fathers:

'Firstly their inadequate husbandry in agriculture sticks out a mile, particularly in the huge area of their 10 million acres of rough grazings – it always has been and so still is. Secondly, in forestry with their 200/300 years practice I have not seen a single private estate with well managed woodlands: so very different from the excellent silviculture found all over Scotland in our state forests with only 50 odd years experience behind them. Thirdly, the sadistic obsession with game resulting in the almost complete degradation of millions of acres of our land.' [7]

There is perhaps more than a grain of truth in McEwan's words, for if the landowner is to manage our food stocks and landscapes, whilst the remainder of us are to be kept tightly penned-in in our 'urban stockades' and away from farmland, then he will be expected to improve his efficiency, raising significantly the present 50 per cent home-production of food and 8 per cent home-production of timber.

Life behind the 'stockades' for the past two centuries has not been an easy survival, as Dickens, Orwell and D. H. Lawrence have testified. Despite the march of science and industrial progress since the last war in particular, there were still over 75,000 homeless households in Britain in 1978 and nearly three-quarters of a million empty homes condemned as unfit for human habitation or in need of extensive repairs. [8] Despite all the rural yearnings of the urban masses, the contrasting survivals of 'town folk' and 'country folk' have been almost equally as difficult and wasteful of human energy and land. The real victims and victors of the debris of survival are the

TABLE 1 LAND USES IN THE UK AND EEC

Land uses	England 000s acres	%	Wales 000s acres	%	Scotland 000s acres	%	Britain 000s acres	%	Northern Ireland 000s acres	%	UK 000s acres	%	EEC %
Crops and fallow	9,936	31·0	264	5·2	1,470	7·7	11,670	20·8	196	5·9	11,866	19·9	–
Temporary grass	2,968	9·3	425	8·3	1,656	8·7	5,049	9·0	668	20·0	5,717	9·6	–
Permanent grass	8,006	25·0	1,915	37·5	1,112	5·8	11,033	19·6	1,199	36·0	12,232	20·5	–
Rough grazing	2,950	9·2	1,480	29·0	11,775	61·8	16,205	28·8	520	15·6	16,725	28·1	–
Other land	588	1·8	82	1·6	–	–	670	1·2	100	3·0	770	1·3	–
Total agriculture	24,448	76·3	4,166	81·7	16,013	84·0	44,627	79·4	2,683	80·5	47,310	79·4	64·2
Urban	3,526	11·0	254	5·0	680	3·6	4,460	7·9	98	2·9	4,558	7·7	6·8
Forestry & woodland	1,895	5·9	504	9·9	1,853	9·7	4,252	7·6	154	4·6	4,406	7·4	21·6
Miscellaneous	2,187	6·8	175	3·4	519	2·7	2,881	5·1	397	12·0	3,278	5·5	7·4
Total land*	32,056	100·0	5,100	100·0	19,065	100·0	56,220	100·0	3,332	100·0	59,552	100·0	100·0
Inland water	175		32		395		602		157		759		

* Not all figures add due to rounding.

Source: *Agriculture into the 80s: Land use*; Agriculture Economic Development Council, NEDO, 1977, page 5, Table 1. 'Britain' column added by the author.

children, so well documented by that poignant commentor on life, Colin Ward. Of the rural child, Ward wrote:

'Once let out of school, his real life begins – wandering by the river banks and up spinney and copse to the hilltops, observing nature with a learning eye, and absorbing the wisdom of shepherd and gamekeeper, forester and farrier, from the lovable old preacher with a heart of gold, and from the scarey old hermit whose tumble-down cottage is really a treasure trove of country lore and bygones.'

And of the town child he wrote:

'Our hero is rather lower in the social scale. Once released from his stern mentors in the boardroom, he is out and down the street like a shot, everybody's friend in the market place, besieging the old lady in the sweet shop on the corner, begging orange boxes from the greengrocer, lifting coal from the railway yard, as a rough-and-ready apprenticeship to the life of the city.'[9]

Survival on the land has been a lesson well-learned in the past, but increasingly forgotten by the present. It is now becoming more difficult for generations of young to learn the natural arts of survival as Britain has become progressively reliant upon artifact and technology. Historically, and particularly since early industrial days, our rural child has grown up embarrassed by his existence and often scorned by the town child for his simpler and less sophisticated lifestyle. The rural child has frequently carried his embarrassment through into adulthood, expressing an apologetic shyness about working the land and consorting with nature. Today, however, the rural child is becoming the envy of increasing numbers of urban emigrés as they too seek what they refer to as the sanctuary of rural life, self-sufficiency and an escape from the urban 'rat race'.

Farming is becoming a respectable occupation in the eyes of townsfolk. As a result of these changing priorities during the late 1970s, agricultural land sustained a value that, for the first time, was regarded by investors as an economic alternative to urban development. As even more citizens besieged the countryside towards the end of the 1970s in search of 'the good life', gaping holes were widening in the fabric of towns and cities. Society was encouraged to strengthen the urban 'barricades', to hold in those who might wish to be free and to protect rural land from further urban encroachment. Our relationship with land has never before been so tenuous. How can we live up to the ideal that every human being should have a roof over his head and a full stomach, when in Britain homelessness continues to rise and imported food becomes increasingly scarce and expensive? There does indeed seem to be a curious mismatch between our human ideals and our use of land.

Concern today focuses upon what, up to now, has been a consistent and endless pattern of urban growth. Population mobility and two-way movement between town and country have never been so high; and fluctuating birth rates and increased longevity makes any kind of land-use forecasting extremely difficult beyond a five year period. Historically the use of land has been constantly changing. Since the early industrial days, when 90 per cent of Britain's population lived and sought their trade in the countryside, times have changed:

'Old patterns of country life are breaking up. Urban values are spreading influence throughout rural areas and exert powerful economic and social pressures on the traditional forms of community

Improved transport and communications have enabled urban development to spread out. (London Transport Poster Collection; photograph by Graham Moss)

life in the countryside. Expansion of the nation's population, increased mobility of the individual, demands of urban development on rural space, technological changes in industry and new methods of agriculture all contribute to the rural transformation, which is now proceeding at accelerating pace in many parts of the country. Urban attitudes towards the countryside are changing. The great majority of people live in towns: much of their food is delivered in a processed form which disguises its origin in the land. The countryside is recognised by the townsman as a source of his physical nourishment more by intellectual effort than instinct, while his demands on the land as a way of escape from urban congestion grow apace. The general situation is one of great complexity and conflict of needs, in which the requirements of those who live and work in the country can be easily lost.'[10]

Over 85 per cent of Britain's population is urban, living within cities, towns and villages or upon their fringes. The remaining 15 per cent live in the countryside. Within a working population of 26 million people, less than three-quarters of a million (2.7 per cent) gain their livelihood from toiling the land directly. In all, about $2\frac{1}{2}$ million people are directly or indirectly involved with agriculture or forestry. Just as in towns there is an intensity of roads and buildings, people and activities, so in the countryside a second agrarian revolution is bringing a progressively intensive and efficient use of agricultural land, whilst accommodating growing numbers of commuters, second home owners, tourists and those in search of recreation.

The consequences of endless growth

By comparison with our mobile society today, patterns of land use during the early stages of the Industrial Revolution were dictated by the limited mobility between home and work and between manufacturer and market. Foot and horse transport brought concentrations of people and industry in frequently unhealthy and inhuman conditions. The use of land during this period was at its most economic and sparing. However, with the emergence of the railway, motor car and telecommuncations, society was able to spread out. Concentration gave way to dispersal and spaciousness. The inter-war period and the 1930s in particular brought a confused sprawl of people and activity around the edges of existing towns and cities at a faster rate than ever witnessed before or experienced since. Urban land uses grew increasingly wasteful, and by the outbreak of the Second World War, land-use controls had become long overdue. By the very intervention of post-war planning legislation that followed, land attained a scarcity value that inflated its price rapidly as controls bit harder and as planning permissions themselves assumed a value, which was reflected in the value of the land. Within the planning framework, society had to survive with land-uses allocated according to forecast demand. The land market became a specialised business — the most successful members being those who achieved an improvement in the officially accepted use of land under the new planning legislation.

In conjunction with planning controls came minimum standards. Housing and industry, roads, communications, open space, in fact almost every activity had to comply with prescribed standards based upon health and safety. As a result, spaciousness increased further bringing an even more extensive use of land:

'Whatever the period adopted, the rate of increase in the urban area has been more than double the growth of population . . . attributed to a general increase in the space standards enjoyed by the population as a whole.'[11]

19

During the 20th century urban development has become increasingly spacious and demanding in its use of land largely as a result of health, safety, building, highways and open space standards. Lydney, Gloucestershire. (Photograph: Aerofilms Ltd.)

By the end of the 1970s it was being suggested that the introduction of planning had merely deferred demand for the development of land, which would work itself out with extremely wasteful consequences over a longer time-scale, than the more rapid rate at which development had proceeded during the inter-war period. In 1901 for example urban development was taking 50 acres for every 1,000 people; by 1931 this had increased to 65 acres; by 1951 to 75 acres; and by 1971 85 acres were being taken for every 1,000 people. By the end of the 1970s, forecasts indicated that demand would average out by the end of the century to about 100 acres for every 1,000 people. The question posed at that time was whether planning and land use standards that demanded such a high level of land use (nearly double the amount of land required at the beginning of the century) was wasteful, and if so, whether development control standards should be reviewed.

In 1973 the *Architectural Review* forced a public debate on what it termed 'Space Left Over After Planning' (SLOAP), in which a searching study criticised the needlessly spacious roads and highways standards, and the often wasteful lay-outs of housing estates and open space. This criticism was applied particularly to the public sector whose standards, it was suggested, were rarely dictated by economy of land use or return on investment. The private sector, by contrast, was trying to force every inch of use from every acre, but it too was being forced into what was referred to in the *Architectural Review* as the 'straight-jacket' of waste:

'England's overcrowding problem is twice India's, four times China's, sixteen times the USA's and thirty-two times the USSR's. All the odder that we still squander land, burying an inexpandable acreage beneath a rash of low-density housing estates and prairie plans.'[12]

The *Architectural Review* also drew attention to the curious contrasts between land wastage at the urban fringes on the one hand and the prediliction for high rise, high density developments on the other. Again the situation was revealing a generally unsatisfactory management of people and land, and an inconsistent approach to land use from area to area throughout Britain.

Land as a commodity

Since the Industrial Revolution land has become an increasingly valuable commodity to be bought and sold like any other expendable consumer product. Today it is big business and a sound investment by any standards, producing increasingly high profits as its value rises from wilderness and agricultural uses towards urban fringe and city centre uses. Rising land values and endless trading are, more than any other factors, responsible for the growing crisis between development and conservation; between the production of food and the seemingly endless need for human settlements; between modern farming and the protection of the landscape; and between sparing use and waste. As industrial society has grown, demand for land has multiplied. Housing and industry, roads and railways, farmland and forestry, reservoirs and canals and open space for leisure purposes have all, at one time or another, staked their claim to land. Progress and new technology have brought changing needs and demands for land. Ship building and coal mining, railway networks and seaport industries, have left behind redundant and unwanted acres as the nature of their business has changed. The energy industries, airports and motorways have all assumed increasing importance. As society has built up its portfolio of land uses, the siege of land as a valuable investment has grown also. The 20th century has seen a relentless demand for land to be used for a multitude of purposes to meet the continually rising expectations of society.

The 'doom' forecast assembled by the Club of Rome and presented as *A Blueprint for Survival* in 1972 was either greeted with disbelief or was ignored altogether. After all, who in their right mind would pay attention to warnings about the future use of land and the limits of natural resources, when in those days life was so sweet and profligate:

'The principal defect of the industrial way of life with its ethos of expansion is that it is not sustainable. Its termination within the lifetime of someone born today is inevitable – unless it continues to be sustained for a while longer by an entrenched minority at the cost of imposing great suffering on the rest of mankind. We can be certain, however, that sooner or later it will end (only the precise time and circumstances are in doubt) and that it will do so in one of two ways: either against our will, in a succession of famines, epidemics, social crises and wars; or because we want it

21

to – because we wish to create a society which will not impose hardship and cruelty upon our children – in a succession of thoughtful, humane and measured changes.'[13]

Land is finite and virtually fixed in supply, gaining only minimumly by reclamation of wetland and sea-bed, or equally losing minimal areas to flooding or erosion. The diversity of location and accessibility, ownership, value and potential use mean that rarely are two pieces of land inter-changeable; each possesses a special character. Competition over well-located and good quality land has been most noticeable in fertile valley areas, which are frequently equally appropriate to both urban development and agriculture. But like any trading commodity that holds the potential of large profits, land is also extremely vulnerable to economic change. Agricultural land values respond to the vagaries of productivity, demand and to a certain extent, trading fashion. Development land investments are even more fragile and, like a barometer, reflect even the smallest changes in the national economy.

Land has always been the basis of a society that has measured its wealth by its land holding. The greatest reward a king could give his favourites was land; the greatest rebuff a man could suffer was to be deprived of land, and worse still his homeland. The greatest power that man has attained has lain in his land holdings; the greatest social division in society has been that between the 'landed' and the 'landless'. The greatest wealth and influence has been wielded by owners of land; the greatest poverty and anonymity has remained among those without land. The easiest way to secure an investment has been through the purchase of land and buildings; the

The demolition of unsuccessful modern buildings means that further needless demands are being made for replacement minerals and building materials – an unnecessary use of materials which involves even further encroachment of mineral extraction upon farmland. (Photograph: Mercury Press Agency)

22

quickest way to bankruptcy has been through a sharp decline in the value of land holdings. Little has changed over the centuries. Those medieval farmers who tended their strips of land well improved their value and reaped due reward; those who left their strips fallow and unkempt reaped minimal value. So it is today. The value of land depends not only upon its location, quality and potential use, but also upon its improved status, to which present planning legislation has often encouraged artificially high valuations by imposing a scarcity brought about by development controls.

The age of profligacy

In 1963, Harold Macmillan, then Conservative Prime Minister, secured his voting public by informing the nation that 'we have never had it so good'. Seemingly to prove the accuracy of his words, Britain set upon a course of massive investment in land and natural resources, as if life depended upon their very depletion. Land values rose as prime building land grew scarce. Building and energy costs soared as mineral extraction could not keep pace with the demand for daily luxuries. Landowners and manufacturers could not believe their fortunes as scarcity brought untold profits — profits that in so many cases were squandered just like the natural resources themselves. Wisdom and caution were thrown to the winds as minerals were torn out of the land without remorse, as vast areas of existing buildings and their residents were replaced by motorways and tower blocks, new city centres and anything that enabled greater profits to be squeezed from a single piece of land. Few could not fail to be impressed and fewer still could avoid involvement in such a period of euphoria.

Despite a minor economic coronary attack towards the end of the 1960s, the blood of industry and finance continued pumping. It was not long before the nation was involved, once again, in another inflationary spiral, only this time of such magnitude that at the beginning of the 1970s land was being bought and sold at inconceivable prices. Investment had never before been so carefree and wanton. Worthless, exhausted mineral extraction land in the metropolitan green belt, for example, was changing hands for as much as forty times its market value; poor-quality agricultural land divided into 'desirable potential housing plots' with little or no chance of gaining planning permission, was being bought at more than 20 times its market value; residential land in the middle of towns and cities was selling for as much as a 100 times the value of good quality farmland. Between the beginning of the 1960s and the middle of the 1970s an acre of urban land had increased in value by an average of 600 per cent. Financial errors were for the time being masked by the ease with which massive profits were made from the sale of land and buildings. As the market became flooded with more consumer products of every shape, size and form, wastage of natural resources had never been higher. This flood of commodities brought in turn an assumed greater demand and pressure upon land and natural resources.

However, like all patients who fail to heed early warnings and specialist advice, Britain suffered almost overnight from an economic relapse, as euphoria gave way to disbelief and as the first energy crisis of 1973 precipitated by the Oil Producing and Exporting Countries (OPEC) of the Middle East, brought Britain to heel instantly. The economy collapsed and land values plummeted. Almost totally reliant upon oil for mobility, commerce and every comfort, Britain had to accept soaring prices that

Where demand for buildings and land is high maintenance is a priority. (Photograph: Shelter)

reflected the OPEC stranglehold. Money became scarce and by the middle of the 1970s the commodity market, including land, buildings and natural resources, had fallen disastrously. Land bought for those astronomical prices at the beginning of the decade was virtually unsaleable by 1974. Many developments already underway were halted, bankruptcy became the order of the day and by 1976, surviving developers were writing off their land and building losses in the hope that, as the economy revived, they could begin again. But in 1979, as their dream was about to come true, a second oil crisis loomed large as the Middle Eastern countries threatened to cripple the mobility of the West again, by raising the prices of oil and energy beyond the reach of most European nations. Although North Sea oil had become, almost overnight, the nation's most valuable resource, Britain fell into the grips of a world recession.

The Conservative Government was returned to power in 1979. Many feared that this would be a recipe for disaster: house prices rocketed by 40 per cent in the first six months of the new Government's life; land values soared to pre-1973 levels and the development market began to regain momentum. However, this activity was short-lived. The British Government was facing a more serious crisis emerging from a stagnating economy; industrial decline; a backlog of run-down and derelict buildings and land; diminishing stocks of farmland and a technological stranglehold that had 20th-century society by the throat.

The crisis looms

Since 1945 people have moved out of urban areas increasingly rapidly, resettling themselves on land elsewhere. Between 1970 and 1975 half a million people moved out of London alone. With the continuing exodus of people on this scale from other cities and declining areas the urban fringe and countryside are facing severe pressures for continued development. Two-thirds of the countryside increased in population by as much as 30 per cent between 1970 and 1980. Rural communities in these areas have grown; villages have become towns, and the village characteristics have often been distorted by large housing estates and congested lanes. On the other hand, less accessible or more remote rural areas have been losing population. For example, the Grampian mountains, the Buchan Peninsular, Angus in Scotland and similar areas in mid and south Wales, and north and south-west England have lost more than one-fifth of their residents in less than a decade. As residents leave these areas, Government investment and transport is withdrawn, and communities decline as schools close and essential services are sacrificed under the most extensive public expenditure cuts to be experienced since the birth of the welfare state in 1947. People moving out of the metropolitan areas and in from the remote rural areas are meeting on land where facilities are still available and where housing, education and employment opportunities offer a more secure lifestyle and improved living conditions. These common areas lie on the edges of cities and large towns. Land uses are also following this two-way movement of people, either in a series of leaps from inner-city to the suburbs, across the green belt and into provincial towns and villages; or by a drift into the suburbs and provincial towns and villages from outlying rural areas. It is these growing areas throughout Britain that are suffering the heaviest pressure for development of land.

Progress has brought increasing reliance upon machines and irreplaceable resources as modern society has delved ever more deeply into its 'glorious bounty' of land, minerals and energy to supply its needs. Buildings and roads, cars and trains, television and films, clothes and carpets, newspapers and food are among the endless daily demands of modern society. Each relies upon natural resources that lie on or below the surface of the land. Farming for example, once at the mercy of the weather and the health of the labour force, is now also at the mercy of oil and science for the production of artificial fertilisers and foodstuffs and an array of automated machinery. Degenerating soil and changing landscapes are two of the many side-effects of an agricultural technology that is squeezing a quart of food from a pint of land. The advent of 'microchip' technology appears to offer slender hope for the future of Britain's declining inner-cities as simple and cheap audio-visual and computer systems point to possibilities of an ever greater dispersal of industry and people into the countryside. Meanwhile a scarcity of energy is slowly limiting personal mobility and is beginning to demand closer relationships between home, work and leisure. Within this 20th-century technological fix, how will we provide more food for an increasing population, from diminishing stocks of farmland? How will we safeguard, at the same time, irreplaceable natural resources; plan for the failure or exhaustion of energy supplies; or simply clear up the debris of successive generations? Urban wasteland, despoiled mineral land, diminishing farmland, the destruction of natural habitats, urban sprawl and the demands upon our landscapes of modern technology are all related, but rarely interchangeable parts of the same

In less popular locations where demand is low there is little incentive to maintain buildings and land. (Photograph: Shelter)

complex chain; beginning with the changing needs of society and ending with an increasingly wasteful use of land. It is often argued that the building of new towns and villages on the scale of Milton Keynes or New Ash Green has been done without sufficient consideration being given to the loss of farmland, or to the future of those existing towns and villages whose extensive pockets of derelict land and deprived populations could have benefited from some of the investment put into these greenfield developments.

What happens to land within either town or countryside has been of little concern to the other. Where the two meet — particularly on the edges of cities and towns, land use tends to be unsatisfactory. 'Green belt' policies have not always checked urban sprawl leaving in its wake a trail of declining inner-city land, and farmland fragmented by isolated housing estates and industrial development, motorway intersections and bypasses. Together with exhausted mineral workings, refuse tips and scrap-yards, they damage and scar the landscape. The building of new and better road networks and public utilities like sewers and water supplies, encourages more creeping development and a continued erosion of farmland, which when developed, affects adjacent farmland leading in turn to further erosion, development and so on.

After more than 30 years of planning, knowledge about Britain's land is still shamefully inadequate. Facts and figures are poor and the information that we have today has been collected in various ways by a host of organisations using different criteria and different definitions of land use that cannot be readily assembled in any comprehensive or comparative way. However, the limited and extremely diverse information currently held points consistently towards a growing crisis, the extent of which we cannot calculate. Land-use information needs to be improved. There is a vast potential for steady and consistent investment and development in Britain's towns, cities and villages, if only comprehensive information were available and private investors and industrialists were guided more positively. Society will always use and discard land in the process of life. Society has now to learn to re-use land. The siege must stop. We should perhaps rekindle the spirit that overtook the nation during the last War. A spirit of an age that promised to clear away not only the wreckages of war, but the cumulative debris of past generations. Since the War a period of uninterrupted peace and creeping complacency has dulled our sensitivity towards land. Are we to await another war before allowing the spirit to return?

Notes

1. Graham Moss, 'A discussion paper on issues related to policies and administrative procedures dealing with distribution of population and allocation of resources', OECD (Paris), 1979
2. Ian McHarg, *Design with Nature*, Doubleday, 1971
3. E. F. Schumacher, *Small is Beautiful: a study of economics as if people mattered*, Sphere, 1973
4. B. Ward and R. Dubos, *Only One Earth*, Pelican, 1972, p.42
5. *ibid.* pp.46-7
6. Oliver Goldsmith, *The Deserted Village*, 1770
7. John McEwan, *Who Owns Scotland?*, 1976
8. Shelter, *Facts and Figures* (booklet), 1978
9. Colin Ward, 'The Opaque City', *New Society*, 10 August 1978
10. 'Living and Working in the Countryside', Countryside in 1970, Second Conference, 1965
11. Countryside Review Committee, 'Food Production in the Countryside', Topic Paper No. 3, Department of the Environment, 1978
12. 'SLOAP', *Architectural Review*, October 1973, p.205
13. Editors of *The Ecologist*, *A Blueprint for Survival*, Penguin, 1972, p.15

CHAPTER 3

Spirit of an Age

'Provision for the right use of land, in accordance with a considered policy is an essential requirement of the Government's programme of post-war reconstruction. New homes, whether of permanent or emergency construction; the new layout of areas devastated by enemy action or blighted by reason of age or bad living conditions; new schools which will be required under the Education Bill now before Parliament; the balanced distribution of industry which the Government's recently published proposals for maintaining actual employment envisaged; the requirements of sound nutrition and of healthy and well balanced agriculture; the preservation of land for national parks, and forests, and the assurance to the people of enjoyment of the sea and the countryside in times of leisure; a new and safer highway, better adapted to modern industrial and other needs; the proper provision of airfields, all of these related to parts of a single reconstruction programme involve the use of land and it is essential that their various claims on land should be so harmonised as to ensure for the people of this country the greatest possible measure of individual well-being and national prosperity.'

The Control of Land-Use, *White Paper, 1944*

Picking up the pieces

Out of the hideous deception of the 1938 Munich Agreement and the ashes of war rose a new determination — a will to be rid of wasteful and uncaring use of land. Above all a will to end urban squalor, to contain suburban sprawl and to clear away weedy agricultural wastes that had emerged during the inter-war depression and which were too infertile upon which to produce food rapidly under crisis conditions. Britain's war-ravaged land was left more vulnerable than ever to misuse; Britain's cities were more over-crowded and damaged than ever; and Britain's people more hungry and reliant upon each other and upon the food of friendly nations, than perhaps at any period of recent history. Although during the war years farming took up the challenge by raising food output from 35 per cent to 55 per cent, this effort was still insufficient. Times were extremely hard. Food rationing arrived as the nation fought for survival. The war years were used to review the whole social and economic structure of Britain and in particular, the condition and state of existing industrial cities and productive rural land. Between 1939 and 1943 Britain became one of the most highly mechanised farming countries in the world and the home-production of many commodities was doubled. Sir Dudley Stamp, Director of the First Land Utilisation Survey of Great Britain, reflected:

'Imports of animal feeding stuffs dropped to about $\frac{1}{10}$th of the pre-war figure, and, broadly, each farm became a self-contained unit, producing what it needed for the support of its own livestock.

(Photograph: Popperfoto)

Every window box, backyard and garden produced food during the war years. (Photograph: Popperfoto)

There was concentration on milk, and the maintenance of priority milk supplies for mothers and children, had much to do with the excellent health record during the war. Beef, cattle, sheep and pigs were reduced in numbers: much unsuitable land was pressed into service, at least temporarily, for cereal production... A rather unkempt and neglected countryside gave place to a neat and trim one, consciously proud of the job it was doing and wearing an air of efficiency. Largely with the use of prisoner-of-war labour a huge backlog of hedging, ditching, and draining was wiped off. Hedges were properly trimmed and laid, often for the first time in years, ditches were cleaned out, reedy

30

pastures drained. Ploughed fields appeared where for years there had only been grass ... The horse gave place to the tractor, the hay wagon to the motor truck. There was much use of common land – some ploughed and cropped for the first recorded time in history – and improvement of hill lands was pushed back to long forgotten upper limits.[1]

As towns and cities put up what defences they could against the strafing German planes and tumbling bombs, every acre of countryside it seemed was put to work. The 'dig for victory' campaign transformed back gardens into piggeries and chicken runs; vegetables sprouted in the most unexpected corners; tomato plants lined windowsills and for the time being at least, a new spirit was overtaking Britain. Reflecting upon the unprepared state of Britain's land before the war, the Government vowed that never again would such a situation be allowed to return. Never again would land be allowed to fall into such disarray. Everywhere, across the face of post-war Britain, opportunities for a renaissance in man's relationship with land were evident. This new spirit was to be enshrined in immediate post-war planning and agricultural policies that were as much an attack on *laissez-faire* and the haphazard use of land that had gone before, as they were upon society's disregard of land as a finite natural food-producing resource.

In towns and cities, urban communities living amid the rubble of war and depression and united by family and kinship ties that had withstood the worst of the Industrial Revolution, were finally and irrevocably split up and resettled in new homes, on new land and among new neighbours. Houses that once rang to the sound of laughter and the songs of Vera Lynn were deserted — broken windows and fallen slates were a testimony to their decline. Streets that had echoed to the sounds of hopscotch, open-air parties and the voice of Churchill were quietened. Patches of cobblestone were torn up and thrown away in accompaniment to the frustrations of the parting epoch. Back gardens once resounding to the chattering fence talk of excited neighbours or the flapping in the wind of smoke-filled washing, lay silent and unkempt — an open temptation to the claims of wilderness. The deserting populations found themselves in new buildings and healthy living environments, with all 20th-century comforts at hand. They left behind them row upon row of draughty outdoor washrooms, and shared toilets, ever-open front doors, and gaggles of entrenched doorstep gossips that had reported upon community life since the beginning of the Industrial Revolution. Countless areas such as these throughout Britain's cities were laid waste. They had become anachronisms as suddenly as the falling bomb had destroyed neighbouring streets, tearing apart the cohesion of generations. Urban renewal had begun in earnest and was destined to leave behind bitterness, hardship and loneliness, as people were transferred into often completely strange environments. Reaction to such community upheaval was very personal. The new life was not always welcomed — leaving the old was often heartbreaking:

'You asking me what I think of Bethnal Green is like asking a countryman what he thinks of the country. You understand what I mean? Well, I've always lived here, I'm contented. I suppose when you've always lived here, you like it.'[2]

Young and Wilmott's now classic story of the break-up of life in East London as a result of a mixture of wartime damage and urban renewal is as poignant today as when it was first produced in 1957. As we shall see, the 'brave new world' that

31

emerged from the post-war spirit did not always live up to expectations. The reluctance of residents of Bethnal Green to leave was born not of reluctance to live in a new 20th-century environment, but of a desire to retain the feeling of community and close kinship ties that had emerged during an era when transport and mobility were severely limited and when generations of family lived altogether in the cramped but happy conditions of a single house:

'I was bred and born in Bethnal Green and my parents and their parents before them: no I wouldn't leave Bethnal Green, I wouldn't take a threepenny bus ride outside Bethnal Green.'[3]

And yet many city families had no choice. Bomb damage had taken away choice and left in its wake either a greater determination for survival or total dejection and hopelessness. Britain's land and buildings, which would otherwise have fallen prey to industrial change, obsolescence or simply old age, were being consciously and systematically destroyed by Hitler's bombs. The public were becoming used to living in a sea of waste, paddling their feet in the rubble of destruction. Their shelter became increasingly a gaping hole in a once unified street, or the fond memory of a row of houses that in an instant had been wiped away.

Elsewhere, decaying areas that had eluded the vengeance of war found their poor state emphasised by surrounding disruption. Squalid housing condtions, so much the clarion call of the thirties, were a part, if only a temporarily forgotten part, of the scene of destruction that greeted the heroes of war as they stepped ashore. Many cities and industrial towns whose buildings had dated from before the middle of the 19th century were:

'... already ripe for reconstruction before the war; obsolescence was bad and housing unsuitable, inchoate communities, uncorrelated road systems, industrial congestion, the low level of urban design, inequality in the distribution of open spaces, increasing congestion and dismal journeys to work – all of these and more clamoured for improvement before the enemies' efforts to smash us by air attack, stiffened our resistance and intensified our zeal for reconstruction.'[4]

Cynics argued at the time that the work of Hitler was advancing the 1930s slum clearance programme by many years. An estimated 500,000 buildings were destroyed in the six years of war. The annual slum clearance rate during the 1930s had been 90,000 buildings. Over a million acres of war-damaged land lay vacant — the spoils of destruction awaiting removal or re-use. Half of the remaining $13\frac{1}{2}$ million houses in 1945 had been built before the turn of the century, while one fifth had been constructed more than a century earlier. In addition, not only was a permanent population of more than one million residents still living in the worst of industrial squalor (their homes were described officially as 'unfit for human habitation') but by 1940, 750,000 war victims were living in temporary pre-fabs covering 16,000 acres of urban land. Many of the pre-fabs are still standing today — more than 40 years later.

War damage, ageing buildings, overcrowding in cities, uncontrolled growth of suburbs, obsolete and declining industry and inadequate services all compounded the immediate post-war problem of waste. However, almost overnight, and largely due to the tireless efforts of Sir Dudley Stamp, a planning system was introduced that won world acclaim and demonstrated how rapidly and effectively governments can act if given initiative and urgency of purpose:

'Land planning has been forced on Britain not by reason of pressure from any particular political group or groups, but by the sheer necessity of using to the best advantage the extremely restricted resources of land.' [5]

An end to uncontrolled development and overcrowding

The 1947 Town and Country Planning Act, conceived during the war years, brought about a remarkable change in private ownership rights. For the first time, land owners were unable to develop their land without public consent and were even in danger of losing it altogether, if they either ignored the laws or stood in the way of beneficial use, or what was to be known as 'comprehensive redevelopment'. Where once land could be developed freely and haphazardly, these new laws required permission to be given by the local authority before land could be changed from one use to another. To ensure a smooth transition from a land market without restrictions to a controlled land market, a central land fund distributed £380 million to landowners who successfully claimed a loss of development value resulting from the planning restrictions. In determining appropriate use, the 1952 Town Development Act required all land uses to conform to 'Town Development Plans', which were to be drawn up by local authorities as guides to the use of land within their boundaries. Rigid 'land zoning' was born and was to bring increasingly hard-faced controls over development, and a planning system that was to become so inflexible as to be unable to respond quickly enough to changing commercial and individual demands, economic trends and community needs.

However far-reaching, these planning restrictions were not guaranteed to contain the urban sprawl which had eroded so much land around the edges of large towns and cities, particularly during the 1930s. The Government accepted that further control over sprawl would be necessary. The idea of placing a 'green girdle' around cities, to hold back further outward growth of built-up areas, was first suggested by Lord Meath in 1901. But it lay dormant until 1955 when the then Ministry of Housing and Local Government drew attention to the 'importance of checking unrestricted sprawl of built-up areas and of safe-guarding the surrounding countryside against further encroachment'. [6]

As a result 'green belts' several miles wide were thrown around existing suburbs, within which land uses were to be limited to agriculture, education, recreation and open space, and to what the Minister described as 'other appropriate rural uses'. Green belts quickly ringed all the main industrial cities such as London, Glasgow, Manchester and Liverpool, and large expanding towns. Until the introduction of the 1947 Town and Country Planning Act, the edges of existing towns and cities throughout the country had spawned great housing estates and dormitory suburbs. It was common practice for speculative builders to buy a farm, erect a few houses for sale, whilst allowing the remainder of the farmland to fall into disuse and to be divided into further building plots awaiting development:

'All this unplanned sprawl produced a crop of new problems – the provision of such essential services as electricity, gas, piped water and main drainage, as well as public transport to minimise the journey to work or access to shopping and recreational centres – and the growth of town planning became inevitable.' [7]

Such was the pressure to accommodate expanding urban populations throughout

'As the dust of war settled it was suggested that the widespread urban destruction had given added impetus to . . . (Photograph: Popperfoto)

. . . the slum clearance programme that had begun in the early 30s and was renewed with vigour after the 1947 Town and Country Planning Act. (Photograph: Shelter)

34

Britain that even the new planning controls were unable to prevent it. Urban sprawl merely leap-frogged the green belt and began all over again on the other side — only this time in the clutches of 'comprehensive policies' which dictated the location and density of development, layout of roads and the provision of day-to-day facilities. Agricultural land soon found itself interrupted by increasing numbers of mineral extraction industries, breakers' yards, riding schools, rubbish dumps and recreational pursuits, and surrounded by scruffy woodland and unusable strips of farmland forming a natural protective strip or 'buffer zone' between the farm and these 'outside' urban activities. But pressure for development of land on the urban fringes was less than it might have been, had the Government's programme of new towns and expanded and redeveloped old towns not been initiated. The 1946 New Towns Act was seen as the most opportune way of improving the conditions of urban areas, of creating better living conditions elsewhere and of relieving the ever-worsening overcrowding and squalor of central areas. Making the most of new uses upon new land, whilst relieving older urban land of its problems of congestion, underlay a policy that emerged from Sir Patrick Abercrombie's 1945 plan for Greater London, in which he set a pattern for dealing with the overcrowded industrial cities throughout Britain. Pledged to the reduction of metropolitan populations in these areas to a maximum of 136 people to each acre (compared with densities of well over 1,000 to an acre in some areas of Glasgow, Liverpool and London), Abercrombie proposed building satellite new towns. The purpose of these new towns was to accommodate urban residents displaced from existing cities, and leaving room for better housing, wider roads, more open space and a stock of spare land that would allow planning to respond to the changing needs of industrial Britain.

This was the momentum upon which the 'great overspill movement' swept Britain, leaving in its wake 34 designated new towns, beginning with Stevenage and East Kilbride in 1947 and ending with Milton Keynes and Telford in 1968. During that period well over 2 million people (almost 4 per cent of the population) were moved, three quarters of a million jobs provided and a third of a million acres of land used, 80 per cent of which was good farmland. In addition, under the Town Development Act 1952, 110 existing towns were designated for expansion, providing accommodation for $\frac{1}{2}$ million people on an estimated 20,000 acres of land surrounding the fringes of cities and large towns. The programme of new and expanded towns had the comprehensive aim of ensuring the 'development of a balanced community enjoying a full social, industrial and commercial life'.[8]

Improving farmland and forestry

If the new spirit wanted to disperse existing industrial communities and to bring a 'sweeter life' to remaining city areas it intended equally to reinforce and bring confidence to agricultural communities whose fortunes had ebbed and flowed over the decades of industrial growth and rural depopulation. Much at the mercy of market demand, fickle government, the vagaries of weather and the surprise of war, the farmer, it was promised, was to see the last of the destructive urban pressures that had so threatened food production and the extreme hardships brought about by a dedicated but inadequate labour force. Henceforth land would be kept in good health, ready to respond to the call of society in the event of another war, or an economic blockade on imported food. The Government recalled that between 1850

As the new spirit invaded agriculture the land army was mobilised. (Photographs: Museum of English Rural Life, University of Reading)

and 1870 high demands for food, skilful husbandry by the tenants, and progressive enlightened management by farmers, produced large and well-managed farms and estates. This was the 'golden age of agriculture'. However, in the depression which followed, the demand for home-produced food dropped, as cheap prairie wheat and refrigerated meat came in from the Americas. Rents fell and buildings were neglected, farms fragmented and thousands of acres of good land went out of cultivation. The temporary stimulation of demand for home-produced cereals by the Corn Production Acts during the First World War produced a slight revival, but the deep depression of the 1930s further damaged the structure of British agriculture.

'Although other factors were in evidence, the main causes of the rise, fall and rise again of British agriculture can be attributed to the derived demand for home-grown farm products in a market guaranteed by the 1947 Agriculture Act.'[9]

Under the 1947 Agriculture Act, land laying fallow or unused and playing host to a rusty hand plough and dead oak, or a dilapidated barn overgrown by weeds and nettles, would be cleared of its debris and put to productive work. Agricultural grants and advice were made available to up-grade farms and to maintain them more efficiently. Building and field layouts were to be improved, fertiliser levels increased and a greater investment made in the purchase and maintenance of equipment and machinery. Land suitable for producing crops would be cleared of grazing cattle, unnecessary plant life, fences and ditches and opened up to the agricultural machines that were arriving. Land treated with fertilisers would be regularly tilled. Marshy land and water bogs were to be reclaimed and drained and brought into farming use as were those extensive areas of upland, deserted well before the Domesday period in favour of the more rewarding valley soils. Less valuable land on the edges of good agricultural land, or on rocky upland, would be opened up to the grazing of animals, serving the lowland cattle markets. Britain's rural areas were to be stripped of their post-depression weedy state and makeshift war-time conditions. They were to be transformed back into a working landscape to meet the needs of the growing population which, by the end of the war, had reached 45 million people — twice the number of a century earlier. Food production, which at that time was barely providing for one-third of the nation's needs, was to be increased. The new agricultural spirit was to bring an impressive rise in the level of productivity. Total agricultural labour productivity was to quadruple during the 30 years after the war.

At the turn of the century only 12 per cent of the acreage of England and Wales was owner-occupied. This figure rose to 36 per cent by 1927 after which it remained more or less static until 1972 by which time owner-occupation had risen to more than 54 per cent and was most prolific among small farms. Larger farms tended to remain tenanted and in many cases co-operative ventures brought mergers among a number of smaller farms. The result of this particular activity was larger fields, often doubling in size in the eastern counties, together with the loss of more than half the hedgerows since the war. The loss of hedgerows, trees and field boundaries reached a peak during the 1960s, bringing a severe reduction in the number of wildlife habitats, which together with the increasing use of pesticides and fertilisers was considered by many to be damaging not only to wildlife, but also to the natural productive potential of soil. However it was largely due to pesticides and fertilisers and the development of disease-resistant varieties of crops that cereal production had doubled by 1976. Wetlands were reclaimed and by the 1970s, 250,000 acres were being drained annually. The demand for new farm buildings such as stock units, silos, and warehouses to keep up to date with other new farming methods, meant that by 1957 the Government was operating extensive grant-aid schemes on buildings that were to make an essential contribution to improving farm efficiency.

However, by the 1970s the new spirit brought with it an increasing divergence between farming on the one hand and landscape and nature conservation on the other, with many observers suggesting that the farmer was no longer a guardian of the countryside, but in fact its potential destroyer:

'All the changes due to modernisation are harmful to wildlife except for a few species which are able to adapt to the new simplified habitats. The reason is very simple: the new agricultural habitats do not contain the basic requirements which are essential for many species. For example the larvae of the common blue butterfly feeds upon bird's-foot-trefoil. This plant disappears when pasture is ploughed and converted into ley or when it is treated with a selective herbicide. Once the plant has gone the butterfly goes too because it is not adapted to feeding upon the plants that are grown in leys or improved pasture. Similarly, most species of birds found on British farms (over 70 per cent) depend on trees or bushes in which to feed and/or nest. When trees are removed the birds disappear; only ground-nesting species like the skylark can remain in a treeless and bushless landscape such as exists in the Fens. If all farms were totally modernised so that they consisted solely of arable crops, grass leys, chemically treated ditches, farm buildings and a few trees and bushes grown for visual amenity, they would support far less wildlife than does the average farm today; about 80 per cent of the bird and about 95 per cent of the butterfly species would be lost from the farm landscape. A proportion of these would survive in very much reduced numbers in gardens, conifer plantations, bunder cliffs, old quarries, etc.' [10]

Interwar propaganda that drew attention to the qualities of the countryside and rural life had a strong influence upon the speed of urban sprawl. (London Transport Poster dated 1920; photograph by Graham Moss)

Reconciling the two extremes of agriculture and landscape amenity was to fall increasingly upon the managers of woodlands and forests, because of three important characteristics. Woodland and forestry can be located upon land that is either poorly located, of poor quality or generally unsuitable for farming; forest and woodland, if carefully managed, can sustain wildlife habitats and can conserve rare species of flora and fauna; and forests in particular are more robust than farmland in providing amenity space for recreation. By 1967 the Government was to call for an integration of land for agriculture and forestry, particularly in the hills. 'There need be no conflict between recreation and tourists on the one hand, and agriculture and forestry on the other.'[11]

The new post-war spirit also brought concern for forestry. The timber crisis of the First World War, when extensive tracts of forest were felled to provide materials for war munitions, led to the establishment of the Forestry Commission in 1919. Despite constant planting during the inter-war period its timber stocks had not matured by the outbreak of the Second World War, which brought an even more serious depletion of privately-owned woodland, to such an extent that by the end of the war Britain had become the least wooded country in Europe. As a result the Government resolved that the more rugged land suitable only for forest or recreational pursuits would be harnessed to replace lost timber stocks claimed by the two World Wars and endless felling over the centuries by an expanding society. The 1947 Forestry Act formed the basis of a concerted policy of afforestation and conservation of timber stocks. Whereas the Forestry Commission have since been charged with the task of encouraging a major increase in home supplies of wood, new policies introduced in 1958 and 1963 were intended to make forestry more of a social service than a commercial activity. For while the Commission was to produce more wood for industry, it was also to provide employment and give greater attention to the appearance of forests and the role of recreation. The growing of trees was seen as more easily integrated with agriculture than almost any other activity and the new spirit of 'one for all and all for one' was to lead, for the time being, to a greater integration of woodland with upland farming and the introduction of commercial shelter belt planting on marginal agricultural land, to provide shelter for animals and crops, whilst making a limited contribution to national timber production.

The renewal of war-damaged areas throughout Britain was hindered by an inadequate stock of timber and insufficient timber imports to enable rebuilding to proceed rapidly. As a result 'dedication schemes' were introduced to encourage private forestry, and the Forestry Commission was granted stronger powers of land acquisition for planting in order to ease the shortage of home grown timber. But it was at leat 15 to 20 years before the first thinnings for pit props were available and at least 50 years before the earliest timber would be available from even the fastest growing species. However, the post-war situation brought, for the first time, foresight and long-term investment programmes that were to benefit future generations. By the middle of the 1970s still only 8 per cent of the land surface of Britain was under forest and woodland, compared with an average of 29 per cent in Europe. At the same time Britain was producing barely 8 per cent of her home timber requirements, importing the remainder, of which nearly 90 per cent came from countries outside Europe. And yet the average planting rate by the state-owned Forestry Commission was 60,000 acres a year after 1945. Private forestry increased spectacularly from under 15,000 acres a year in the immediate post-war years to over 60,000 acres a year at the end of the 1970s.

Planning and agriculture

The new planning laws were restricted to urban developments and only encroached onto farmland where non-agricultural, residential buildings were proposed. In general, the farmer was to continue as manager and planner of the landscape. He would be able to change his field shapes and textures from arable or grazing to woodland and then back again without any need for change of use planning permission, required, under the 1947 Town and Country Planning Act, for non-agricultural development. However, later in its life the Act was to increasingly deny farming its essential labour accommodation, whilst dictating the colour and shape of farm buildings adjacent to main roads. Although the real role of planning in the countryside was to ensure the adequate provision of services like schools, doctors and public transport, it was also empowered to maintain roads and other facilities essential to the agricultural sector and other indigenous rural industries. The Ministry of Agriculture, Fisheries and Food advised on all aspects of agriculture and was able to intervene where land was to be taken out of agricultural use for forestry, leisure or urban development. Yet the 1947 Agriculture Act had few powers over supposedly operational agricultural and forestry land, which was in fact ignored or left in a general state of dereliction. Similarly the Town and Country Planning Act had no direct powers to combat wasteland. In both cases derelict land could, in effect, lie idle and unused indefinitely unless the local authorities used the compulsory purchase powers granted under the 1947 Planning Act, which they could do only if the land was required as part of the local development policy.

Planning for amenity and recreation

The new spirit acknowledged both the needs of the farmer and the more recent need for recreation and leisure space which was a result of increased mobility between towns and within the countryside. Farming was less robust and less able to cope with 'visitor invasion' in 1948 than it had been before, and it was acknowledged that some kind of two-way control was required to safeguard farmland and agricultural productivity, while permitting access for recreational and leisure purposes. In 1945 John Dower had already drawn attention to the growing conflicts between the conservation and use of the countryside in his recommendation for the introduction of national parks which he defined as 'extensive areas of beautiful and relatively wild country':

> that the characteristic landscape beauty should be strictly preserved;

> that access and facilities for public open-air enjoyment should be amply provided;

> that wildlife and buildings and places of architectural and historical interest should be suitably protected; and

> that established farming should be effectively maintained. [12]

40

Even the theatre perpetuated the ideals of spacious living held by John Ruskin and Ebenezer Howard and the strong belief in the quality of life sought by the Garden City and later New Towns movements. (Photograph: Popperfoto)

41

By the beginning of the 1960s rural recreation was to become an important force, during a period when 'Britain had never had it so good' and when increasing prosperity, the five-day week and longer holidays were to place more free time at the disposal of the majority of the population than ever before. Participation in leisure activities in the countryside began to increase in proportion to rises in income and car ownership. This trend had been recognised earlier with the introduction of a National Parks programme within the 1949 National Parks and Access to the Countryside Act.

As the pressures grew, the Countryside Act was introduced in 1967, giving local authorities the power to make recreation provision across the board in the country-side, in the shape of country parks, caravan and camping sites, picnic areas and improved access. The Act also provided finance to both public and private sectors for this purpose. The Countryside Commission was introduced at the same time to co-ordinate this activity throughout Britain. With 45 per cent of the population having access to a car by the middle of the 1960s, the Commission argued that a balance between the flow of vehicles and the carrying capacity of the countryside was likely to be a more effective form of management than a host of negative planning controls placed upon individual areas of land. Southern England in particular suffered from congested motorways, and in the upland areas of northern Scotland both double and single track roads were overcrowded. The new spirit of freedom reached its ultimate in spring 1973, when the M61 Motorway first came to a standstill as a result of demand to visit the Lake District. Further south, so many people now visit the Chilterns that in numerous places such as Ivinghoe Beacon, the underlying chalk has been exposed by the endless trampling of feet.

Post-war Britain, therefore, acknowledged that population and human activities had increased sufficiently for controls to be placed upon land to ensure its best and most beneficial use. Whilst planning was to become increasingly powerful and legislative, it was not always to be totally successful. By the middle of the 1960s there were already serious warnings being voiced about the wastage of minerals and derelict exhausted mineral land; about the continuing poor conditions of inner-city residential areas and increasing amounts of vacant land; and a general disquiet about the growing trend for high-rise residential living and all the social problems that were emerging. Whilst it would be difficult to assess what might have been without this new spirit of land-use, observers in many parts of Britain and Europe were, by the middle of the 1960s, awakening to an apparently increasing stock of derelict and waste land.

Notes

1. L. Dudley Stamp, *Man and the Land*, Collins, 1969, pp.238-9
2. M. Young and P. Wilmott, *Family and Kinship in East London*, Pelican, 1957, p.113
3. *ibid.* p.113
4. J. H. Forshaw and P. Abercrombie, *County of London Plan*, Macmillan, 1943

5. Stamp, *Man and the Land, op cit.* p.241
6. Circular 42/55, Ministry of Housing and Local Government, August 1955
7. *op. cit.* p.236
8. Abercrombie Committee Final Report, Cmnd 6876, 1946
9. 'The Future Pattern of Land Ownership and Occupation', a discussion paper of the Land Agency and Agriculture Division, The Royal Institution of Chartered Surveyors, 1977
10. *Nature Conservation and Agriculture*, Nature Conservancy Council, 1977
11. The Development of Agriculture, Cmnd 2738, HMSO, 1967, p.4
12. National Parks in England and Wales (Dover Report), Cmnd 6628, Ministry of Town and Country Planning, HMSO, 1945

CHAPTER 4

The Dawn of Dereliction

'... the face of the world is riddled with abandoned mineral workings, pocked with subsidence, dashed with quarries, littered with disused plant and piled high with stark and sterile banks of dross and debris, spoil and slag.
These deformities of nature do more than mar the view. Their grim desolation dulls the spirit – as their dust and fumes defile the fabric – of the human settlements that straggle along. Smouldering pit heaps foul the air, poisonous chemicals pollute the waterways and treacherous pits endanger the lives of adventurous children. Neglected wastes breed vermin and disease. Their very existence fosters slovenliness and vandalism, invites the squatters' shack and engenders a "derelict land mentality" that can never be eradicated until the mess itself has been cleared up. Dereliction, indeed, breeds a brutish insensibility bordering on positive antagonism, to the life and liveliness of the natural landscape it has supplanted. It debases as well as disgraces our civilisation.'

The Civic Trust, 1964

The awakening

Many of the destroyed acres that emerged from the dust of war lingered long into the post-war years as fallen bricks and vegetation began to form a patchwork of unkempt and derelict land that in a number of Britain's cities is still evident today and difficult to explain away to our children, as I have found to my own embarrassment. How can land be ignored for so long, they ask? Why hasn't somebody done something? The types of questions that have perhaps passed through all our minds as we have parked our car within the weathered ruins of a 'temporary' bomb-site, or as we contemplate the basement depths of an overgrown gap in an otherwise fluent streetscape of Victorian houses. To extend the children's questions into the future, why should we tolerate such complacency, and why has it taken well over 30 years to acknowledge and take action over decay and dereliction?

In its consideration of the problem of post-war reconstruction, the 1942 Uthwatt Committee concluded that:

'... the simplest and only effective method of achieving the desired results is to confer on the planning authorities compulsory powers of purchase much wider and more simple in operation than under existing legislation, over dry land, which may be required for planning and other purposes.'[1]

These recommendations were incorporated in the 1947 Planning Act and produced the earliest comprehensive legislation aimed at the renewal of buildings and land uses falling redundant due to old age, changing patterns of industry or war damage. Initially consideration of these areas tended to be limited to the built-up

(Photograph: Shelter)

Steady decline of traditional urban industries has, since the war, created empty and lifeless environments in most of Britain's cities and towns. (Photograph: HMSO)

areas of towns and large cities — only a small part of the picture of dereliction which began to emerge at that time. An equally insidious, but more dispersed aspect of wasteland was also arousing public concern, as Jacquetta Hawkes emphasised in 1950:

'The present derelict parts of industrial Britain assume a degraded ugliness never before known. Who can ever express the desolation of these forlorn scenes? The grey slag heap, the acres of land littered with rusted fragments of machinery, splintered glass, tin cans, sagging festoons of barbed wire; vile buildings, more vile in ruins; grimy stretches of cement floors, shapeless heaps of broken concrete. The air about them still so foul that nothing more than a few nettles and tattered thistles will grow there; not even roseberry and ragwort can hide them with a brief mid-summer promise. This is the worst that has happened to land.'[2]

This kind of dereliction, involving mineral extraction and often unavoidable damage to the landscape, is more commonly found in the open countryside surrounding towns and cities. It is one of the oldest forms of land despoilation, dating back to the first tin mines sunk by Iron Age man. It has increased as successive generations have dipped into the 'glorious bounty' of minerals as eagerly as a child plunges his hand into a lucky dip, scattering all the sawdust spoils around him, but caring not to clean up the mess in his excitement. Since the Industrial Revolution we have left holes and heaps as peat and coal have been taken for energy; as sand and gravel have been excavated for buildings and roads; and as chalk, clay and all manner of minerals have been hewn from the land.

Until the Second World War, derelict land — defined as land so damaged by industrial or other development, that is likely to remain out of use unless subjected to

46

special treatment — was commonly believed to be a legacy only of the Industrial Revolution. But early post-war surveys indicated that extensive areas of land used for surface mineral workings such as sand and gravel extraction, and the tipping of colliery spoil were becoming derelict each year. Operators were not required to reclaim the landscape of exhausted mines and hence the areas of permanent dereliction were mounting up. Little thought was being given either to the procedures requiring the reinstatement of such land or to the extent and speed with which these mineral resources were being mined and depleted to keep up with a consumer society growing in numbers and expectations, and more accustomed to throwing away than to salvaging and re-using. The result, at its most bizarre, has been seen in the demolition of hundreds of thousands of buildings, many with a long and still useful life left in their fabrics — their re-usable materials smashed and splintered as they have been bulldozed remorsefully into the ground to make way for mass redevelopment schemes. In their place have been erected sparkling new tower blocks and housing estates which in many cases have fallen into disrepair and into decay within 20 years of their completion.

Belief in an endless source of raw materials has created a 'disposable society' which accepts waste and built-in obsolescence as readily as it accepts dereliction and rubbish dumping. An attitude of mind of which George Orwell wrote in 1937:

'In a crowded dirty little country like ours one takes defilement almost for granted. Slag heaps and chimneys seem a more normal, probable landscape than grass and trees.'[3]

In its destructive mood society can be readily imbued with what the Civic Trust described in 1964 as a 'derelict land mentality' that scorns those who seek an alternative and simpler society based upon the re-use of land, buildings and waste materials and the provision of energy from natural sources. In 1946 a pioneer survey of derelict land in the Black Country and subsequent surveys of North Staffordshire and East Shropshire coalfield, by Professor S. H. Beaver, shocked politicians with its findings.[4] In the Black Country one in eight acres was found to be so damaged or affected by 'chronic dereliction' as to require urgent attention. Although various official references to derelict land appeared in reports relating to specific problems of mining subsidence and reclamation of ironstone workings during the inter-war period, these reports did not shed much light upon the problems of dereliction. Indeed in 1936 the Commissioner for England and Wales had observed that the clearance of derelict land would not be encouraged unless it offered economic advantages. However, there were at the time no land-use statistics on the growth of dereliction, that is, until 1948 when John Oxenham found that 120,000 acres of mineral land, a total area equivalent to $1\frac{1}{2}$ times the size of the Isle of Wight, were lying derelict or damaged in England and Wales.[5] This was the first attempt at estimating an overall total of derelict land, and was a powerful indication of the need for a more complete survey of dereliction. As a result the Government resolved to study the matter more deeply.

A confused state

By 1954, a national working party, set up by the Ministry of Housing and Local

Government to report upon the problems of derelict land, confirmed Oxenham's figures. 126,000 acres of land were found to be so damaged by industrial activity as to warrant reclamation, of which 50,000 acres were spoil heaps, 53,000 acres were excavations and holes and 23,000 acres were other forms of dereliction like abandoned woodlands and derelict industrial villages. Durham and Yorkshire, Staffordshire, Lincolnshire and Cornwall were among the most severely affected counties. However the Government appeared to have scared even itself and the figures were quickly withdrawn. It was argued that the information, although helpful to individual authorities, was not considered reconcilable on a national basis, since local authorities' returns were based upon differing time scales and rarely included action taken to reclaim or to treat derelict land. It had been the original intention, as set out in the Government's 1956 memorandum entitled 'Derelict Land and its Reclamation', for derelict land information to be collected and included in the first Development Plan Review in 1960, containing a fully documented survey of all derelict land and a programme for its reclamation.

Although the Government abandoned this first attempt at setting up a National Derelict Land Survey, its 1963 report, 'New Life for Dead Lands', acknowledged that there was a case; 'a desolate and unkempt land may not be only a symptom of obsolescence, it may be the cause of it'.[6] This report put the total area of dereliction for England and Wales at about 150,000 acres of which 60,000 acres consisted of spoil heaps, 60,000 acres of excavations and 'holes in the ground' and 30,000 acres of other types of dereliction. These details also confirmed Oxenham's figures produced fifteen years earlier. Again because of the imprecise definition of derelict land these statistics were seen to be totally inadequate to allow a clear picture to be drawn of the rate at which land was being consumed. In urging a full derelict land survey to be commenced and up-dated annually, Sir Keith Joseph, then Minister of Housing and Local Government, stated in 1963 that the nation should turn its attention to:

'. . . land which we and our forebears have exploited in the interests of industry and other uses, only to leave it in many cases, idle, forlorn and ugly. Substantial areas of dereliction up and down the country testify to our apparent unconcern for beauty, and suggest deference to waste. Wherever possible, derelict land should be reclaimed for building, recreation and agriculture.'[7]

A large proportion of derelict land (particularly waste tips and abandoned industrial land) was concentrated in relatively small parts of the older industrial areas of the north, the Midlands and South Wales. The Hunt Committee, set up in 1969 to study older industrial areas of Britain, considered that this sporadic dereliction hindered a more rapid rate of reclamation. However, small local authorities with small resources of money, staff or expertise often found themselves with large problems of derelict land. As a result of its findings the Hunt Report called in vain for the establishment of a Derelict Land Reclamation Agency.

By the end of the 1960s railway and colliery closures, in addition to continued new mineral workings, were contributing to a gradual rise in the rate at which land was falling derelict. In 1964 the first officially accepted derelict land survey indicated that there were 85,000 acres in England alone. But local authorities had no statutory duty to reclaim derelict land or to improve its appearance. Much depended upon the

48

As individual communities have become 'surplus to requirements', housing and the surrounding environment have frequently been allowed to fall into disrepair, the improvement of which few residents have been able to afford and towards which not all local authorities have been prepared to allocate public funds. (Photograph: Architectural Press Ltd.)

energy of individual local authorites. However after 1964 incentives were made available for derelict land to be reclaimed, either during the normal course of development, or through compulsory purchase. The National Parks and Access to the Countryside Act 1949 had already included specific powers for the acquisition of derelict mineral land and the restoration and improvement of such land, whether or not it was owned by a local authority.

From 1964 onwards, comprehensive information was to be compiled about derelict land in a form which would enable it to be up-dated year by year. While local authorities would be required to keep to the original definition of spoil heaps, excavations and pits and other forms of dereliction, this time they were to *exclude* specifically from their returns:

land such as tipping sites on which development has not been complete

land subject to conditions attached to planning permissions or other arrangements for restoration

land which may be regarded as derelict from natural causes such as marshland and neglected woodland, and

war damaged land, 'in-filling' sites awaiting redevelopment and urban sites cleared with a view to redevelopment as part of the programme or urban renewal.

Not surprisingly the results of the first survey produced in 1964 indicated that what the Government referred to as 'hard core' dereliction was less than half the previous survey total in 1955. While concern among certain public bodies had been appeased, the new definitions inflamed critics, who saw these latest statistics as white-washing of more severe problems.

The Civic Trust immediately gave warning that the new definitions would be inadequate and that in practice industrial developers would not be treated strongly enough for fear that they may move elsewhere and take with them jobs and possible prosperity. These views were reinforced by a 'Countryside in 1970' study, 'Reclamation and Clearance of Derelict Land', which recommended certain additional categories of land that should be added to the 'hard core' of dereliction:

'Even if we ensure that in future the planning conditions covering current industrial operations are realistic, are carefully drawn up and are complied with, there will still be additions to this "hard core" which will have to be dealt with in due course as follows:

(a) land now being actively damaged by development which escapes planning controls;

(b) land now in industrial or other use (e.g., a factory) which does not have to be restored when it ceases to be so used;

(c) land which requires or will require further treatment because the planning conditions imposed in the past have been inadequate or incapable of fulfillment.

We recommend that land in these categories be included in any future survey of derelict land as it will sooner or later constitute an addition to the hard core of dereliction.'[8]

These recommendations were largely ignored and the Derelict Land Survey as commenced in 1964 and still undertaken today is based upon similar definitions which give an entirely misleading picture, as recent evidence confirms, and which is discussed in detail in Chapter 5.

By the end of the 1960s public concern for waste and derelict land was mounting. In 1969, John Barr wrote in his petulant book *Derelict Britain* that the official derelict land survey:

'... could include all such testimonies to man's ill works, but it doesn't. For the purposes of entertaining grants for reclamation or improvements of derelict land, the Government appends to its definition a cluster of exceptions which effectively removes at least half the nation's dereliction from any consideration.'[9]

John Barr, together with other literary contributions to the debate like *Battle for the Environment* by John Aldous and Kenneth Wallwork's definitive work *Derelict Land*, indicated that reconciliation between economic and amenity interests in mineral working and the reinstatement of derelict land were quite properly the responsibility of planning authorities. As long as industry is not required to clear up and reclaim the landscape after its activities have been exhausted, then despoiled land will continue to grow.

Taking a lead in establishing a system for land reclamation, the Ironstone Restoration Fund, set up under the Mineral Workings Act of 1951, made finance

50

available for the reclamation of Midlands limestone fields where workings involved untidy and damaging open-cast methods. Generally ironstone operators and land-owners made a contribution to the Fund for each ton of ironstone extracted by open-cast working — an example that could well be followed by other mineral extractors. Even open-cast coal mining, which began during the war under emergency legislation, continued to be free from interference until 1958 and, even then, development was outside planning control. It is only recently that these land-use activities have come under the scrutiny of local authorities and more importantly the Secretary of State for the Environment. The Vale of Belvoir Inquiry in 1980, in which more than 100 acres of prime agricultural land were to be opened up for coal mining, is a recent testimony to the determination of nationalised bodies like the National Coal Board to press on in the face of massive opposition. And yet it is estimated that if the tips for this project were dumped in central London, they would bury Buckingham Palace and St. Paul's Cathedral and all the land in between in a belt over a mile wide from the Thames Embankment to Russell Square.

Other forms of dereliction

Mineral excavations have not been the only activities to contribute to landscape dereliction. Dumping of solid wastes and spoil from mining activities has produced countless mountains of coal sludge, brick and limestone wastes, slate and rubbish tips, slurry ponds and piles of shraff (waste) surrounding the pottery areas of Britain. In October 1966 the full extent and potential horror of waste tipping was brought home to the residents of a small Welsh valley village, Aberfan, when 116 children and 28 adults were killed by a hill of coal sludge that slid down upon the village school, burying all in its wake. In one short sharp catastrophic moment, the future generation of the village had been wiped out. Whilst accidents on this scale are not common among the pits and heaps of the mineral industry, in his post-mortem on Aberfan and his analysis of the 60 varieties of land despoliation brought about by new technology John Barr wrote:

'This dereliction kills vast acres of a small nation; at its ugliest it kills the spirit of the people who live amidst it, but it seldom kills in the way of Aberfan – at least not in the hundreds at one moment's blow, only a yearly trickle of too adventurous children who shouldn't have been playing round some abandoned mineshaft or steep-sided quarry.'[10]

Successive generations born into such derelict and wasting landscapes as the industrial areas of South Wales, the brickfields of Bedford, the china clay pits of Cornwall or the coalfields of Durham, may have known nothing better than dereliction. The mere fact that their free time is spent playing tag around mineshafts, scrambling up and down spoil heaps and steep-sided quarries, makes their world a game of chance within an environment at its most base and uncaring.

Elsewhere families of children, communities of wildlife, fields of farm animals and droves of picnickers and tourists spend time on land in industrial areas that is being gradually poisoned by toxic industrial waste released into the air or local water courses. Metal and plastic industries, aluminium smelting and nuclear power stations and many other installations can yield toxic or potentially contaminated waste that presents severe problems of disposal. Chemical or filtration treatment

51

Declining or exhausted mineral industries have been allowed to leave land in a despoiled and derelict condition, while further mineral workings have been permitted elsewhere upon land without adequate environmental or reclamation safeguards. (Photograph: Architectural Press Ltd.)

of toxic industrial waste, recently developed, is expensive and leaves an isolated solid toxic residue that is equally difficult to break down or to jettison with safety. The advent of plastic has caused the most complex problems of disposal. Its low-value waste and the extreme difficulty of breaking down plastic into disposable form have led to endless piles of plastic bottles and boxes, cellophane and paperbags, discarded by carefree users. Idle and derelict land particularly attracts illicit dumping of these low-value commodities. Piles of rubber tyres, plastic containers, discarded beer cans, and redundant cars scar pockets of land ranging from the depths of the city to the most open expanses of countryside, adding to the severe problems of handling illicit waste, which is so often outside the responsibility of officials and 'designated' rubbish tips. However Britain's wasting land does not stop here.

Disused industrial buildings have emerged with increasing speed since the war, as changing technology has brought more concentrated and efficient industrial activities and plant requiring less land and fewer buildings. As a result, derelict and abandoned sites have sprung up on land within traditional industrial cities and their fringes. Textile mills and coal mines, abandoned military installations and military airfields, have all brought the general dereliction which hangs round declining industry — few areas of land in urban Britain have escaped this mounting catalogue of wasteland.

By the beginning of the 1970s traditional transport installations, particularly railways and shipping activities had been overtaken by more efficient and streamlined communications such as container-freight requiring less land. Abandoned docklands and obsolete canals, disused railway lines and goods yards all contribute

IDLE LAND
MEANS IDLE MEN

The modern block of buildings marked "A," consisting of showrooms and warehouses, forming No. 7, Aldersgate Street, is rated at £2,677 per annum. The vacant site marked "B," forming Nos. 4 & 5, Aldersgate Street, is rated at nothing. Block "A" occupies a site of about 10,000 sq. feet and pays £870 in rates. The vacant site "B" extends to 12,700 sq. feet, and pays nothing. It has been vacant for several years.

VOTE PROGRESSIVE
Rate Land Values and Prevent Unemployment.

By 1980 urban wasteland had become a political issue, just as it had been more than a century earlier. (Photograph: Museum of Rural Life, University of Reading)

For twenty years after the 1947 Town and Country Planning Act, redevelopment dominated planning and investment. Conservation and the reuse of existing buildings and materials was rarely given sufficient consideration. (Photograph: Joseph McKenzie)

noticeably to a more widespread dereliction, the extent of which is either unknown or not acknowledged. By the end of the 1970s, Britan's landscape was subjected to four specific types of land dereliction caused mainly by the following:

exhausted mineral excavations and abandoned workings

redundant, disused and abandoned buildings and land

industrial and domestic waste dumping

disused and abandoned transport installations and land.

In 1969 the Hunt Committee studying industrial decline concluded that slow economic growth and these various forms of dereliction were most noticeable among early traditional industrial areas:

'... *associated with unused or underused labour resources, low earnings, a concentration of industries with a declining labour force, poor communications and a run-down physical environment making areas unattractive for new economic growth, and net outward migration.*'[11]

The cost of indifference

The complacency of an inadequate official approach to the growing pattern of derelict land was again given a sudden and violent jolt by the Civic Trust in 1977. While the Department of the Environment contemplated the extent of its official derelict land, the Civic Trust announced that there was a further category of 'dormant' or waste land of which there was at least a quarter of a million acres lying throughout our cities, towns and villages. Dormant land was described as land undamaged or only slightly damaged, which could be made useable without great works of reclamation and included demolished buildings, bomb sites, abandoned allotments and unused bits of land left over after development. Some of this land is vacant, some is in temporary use, for example, as car parking or storage. Results from the privately sponsored Second Land Utilisation Survey also published in 1977,[12] more than confirmed the Civic Trust's figures. However it estimated that in 1963 waste and scrubland, similar to the Civic Trust's dormant land, exceeded 346,000 acres and that the survey's 1977 forecast expected this figure to have increased to $\frac{3}{4}$ million wasting acres. If the Second Land Utilisation Survey figures eventually prove to be the more accurate, then Britain's urban wasteland alone could, by the beginning of the 1980s, be approaching a million acres.

The figures, however, are only the tip of the iceberg. There are also extensive areas of land affected by noise from aircraft, traffic and industrial processes, and by fall-out from waste discharged into the air and by seepage onto land of liquid waste released into water courses. In addition, fringe land on the edge of dangerous industries, motorways, railways and canals; military land lying idle and used only for intermittent training; and fragmented land severed by motorways and railways or lying trapped in the green belt, are all rarely able to be put to efficient urban use or productive agricultural use. All these land uses and more create an idleness that is vulnerable to attack from tin cans and rubbish, from weeds and nettles, and which carry little incentive for development or even reclamation. The ultimate irony is that as we watch urban land wasting way, it is being steadily replaced by more expansive urban development upon good agricultural land. As the Civic Trust pointed out:

'Land is being taken from farming at the rate equivalent to the loss of the whole of Bedfordshire every four years, and thousands of buildings – many of them with a useful life left – continue to be demolished yearly to give space for new development. At the same time, this Report estimates that at least a quarter of a million acres in Britain lie dormant.'[13]

Under present legislation derelict land is likely to continue to grow, caught as it is in a technological fix where progress means increasing reliance upon the exploitation of existing resources of land, minerals and energy. The despoliation of the Vale of Belvoir to supply coal, the laying waste of more coastal land (often good agricultural land) for oil refineries, petrochemical works and nuclear power stations; oil spillage and nuclear accident; contaminated landscapes and infected livestock are a risk facing society whose demands and expectations are out-reaching its ability to cope with technological side-effects. Under such circumstances how can we safeguard irreplaceable natural resources; plan for the failure or exhaustion of energy supplies, or more simply begin to clear up the debris of successive generations?

This dawn of dereliction and waste is made all the more shocking because, apart from the privately sponsored Second Land Utilisation Survey, no British Government to date has taken the plight of land seriously. Statistics quoted and included in the Department of the Environment's own official derelicted land returns are considered by many local authorities themselves to be grossly inadequate. The seemingly impossible task of defining idle, waste or derelict land has all too frequently been used as an excuse for not coming to terms with the problem. Britain has not yet begun to tackle its wasting acres, which will be a damnable inheritance for succeeding generations. To understand the reasons why this situation has occurred and the facts behind the growing crisis of land in a changing society, it is necessary to explore a series of issues in greater depth.

1. Report of the Uthwatt Committee on Compensation and Betterment, Cmnd 6386, HMSO, 1942
2. Jacquetta Hawkes, *A Land*, David and Charles, 1951, p.208
3. George Orwell, *The Road to Wigan Pier*, London, 1937
4. S.H. Beaver, *Derelict Land in the Black Country*, Ministry of Town and Country Planning, 1946
5. John Oxenham, 'The reclamation of derelict land', *Journal of the Institute of Municipal Engineers*, Vol.75, No.3, 1948
6. *New Life for Dead Lands – Derelict Areas Reclaimed*, HMSO, 1963
7. *ibid.*
8. 'Reclamation and Clearance of Derelict Land', Countryside in 1970 Conference Paper, Study Group 12, 1965, p.12.7
9. John Barr, *Derelict Britain*, Pelican, 1969, p.39
10. *ibid.* p.13
11. Hunt Committee Report, *The Intermediate Areas*, HMSO, 1969
12. Alice Coleman, 'Land Use Planning — Success or Failure?', *Architects' Journal*, 19 January 1977
13. The Civic Trust, *Urban Wasteland*, 1977, p.6

PART 2

THE GROWING CRISIS

'Never has the land of this country been more vulnerable to misappropriation and misuse than during the past 30 years. Our planning system, arguably the most all-embracing in the Western world, has almost totally failed to achieve any compatibility of planning aims. Good agricultural land is being turned over to urban use and road building at an increasing and alarming rate; the countryside is more and more infested by diffuse urban sprawl – the rurban fringe; farmland which has taken over 5000 years to build up could be totally destroyed in a mere 200 years (Grade 1. farmland will vanish within 50 years); wasteland, derelict land and scrub are advancing like a cancer across the face of what was once good productive soil; the galloping consumption of land needed for agriculture has, paradoxically, not lessened, but rather increased, the problems of our inner cities.'

Alice Coleman, 'Land Use Planning – Success or Failure', Architects' Journal, 19 January 1977

Glasgow's new skyline. (Photograph: Joseph McKenzie)

CHAPTER 5

Mineral Extraction and Despoiled Landscapes

'The derelictions of the Industrial Revolution produced around the world in only 200 years, have received little consideration or idealism. I never quite understand why, when they have occurred, industry, government and folk should endure them with such callousness, fatalism and insensitivity.'

Sir Frank Fraser Darling, 1963

An uneasy alliance

The history of mineral extraction is also the history of man's changing and rapidly increasing dependence upon different sources of raw materials, exploited to meet the needs of successive generations. It is the history of a society that was once perhaps exclusively dependent upon renewable resources, but is now engaged in uneasy alliance with a wide range of non-renewable and diminishing raw materials. We rely upon this alliance more than we dare admit to provide our daily comforts and to meet future expectations. So much so that mineral workings claim an estimated 13,000 acres of new land every year in Britain (see Table 2) of which at least half are not restored to any beneficial use, either because of weaknesses in present planning legislation, or because the scale of modern extraction makes restoration impractical within present economic priorities. Mineral working is indeed one of the largest current contributors to the stock of despoiled and derelict land in Britain, but its extent has been consistently under-stated within Government statistics. In England in 1974 there were, according to the Department of the Environment,[1] 114,000 acres of derelict mineral land and abandoned workings and a further 28,000 acres being used as refuse tips. However it was suggested by a number of commentators, including county and local authorities, that by taking account of a wider, and in their opinion, more realistic definition of despoiled land, these official figures would be at least double. Also by 1974 the area of new workings in England for which planning permission had been granted, was 236,000 acres (52,000 acres without restoration conditions) of which 122,000 acres were affected by spoil heaps, buildings, lagoons, excavations and pits. In 1979 the Department of the Environment indicated that the extent of operational and exhausted mineral land and waste tipping of all kinds in Britain covered 350,000 acres (250,000 acres in England, 53,000 in Wales and 46,000 in Scotland). Reclamation of exhausted or abandoned mineral land averaged 7,000 acres annually during the period 1971-8 (33,000 in England 5,000 in Wales and 11,000 in Scotland).[2]

Although most mineral extraction is deemed to be in the national interest, there is

60

(Photograph: Roy Morgan)

a growing belief that much of it is merely supporting an existing economic system. If this is the case then the emerging figures reflect a rapid growth in land despoliation that is hard to justify on grounds of social need alone. Whatever the issue, despoliation can only grow worse under present circumstances as high levels of extraction continue and as industrial operators remain reluctant to restore their damage or to minimise their initial impact by 'landscaping as they excavate'. But society is still deeply imbued with past freedom and seems disinclined to impose costly conditions upon mineral extraction, which may be seen to inflate the price of the end product or to deprive an area of potential employment. However economically or socially desirable this approach may be, the mineral industry has an inbuilt momentum that is difficult to control even with the strongest of local planning conditions. In the end control can come only from a clearly defined Government policy for the various extractive industries. As yet such a policy has not emerged.

Unearthing the bounty

Mineral working in Britain dates back to pre-Roman times, but no other period can compare with the last half-century, either in the extent and speed with which the mineral industry has spread across the face of Britain or in the extent of damaged land that remains unrestored or difficult to restore under modern extractive

61

TABLE 2 SUMMARY OF ESTIMATED ANNUAL LAND TAKE ASSOCIATED WITH MAIN MINERALS WORKED IN BRITAIN

Mineral	Geological origin	Geographical distribution of workings	Land take (per year at mid-1970s output levels, in acres)	Type of working	Extent of present restoration	Uses of mineral	Main conflicts with
Sand and gravel	Glacial, fluvial and Triassic deposits	Widespread in England	5,000	Wet pits 60%	Less than 50%	Concrete, roadstone	Agriculture, amenity
Limestone	Carboniferous, Jurassic, etc.	Pennines, Mendips, S. Wales, Central Lowlands of Scotland, etc.	600	Deep quarry	Negligible	Concrete, roadstone, agricultural lime, iron and steel and chemical industries	Amenity
Igneous rocks	Many deposits, from pre-Cambrian to Tertiary	S.W. Peninsula, Welsh and Scottish Highlands, Mendips, Charnwood Forest	400	Deep quarry	Negligible	Roadstone, concrete	Amenity
Sandstone	Many deposits, from pre-Cambrian to Jurassic	Widespread in British highlands; Norfolk, Surrey	125	Deep quarry	Negligible	Roadstone, concrete	Amenity, agriculture
Chalk	Cretaceous	Shallow uplands of S. and E. England	150	Deep quarry	Negligible	Cement, agricultural lime, iron and steel industry	Amenity, agriculture

Brick clay	Carboniferous, Jurassic, Cretaceous	Widespread, but especially in Oxford Clay area	100 (in main producing area)	Deep pit	Negligible	Bricks	Amenity
Coal: Open cast	Carboniferous	Midlands, S. Wales, Lancs., Pennines, Central Lowlands of Scotland, N.E. England, Yorkshire	5,000	Deep pits	All workings restored	Domestic and industrial fuel, electricity generation	Agriculture, amenity during working
Deep mining	"	"	700 (for waste disposal)	-	Contouring and planting increasing	"	Agriculture, amenity; subsidence problems
Iron ore	Carboniferous, Jurassic	Northants., Lincs., Cumberland	120	Open-cast, mined	All open-cast working restored	Iron and steel industry	Agriculture, amenity during working
China clay	Kaolinised granites	Cornwall, Devon	250-400	Open pits, waste mountains	Negligible	Paper industry, earthenware and bone china; filler for chemical industry	Amenity

TOTAL LAND TAKE PER YEAR   12,445-12,595

Sources: Annual land take figures assembled from information provided by the following: J. Blunden, *The Mineral Resources of Britain*, 1975; Civic Trust, *Derelict Land*, 1964, and information received from the Sand and Gravel Association.

Note: Minerals not included are those with a relatively low current land take (if not a negligible land take) such as slate, ball clay, fullers earth, salt, gypsum, tin and Fluorspar.

Mineral working dates back to the earliest civilisations. Wheal Jane tin mine, Cornwall. (Photograph: The Guardian)

conditions. Even the narrower individualism of the Victorian age (during which the output of minerals such as coal and iron ores considerably exceeded present levels) failed to produce anything approaching the widespread devastation brought by mineral extraction to the landscapes of contemporary Britain. Derelict and despoiled land left in the wake of mineral workings is not, as we would perhaps prefer to believe, predominantly the legacy of past avarice, but is rather the outcome of recent progress in extractive technology and society's insatiable demands for minerals of every kind.

It is noticeable that the mineral industries with the fastest rates of growth of output over the last 50 years have been those born of the demands of earlier urban and more recent suburban growth. These are required for the continued well-being of the network of production and delivery industries involved in supplying goods and energy to a progressively urbanised and growing population. Although the remarkable increase in demand for minerals in the last half-century has been matched by technological innovations needed to extract and deliver them, the decreasing flexibility of these capital-intensive technologies and the changing accessibility of the resources themselves threaten to undermine the raw material basis of future expansion. As remaining mineral supplies become more difficult to extract and their proximity to major markets diminishes, so every ton of mineral delivered will require generally more energy for extraction, processing and transportation, and will thereby impose further pressures upon land where energy-producing minerals are extracted and processed. This self-sustaining spiral of demand has culminated in a six-fold increase since 1920 in the annual output of minerals, with the exception of coal.

The implication for land use of this upsurge in demand is that virtually every mineral for which output has increased is extracted by 'open' methods of working, which inflict the worst kinds of damage upon the landscape, and generally reduce the possibility of restoring it to beneficial future use. Recent improvements in the capacity and size of machinery used to strip and dump overburden and soil, and to gouge minerals from the earth, have serious consequences upon the extent of damage and the degree of restoration necessary to reinstate land after mineral working. Using open-cast methods the depth of overburden stripped for ironstone excavation, for example, has since 1900 increased from 3 feet to more than 130 feet; deposits of coal can be worked to depths over 650 feet; and soft materials (like china clay, excavated at depths of 350 feet) can now be worked economically at increasing depths. Open methods of working minerals are on average ten times more productive than deep mining. An estimated increase in output of 500 per cent has been recorded for open-worked minerals since 1900, compared with a 45 per cent decrease in output from deep mines.[3]

Sand and gravel, limestone and china clay extraction

Traditionally, mineral working and consequent dereliction were highly concentrated around Britain's coalfields. Improved communications and a dispersed pattern of mineral working have largely been a result of exhaustion of mineral reserves with longer histories of extraction and upon the dispersed location of minerals for which recent demand has been increasing at a high rate. Both these factors can be seen in operation in the sand and gravel industries, where production has increased from 2 million tons in 1922 to more than 100 million tons a year since the mid-1960s: such a sustained rate of extraction has exhausted many sites close to major markets and placed a premium (in an industry where transport costs can make or break an operator) on remaining working sites within the economic radius of operation. This has brought further land-use conflicts in areas where competition for land may already be fierce. Near London, for example, the sand and gravel industry is spreading over the 8,000 acres of high quality agricultural and horticultural land recommended for conservation by the Sand and Gravel Advisory Committee in 1948. Planning authorities are likely to become increasingly reluctant to allow mineral industries to make such inroads into the landscape, since the proportion of exhausted pits being filled in is generally less than 50 per cent, as low as 20 per cent in some areas.[4]

Limestone production, which has increased ten-fold since the early 1920s, generates land-use problems of a different nature. Although extraction rarely competes for land of high agricultural value, the method of working — in deep pits with little overburden and usually in remote locations — means that only limited back-filling and restoration is possible. By 1970, out of 700 acres taken annually in England and Wales for limestone and chalk production, only 35 acres were restored to beneficial use: a proportion that is likely to decrease further as production is concentrated on fewer, longer-term and larger quarries operated under out-dated planning controls.[5] Production tends to be concentrated in upland areas of high scenic value. There are, for example, active limestone quarries within the boundaries

65

TABLE 3 MINERAL WORKINGS IN NATIONAL PARKS AND AREAS OF OUTSTANDING NATURAL BEAUTY IN ENGLAND IN 1974*

	Areas affected by spoil heaps and tips, plant, buildings and lagoons (acres)	Excavations and pits excluding lagoons (acres)	Total (acres)
National Parks			
Dartmoor	257	325	582
Exmoor	0	0	0
Lake District	70	238	308
Peak District	250	490	740
Northumberland	20	12	32
North York Moors	22	205	227
Yorkshire Dales	38	202	240
AONBs	1,075	4,812	5,887
Total	1,732	6,284	8,016

*   Amount of land covered by permissions for surface mineral working and mineral waste tipping in progress or to be commenced in 1974.

Source: Survey of Derelict and Desoiled Land in England 1974 – Mineral Working, Department of the Environment, Table M3, page 87.

of five National Parks, with over 30 quarries alone in the Peak District National Park. Large quantities of limestone are also won from Areas of Outstanding Natural Beauty or Great Landscape Value. In 1971 the Somerset County Council reported upon the impact of increasing production in the Mendips. An anticipated six-fold increase in local production of aggregate, mostly limestone, by the year 2010 was considered likely to generate altogether formidable planning problems — noise, vibration and dust; heavy traffic on narrow country lanes running through small settlements; the visual impact of processing plant for aggregate crushing and coatings, or of complexes of cement works or lime kilns up to 100 feet in height; and the possibility that new methods of working, specially designed to contain the spread of such problems, could directly conflict with other goals, such as the preservation of water quality. John Blunden has concluded that:

'. . . unless rapid advances are made in overcoming the problems of sub-water excavations or deep-mining the conflicts arising from continued surface working of limestone to meet estimated demand by the end of the century, are likely to be of the utmost gravity.'[6]

In areas where limestone, sand and gravel supplies are short, sandstones and igneous rocks have been increasingly quarried as aggregate, and have contributed further to an extensive pattern of deep pits with low reclamation potential.

66

Lime quarry and kiln at Batts Combe, Somerset. (Photograph: Amey Roadstone Corporation Ltd.)

The extraction of china clay, Britain's major mineral export, also poses intractable difficulties of restoration. In this case, however, the problem is not one of a shortage of suitable filling material. Some 8 to 10 tons of waste are produced for every ton of saleable product, and about 25 million tons of waste are dumped next to the workings every year in tips that reach 150 feet in height. But restoration is not simply a matter of shoving tips into holes, as the Civic Trust noted in 1964; the uniqueness of the deposits and their often great depths, frequently militate against the filling and restoration of currently unworked, but bountiful pits. Moreover, many customers of the china clay industries require delivered products of increasingly fine specification for their own refined technologies, which has meant that a large number of pits, with deposits of different quality, have to be kept open to guarantee the future availability of clays for complex product blends. This and the trebling of china clay output since the war produced a unique landscape in the working areas of Devon and Cornwall. Steep-sided pits, some being worked and others not in use, can be as much as 350 feet deep. Clusters of conical or elongated tips of waste surround the pits. Tracts of neglected land not yet worked, or land sterilised for other uses by having fallen

Typical sand and gravel extraction activities. (Photograph: Amey Roadstone Corporation Ltd.)

within the industry's 'Consultation Areas' are all too evident.* One such area alone, near St. Austell, covers 20,000 acres, and within its long-term development plan the industry has envisaged a quadrupling of its land requirements within the area.

The effects of coal mining

While the restoration of open-cast coal and ironstone production is enforceable by legislation, it is difficult to find any records of restoration technology which match the progress made in extractive technology used for open methods of working. Technological development in other methods of mineral working has also had a serious impact upon Britain's land. Deep mining of coal, for example, has undergone major technological changes since the war, particularly in the mechanisation of cutting and coal preparation, and in the extension of the 'longwall' method of mining. In both cases, technological and productivity gains have brought substantial environmental losses. Mechanisation at the coal face and pithead, in conjunction with the working of poorer seams, has gradually increased the proportion of waste to saleable coal brought to the surface, from 1 part waste to 5 parts saleable down to 1 to 1.25 at some of the most recently opened pits; about 60 million tons of waste are brought to the surface annually for disposal. In the early 1970s, the National Coal Board was disposing of 65 per cent of its 'land-dumped' wastes on tips not subject to

* 'Consultation Areas' are zones within which further reserves of the mineral occur, and where all proposals for development are automatically referred by the local planning authority to the china clay industry for comments; disputes are referred onward to the Secretary of State for the Environment.

China clay workings near St. Austell in Cornwall create a landscape that could be part of a Jules Verne novel. (Photograph: Aerofilms Ltd.)

planning control, and although this proportion is now decreasing, the industry has fully exploited a freedom which has resulted in thousand of acres of untidy and rubbish-strewn landscapes.

Over 35,000 acres of land now lies sterilised beneath coal tips, with a further 700 acres being added every year. As the cost of oil continues to rise and less accessible coal reserves become economic to mine, individual counties will inevitably face difficulties in meeting the land requirements demanded by the coal industry. By the end of the 1970s the Vale of Belvoir and the South Downs were two of the many potential new coal mining areas of Britain whose landscapes faced the worrying effects of the impact of not only extensive open-cast workings, but more seriously the disposal of bulky quantities of coal waste. In 1966, for example, when 2,200 acres of Nottinghamshire were covered by spoil heaps created from all kinds of mineral workings, it was estimated that a further 12,500 acres would have to be found by the end of the century for the annual disposal of 13 million tons of coal waste alone:

'. . . *although the . . . newest collieries have been built entirely within the context of planning controls, the planning authorities' power to insist upon the shaping and planting of new heaps is insufficient to deal with the main problem when such large quantities of waste are involved.*'[7]

Seven million tons of coal waste are disposed of commercially each year by the recently formed Minestone Executive, and yet the planning system has insufficient power to persuade the National Coal Board to consider the possibility of 'backstowage' of waste, to lessen the destructive effects of its operations upon land. Although this system of filling tunnels immediately after exhaustion is widely used in western Europe, no thorough analysis of its advantages and costs has been published by the National Coal Board. Such an analysis, had it been made, should certainly have incorporated the extensive costs of subsidence to local communities. Again it is modern techniques rather than primitive practices that have been responsible for increased damage to the land, encouraged in no small measure by legislation which in Kenneth Wallwork's opinion 'set the seal of responsibility on coal-mining subsidence'.[8]

By allowing compensation for damage at the surface, rather than seeking to remove its cause, the 1950 and 1957 Coal Mining (Subsidence) Acts also gave powers to the National Coal Board to impose stringent construction standards on new development in areas likely to be affected by subsidence. Land threatened by subsidence is effectively sterilised for development purposes for 10 years after mining ceases. Compensation for damage caused by subsidence can only represent a fraction of the total costs to the community in terms of land taken out of active use either for urban development or agricultural purposes.

Brine pumping*
Another illustration of the way in which planning control has been overtaken by technological change comes from the brine-pumping industry of Cheshire, and from the failure of the former Ministry of Town and Country Planning and Cheshire County Council to anticipate the degree of subsidence likely to be created when granting extensive permissions for working by older extractive techniques in the early 1950s. Once established, this 'natural brine-pumping' method has been freely used to meet rising demand from the local chemical industry, with the local authority standing by almost powerless to impose conditions concerning subsidence, even though it knows that a costlier, 'controlled pumping' method would by comparison cause little or no known subsidence problems. Consequently, the local authority faces an extension of the 'yellow area' defined by the Brine Pumping Compensation Board, within which there is a higher risk of subsidence, and within which development can proceed only after consultation with the Board. The Brine Pumping (Compensation for Subsidence) Acts of 1891 and 1952 have, as in similar legislation for coal mining, cushioned extractors against the true costs of their activities.

The controversy of mineral land
Although the 13,000 acres of land a year being taken by the mineral industries in the 1970s is comparable with the 12,000 acres a year estimated for the late 1940s, significant changes have occurred within these totals. According to the Civic Trust, in 1958 open-cast extraction of coal and ironstone in England and Wales was taking

---

* The removal of solid salt from below the ground by steam and liquid pumping processes. The salt is used in certain chemical industries and bulk uses such as treatment of roads during icy weather.

Open-cast coal mining and modern forestry near Glyn Neath in Wales have an uncompromising effect upon the landscape. (Photograph: Coal News)

7,300 acres of land each year, of which over 95 per cent was restored to productive use after completion of working.[9] By 1977, the proportion of land taken annually had dropped from 7,300 acres to 5,000 acres, having fallen considerably lower in the intervening period. On the other hand, expansion in the production of minerals for aggregate had more than doubled its land requirements, from 2,700 acres to more than 6,100 acres annually during the same 20 years. Sand and gravel production,

71

Slate workings at Blaenau Ffestiniog, Wales. (Photograph: Aerofilms Ltd.)

Fletton brickfields interrupt an otherwise flat and featureless landscape near Peterborough, Cambridgeshire. (Photograph: Aerofilms Ltd.)

which now consumes an estimated 5,000 acres of land every year, is becoming increasingly reliant upon sub-water workings for its output. As a result, more than 2,000 acres of agricultural land are converted annually to permanent water. Equally, where chalk and the hard rock aggregate minerals demanded 800 acres of land each year in the late 1950s, the figure has now almost doubled, the single constant factor being that 3 per cent of the land only has consistently been restored. Consequently by the end of the 1970s at least half of the land used for mineral workings was being left unrestored every year. It is a salutary thought that in most cases the expanding mineral industries are taking land permanently out of agricultural use or are inflicting irreversible damage upon its amenity value. The figure for unrestored land is compounding annually and together with the rising cost of restoration is building up a massive financial debt which will one day have to be met by society.

The problem of land left blighted by mineral working is therefore an escalating one, accumulating over decades of industrial expansion and, more recently, of inadequate planning controls. The statistics on derelict land collected annually by the Ministry of Housing and Local Government (MHLG) and the Welsh Office from 1964-71 confirmed this trend, notwithstanding the intervening efforts at restoration made by local and central Government. The area of land lying officially derelict in England and Wales increased at an average of 2,550 acres annually during the period 1964-71, despite the fact that restoration was running at an annual average of nearly 3,100 acres. If official total estimates of 18,000 derelict acres in Wales and 17,000 in Scotland are added to the 114,000 acres for England, it would appear that the total area of derelict land in Britain at the beginning of the 1970s constituted 150,000 acres. At the average annual restoration levels of the period 1971-8 it would take over 22 years to clear the existing stock of dereliction, even if no further additions were made to it.[10] However the inadequacy in the definition of dereliction used over the years by the Department of the Environment, and discussed in Chapter 4 above, cannot be ignored. In the late 1960s both the West Riding of Yorkshire and Bedfordshire surveys suggested that the area of disused 'spoiled and degraded' land was $2\frac{1}{2}$ times greater than that recorded by central Government statistics. The area 'officially' derelict in Bedfordshire in 1968 was 619 acres compared with the local authority estimate of 1,400 acres; in the 1974 Department of Environment survey, the figure for dereliction in the county had fallen to 225 acres, although the actual area of degraded land is likely to have increased considerably. In this context it is worth recalling that reclamation grants are available only for land within the officially defined derelict figure.

The seriousness of the cumulative effects of three decades of inadequate controls was revealed in a survey undertaken for the Stevens Committee, and reproduced in its 1976 report, *Planning Control over Mineral Working*. Almost one-third of the area worked under the permissions granted since 1943 was likely to become derelict because of inadequate restoration conditions. Nearly two-thirds of the area, where mineral working had terminated and where the original planning permission contained requirements for restoration, still remained unrestored. It may be true that some small proportion of these areas has been restored subsequently by other agencies, or has been weathered into a more acceptable condition by the processes of nature. However, two conclusions can be drawn from the findings of the Stevens Committee:

There can be no excuse for leaving abandoned, damaged mineral extraction land...

74

. . . when the scale of modern earth moving machinery and geological knowledge can help to reclaim despoiled landscapes in a spectacular and effortless way. (Photograph: Lancashire County Planning Department)

dereliction resulting from earlier planning permissions granted particularly during the first decade after the war, will continue to accumulate as long as local planning authorities are unwilling to risk or even incur massive compensation claims from operators whose planning permissions are either amended or revoked; and

although some mineral operators may restore land from goodwill, or for public relations purposes, the inadequate advice and resources made available to mineral operators from local authorities or central Government represents a missed opportunity of further restoration.

It is evident from the 1974 *Survey of Derelict and Despoiled Land in England* that nearly 32,000 acres will probably become derelict because no restoration conditions whatsoever had been included in permissions up to that time. Moreover, a further very considerable area of dereliction will inevitably accumulate as a result of inadequate restoration conditions, or the failure of planning authorities to ensure that conditions are adhered to by mineral operators. It is becoming vitally important for central Government to make available to local authorities the expertise necessary for drafting, monitoring and enforcing planning conditions concerning restoration:

'. . . amongst county council staff associated with planning control over mineral working we met only one mining Engineer . . no mineral Surveyors, no experienced mine or quarry managers, none with the practical knowledge of mineral economies . . . [it] was quite clear to us that many of the past failures of planning control in relation to mineral working were directly attributable to lack of necessary professional skills in local planning staffs, and that many failures would continue to occur unless this lack was remedied.'[11]

Even if expertise were made available to planning authorities, the major recommendation on planning procedure, that of introducing a quinquennial review of planning conditions in the light of changing operating circumstances and of individual operators' records of compliance with conditions, is likely to have little effect on dereliction arising from current permissions, because any new conditions imposed would have to be based on the operators' agreement as to the 'reasonableness' of their cost. Indeed, if the recommendations of the Stevens Committee on the extension of 'consultation areas' and of 'buffer zones' between workings and incompatible development are acted upon, the outcome is likely to be an extension in the area of sterilised land. The creation of temporary dereliction through the suspension of workings on individual sites is a trend which will increase as economic forces favour production at fewer, larger sites and the holding of partially worked or unworked sites as reserves, referred to as 'operational land' whether it is tended or left derelict.

Although the output of most of the mineral extraction industries with high rates of increase in production has levelled off in the last 5 years, the pressure to work other minerals with extravagant land requirements, such as copper and oil shale, is likely to re-emerge as world and local scarcities develop.* Arguments of national or local interest will be liberally rehearsed over every major proposal for more mineral extraction, even though central Government has still to clarify the wider responsibilities of mineral operators. In particular, responsibility for the restoration of workings has not yet been clearly apportioned to operators, even though such foreknowledge would help to reduce the cost of restoration.

John Oxenham whose original work in 1948 was born of years of experience of the achievements, failures and possibilities of reclamation summarised the situation in 1970:

> '*On the grounds of equity, there is no doubt that those who created the dereliction should remedy it. The costs of reclamation should be a charge upon the industry concerned and any contribution or grant made by the state should be recognised as what it really is – a subsidy to the industry. If the working of any mineral cannot bear the expenses of land rehabilitation then it is submitted that the conservation of land and amenity demands that the mineral should not be extracted.*[12]

Oxenham's conclusions are more relevant than ever. So a sensible and practical suggestion made by John Barr for a National Land Reclamation Agency with a fixed, long-term budget, and for a minimal restoration levy on all mineral operators, is still worth considering. Mineral excavation has a serious impact upon land and the countryside, and will come progressively into conflict with farming as lower grade, more dispersed mineral deposits become increasingly economic to mine. However, the mineral industry is only one of the many conflicts within the countryside which is resulting in idle and derelict acres.

---

* The Zuckerman Commission's *Report on Mining and Environment*, 1972, indicated that a hypothetical open-cast copper working might have a landtake of 1,500 to 3,000 acres over a working life of 15 years; the pit would almost certainly be unrestorable. In addition, the Government paper *U.K. Oil Shales*, Past and Possible Future Exploitation, 1975, estimated that working in the Kimmeridge oil shale deposits over 30 years would require nearly 14,000 acres of high quality land for working areas and shale dumps.

Notes

1. Department of the Environment, *Survey of Derelict and Despoiled Land in England 1974,* HMSO, 1975, Tables 51 and 52
2. Statistics taken from the Department of the Environment, *Digest of Pollution Statistics No. 2,* HMSO, 1979 and *Progress in Pollution Control: Pollution Paper No. 16, the UK Environment,* HMSO, 1979
3. K. Wallwork, *Derelict Land—Origins and Prospects of a Land-Use Problem,* David and Charles, 1974, p.185
4. J. Blunden, *The Mineral Resources of Britain,* Hutchinson, 1975, p.62
5. *ibid.* p.92
6. *ibid.* p.100
7. *ibid.* p.62
8. Wallwork, *op. cit.* p.185
9. The Civic Trust, *Derelict Land,* 1964, pp.21-24
10. *Progress in Pollution Control, op.cit.*
11. *Planning Control over Mineral Working,* Report of the Committee under the Chairmanship of Sir Roger Stevens, HMSO, 1976, pp.203-8
12. J.R. Oxenham, 'Land Reclamation', *Journal of the Institution of Municipal Engineers,* 1970, pp.264-7

CHAPTER 6

Conflict in the Countryside

'The total area of land in the United Kingdom is about 47,000,000 acres. Between 1971 and 1978 the average recorded loss of land from agriculture was about 125,000 acres a year. About half, mainly of poorer quality and in Scotland, was transferred to forestry and woodland. The remainder went to urban, industrial, highway and recreational uses and other purposes. Better quality land, because it is usually fairly flat and well-drained, often tends to be lost to this kind of development. There is, however, uncertainty about the area and quality of the land that has been transferred to urban use and action is being taken to obtain better information about land going out of agricultural use.'

Farming and the Nation, *Government White Paper, 1979*

The dilemma

Britain produces little over half of her own food needs, relying for the remainder, in the past, upon relatively cheap produce from the Commonwealth countries, and more recently upon other food-exporting areas like America, Holland and the tropics. Looking towards the future, there are signs that we may be unable to rely upon such a high level of food imports, as other nations cease to be food exporters and as imports become progressively more scarce and expensive. It seems inevitable that unless we produce considerably more food from our present land stocks, change our dietary habits, bring further areas of land into efficient agricultural use, reduce the present rate of farmland loss to urban development and harness the food-producing potential of our oceans, we will be forced to join the long queues waiting for dwindling supplies at the world food market.

On present trends, the outlook is bleak. Demand for food is expected to increase world-wide by 10 per cent before the end of the century, as populations grow and as developing countries are increasingly able to compete for available food supplies. In 1975 the Club of Rome, an international group of world renowned specialists in subjects relating to human survival, together with the Food and Agriculture Organisation of the United Nations, warned that future food supplies per head would decline and would be insufficient to meet the demands of a rapidly growing world population. It is therefore not unreasonable to assume that food and farmland are perhaps destined to become the world's most scarce and valuable resources during the coming years, particularly in countries like Britain where population density is high and where good quality farmland covers little over a third of the total land surface.

Productive British farmland is being lost to non-agricultural use each year at a rate equivalent in area to the County of Gloucestershire every five years; of this figure

(Photograph: Architectural Press Ltd.)

TABLE 4   AGRICULTURAL LAND AREA BY GRADE

Agri-cultural land classifi-cation grades*	England		Wales		Scotland		Northern Ireland		UK	
	000s of acres	%	000s of acres	%	000s of acres	%	000s of acres	%	000s of acres	%
1	806	3·3	8	0·2	49	0·3	-	-	863	1·8
2	4,083	16·7	96	2·3	383	2·4	89	3·3	4,651	9·8
3	13,203	54·0	729	17·5	2,175	13·6	1,128	42·0	17,235	36·4
4	3,838	15·7	1,842	44·2	1,631	10·2	1,313	49·0	8,624	18·3
5	2,518	10·3	1,491	35·8	11,775	73·5	153	5·7	15,937	33·7
Total †	24,448	100·0	4,166	100·0	16,013	100·0	2,683	100·0	47,310	100·0

* Ministry of Agriculture, Fisheries and Food grades for England and Wales; Scottish and Northern Ireland equivalents.

† Not all figures add due to rounding.

Source: Agriculture into the 80s – Land use, Agriculture Economic Development Council, NEDO, 1977, page 5, Table 2.

TABLE 5   AGRICULTURAL LAND USE CLASSIFICATION FOR ENGLAND AND WALES

Grade 1   Land with very minor or no physical limitations to agricultural use. Capable of growing most crops including the more exacting horticultural crops.

Grade 2   Land with some minor limitations which exclude it from Grade 1. Capable of growing a wide range of crops.

Grade 3   Land with moderate limitations due to the soil, relief or climate, or some combination of these factors which restrict the choice of crops, timing, cultivation or level of yield. Grass and cereals are usually the principal crops:

Subdivisions   (a)   better production than (b)
(b)   average production
(c)   poorer production than (b)

Grade 4   Land with severe limitations due to adverse soil, relief or climate or a combination of these. Generally only suitable for low output enterprises.

Grade 5   Land generally under grass or rough grazing, except for pioneer forage crops and including land unfit for vegetation such as bare rock outcrop.

almost one-third is lost permanently to urban development, a high proportion of this loss occurring at the urban fringes. Agriculturists feel that the problem lies in the quality of farmland which is being lost, rather than its quantity. In some parts of the country the loss of top quality farmland (Grades 1 and 2 of the official agricultural land classification and their equivalent in Scotland), has been disproportionately high, despite the fact that these grades constitute only 12 per cent of Britain's farmland and are vital to food production.[1]

Towards the end of the 1970s, growing concern over the rate at which farmland was being transferred to other uses was not shared by everyone. Robin Best, a leading land-use statistician, suggested that the problem was 'simply in the mind; it is not out there on the ground'.[2] Best argued that other European countries like the Netherlands, Belgium and East Germany, with higher population densities than Britain, were releasing a higher proportion of land to non-farming uses. Pro-European commentators argued that the vast land resources of our European partners were more than adequate to meet our needs. Others suggested that even the smallest changes in our dietary intake could reduce significantly the demand for food, which could be assisted by the agricultural community working towards more specific types of production. In short the various protagonists were arguing that the conservation of farmland was only one of a number of 'food-producing' alternatives open to us. Total self-sufficiency in Britain under our present dietary habits is just not possible. 20 per cent of the major foodstuffs on which we rely cannot be grown in Britain. So at best we may be able to achieve between 70 and 80 per cent self-sufficiency and even this would require extensive investment and rationalising of land uses and patterns of ownership among smaller farm holdings.

The Government has, since the last War, encouraged greater self-sufficiency through subsidies for production of particular commodities, a policy that was further reaffirmed in the 1979 White Paper, *Farming and the Nation*. Greater home production of livestock and dairy products would reduce the high cost of imports, particularly now that cheap supplies from the Commonwealth are no longer available. Britain, after all, has a climate well-suited to the production of rich grasses and therefore to the rearing of animals, which should play a vital role in future agricultural development policies. It would be possible for a quarter of the food imported to be produced at home, given more economically favourable conditions for farmers to do so. However this degree of expansion and intensification cannot take place without increasing conflict with other land users.

Modern agricultural techniques, used to keep pace with food demand, have resulted in the loss of a quarter of all Britain's hedges since the war, and by 1979 an estimated 3,000 miles were being grubbed-up annually. Since 1945 one-third of all hedgerows, trees and small woodlands have disappeared. The forestry industry produces only 8 per cent of Britain's timber needs and has seen the loss of thousands of acres of private forests in recent years, and 6.5 million elm trees during the ten year period after the outbreak of elm disease in 1969. In addition traditional drystone walls and old farm buildings have grown increasingly redundant and derelict.

The dilemma, however, is wider than a debate on the loss of agricultural land, hedgerows and trees, and the increase in derelict structures. The countryside today is an arena of competing interests between food and fibre production, forestry and wildlife conservation, recreation, water storage, housing, mineral extraction and

Modern agriculture has brought building shapes and field sizes that are often in conflict with the traditionally accepted image of the countryside. (Photograph: Farmers' Weekly)

other local industries. The effect of this competition upon the traditional landscape is often severe, as Nan Fairbrother reminds us:

'To many of us in Britain our countryside is the most beautiful landscape in the world: farms and villages and local towns; fields, woods, leafy lanes, changing coasts and open hills – all evolved as a varied and harmonious whole by a long living-together of man and nature in a gentle climate. But the modern world is now destroying this countryside inherited from the past; exploding the towns, swamping the villages, tearing up the farmland and splattering the old harmonious landscape with alien intrusions.'[3]

Changing agricultural techniques

At the beginning of this century British farming was 41 per cent self-sufficient, providing food for 15 million people. Today agriculture feeds almost 27 million people and is 46 per cent self-sufficient. British farming is one of Europe's most efficient industries. Food production has, since the turn of the century, doubled, and yet it has barely been able to maintain the early levels of self-sufficiency because of a relentlessly rising population. Agriculture has been a victim of diminishing returns, particularly since the 1947 Agriculture Act. In addition, rising expectations of quality and choice, the increasing rate at which each of us has been consuming food, and the continuous loss of farmland means that agriculture will continue to chase an elusive target. British farming contributes $2\frac{1}{2}$ per cent of the gross domestic product and is paralleled in the efficiency of its labour only by the electrical industries. Since 1950 the agricultural gross product in Britain has increased by 75 per cent, while the work force employed directly on the land has fallen by less than half — to about $2\frac{1}{2}$ per cent of the nation's working population. This figure rises to 10 per cent if employment created by all the associated agricultural service industries is also taken into account.

Investment in new agricultural technology and farm buildings has enabled farmers to maintain, with startling success, the agricultural momentum of the immediate post-war years. Over this period, production has been carried out on a shrinking factory floor with a declining labour force. This phenomenon has come about through considerable changes in agricultural techniques since 1947, which have enabled farming to emerge from a depressed and declining business into an increasingly commercial and profitable industry. These changes have emerged as a result of a combination of factors including new forms of energy, capital investment, improved labour productivity and management. The majority of energy has now ceased to be supplied by horses and human muscle, as important fossil fuels have taken over. The number of tractors in use has increased significantly since the War and other more recent types of sophisticated machinery have been able to carry out an increasing variety of tasks. Mechanisation has assisted this remarkable increase in labour productivity, which during the 1970s was rising by 7 per cent a year — twice the rate of the rest of the economy. Today's farm worker is no longer regarded as a general hand, but an increasingly skilled operative. While there is less drudgery in farming today, there are also less workers.

'When I started in 1929, a 250 acre farm would have eight workers, now a 2,000 acre farm has the same number.'[4]

Capital investment has also meant new buildings for intensive production, such as poultry units for as many as 20,000 birds or 'zero' grazing houses with bought-in feed for permanently enclosed animals, pig farms and milking units; this in turn has led to farm amalgamations. By the end of the 1970s a third of all farm holdings were over 300 acres in size, with 17 per cent of all holdings producing 60 per cent of agricultural output. Management changes have also transformed agriculture into a more commercial undertaking, increasing production and redirecting investment. The profitability of modern farming in lowland areas has been the outcome of the Government's continuous support since 1947 and has made Britain one of the most highly organised and advanced agricultural nations in the world.

Lowland progress

The 1947 Agriculture Act did much to smooth out the fluctuations, depressions, instability and stagnation that had plagued British farming until the war years. This Government aid was a response to the waste and dereliction wrought by the inter-war agricultural depression in particular, when prime farmland was sold off at minimal prices for urban development, leading to wasteful and over-spacious sprawl and ribbon development. The depression had also resulted in extensive areas of farmland being left uncared for and virtually derelict. New technology, structural capital and management changes have transformed lowland agriculture over the last 30 years, and Government moves during the 1970s to improve the level of self-sufficiency emphasised the importance of agriculture to the national economy. By 1980 lowland areas showed considerable evidence of progress. Mixed farms have given way to specialised concentrated units with arable activities dominating the

The rural economy is no longer able to survive on farming and forestry alone. Tourism, leisure and other non-agricultural industries, and commuting and second-home activities are all relatively dominant new roles that rural communities are assuming. While these activities may bring social conflict and argument over the use of land and buildings, they have enabled many communities to survive change. Long Parish, Hampshire. (Photograph: John Topham Picture Library)

south-east and east of Britain and livestock production much in evidence in the north and west. Chemicals have replaced the function of agricultural rotation. Larger units are being farmed more intensively with more business expertise by farmers using a diminishing labour force. Agricultural service industries and associated businesses have been located in market towns or on the edges of large urban centres rather than in the smaller rural settlements.

Traditional communities have been the cause of concern since the middle of the 1970s. Unable to rely upon farming or forestry for their social and economic well-being, they have gradually changed and expanded into commuter or tourist centres. Elsewhere, rural settlements have had difficulty in finding their new roles, particularly in the more remote or less accessible areas, where populations tend to be predominantly aged and possessing few younger generation residents to add life and diversity. Even in the richest agricultural areas like the fenlands, where 'alien' land owners such as major retail houses and pension funds find agricultural land an attractive investment, rural communities have found change difficult to accept. The headmaster of an East Anglian village school remarked that when he walked down the street the faces he saw were those of his slower pupils. In these areas, often readily accessible to a large town, 'tradition has people by the throat, whilst agricultural mechanisation is emptying the land'.[5]

Planned expansion and the emergence of official structure plans have brought pressures for the transfer of increasing areas of land from agriculture into housing, roads, services and industry, particularly around selected key settlements, into which essential services, investment and people have flowed, often at the expense of

84

outlying rural communities. By the end of the 70s Britain's rural communities were facing a prospect of growth or decline and in many areas were being regarded as wasting investments of land, people and buildings.

Despite the plight of many communities, agriculture has tended to prosper, particularly in rural areas with good communications where mobility of labour and the inherent natural qualities of land have been most evident. Urban development has been significantly slower in areas where these conditions are deficient. The lowlands are often equally suited to urban development and agriculture and these contrasting demands have led to severe land-use conflicts. Some of the best quality land in England and Wales is located on the edges of urban areas where these conflicts are at their most severe. In the past, planning authorities have not always taken sufficient account of the quality of agricultural land as a factor in the control of urban development, and if present trends continue the future could be even more problematic:

'If present economic conditions persist, authorities are likely to be more than usually attracted to land which is least costly to develop (i.e. farmland of higher quality).'[6]

Not only does development take land out of agriculture around the edges of towns and cities, but it also affects the efficiency of surrounding farmland because of the fragmentation of land uses, and the increase of dereliction, trespass and vandalism. Lowland farmers caught in this situation are frequently the smaller landowners, rarely able to acquire a similar holding elsewhere in a more dominant agricultural area. They cannot readily leave farming. Not only do they have to change their occupation, but they may also have to learn another business and redirect their investments in a totally different way. Urban fringe farmers are often as vulnerable as their upland counterparts caught in a spiral of decline, one from urban pressures, the other from a tradition of hardship and isolation.

Upland decline

Problems of lowland farming, as we have seen, frequently relate to conflicts of over-development; the problems of upland farming, however, are far more concerned with lack of development. While the lowlands have prospered, the hills have been left behind; they have rarely been able to take advantage of modern agricultural technology; soils, climate, orientation, land form and access are so often against productive use of the uplands.

Hill farming can no longer support communities in the way that it has done in the past. Although improvements in communications and income from agriculture have occurred, upland areas have so often been caught in a vicious spiral of depopulation, declining services and a general lack of improvement in agricultural resources. As a result land has become increasingly uncared-for and uneconomic:

'It is clear that in many parts the outstanding problem is that of size of the hill farms. Although the average size is increasing, these farms are very often too small to afford a satisfactory living to their present occupiers and their families; still less an attractive prospect for the next generation of hill farmers.'[7]

In a bid to make better use of the frequently underused and wasting uplands, the

Despite a mixture of farming, forestry and grant-aid, the uplands remain a difficult landscape to work efficiently and productively. Poor climate, orientation, soil and drainage together with excessive slope, rocky outcrop and remoteness contribute to the problems of working the land and living in the uplands. (Photograph: John Porteous)

Government called in 1965 for integration of land for agriculture and forestry in the hills, so that these activities could become complementary and not antagonistic to one another. But this was more easily said than done, for there are social problems of loneliness, poverty and relentless hard work in a difficult climate, which add to the existing problems of inhabiting and working the uplands. The situation has become even less attractive as urban comforts have drawn people from the uplands. The Select Committee on Scottish Affairs in 1972 had no illusions as to the importance of hill farming in providing initial grazing land for livestock destined for the lowland livestock markets. However, it conceded that the social justification for communities to continue in the hills is far less forcible.[8] The hill farmer is expected to rear sheep, and also cattle if he is fortunate, on minimum quality grazing land, with little if any arable land to assist with animal feed. All too often the difference between the hill farmer continuing his often precarious occupation or turning his land over to forestry or the claims of wilderness, lies in his ability to judge the fine line between the physical potential of the land and the economic return this will bring. An understanding of this relationship distinguishes the successful upland farmer from his less successful neighbour; distinguishes a tidy, ever-changing upland farmscape from an expanding wilderness. Increasing numbers of upland farmers and hill populations have, particularly since the last war, turned away from full-time agriculture, supplementing their income from other sources such as forestry, tourism, or, where possible, industrial work. In the Scottish Highlands, for example, 96 per cent of all crofts are farmed on a part-time basis with 80 per cent entailing less than two days work a week. Managing second homes and holiday flats, operating caravan sites and pony-trekking, for example, provide a significant portion of income to the upland residents in National Park areas.

Despite grants and subsidies for agriculture in these less favoured areas, hill farming in its present form is rarely attractive to coming generations. The future of the uplands cannot rely upon farming alone. Modern agricultural practices involving high capital investment for high value and intensive output has made the traditional hill farming system of low investment for low output on extensive areas of poor land increasingly uneconomic. Flocks of sheep tend to be restricted to lower or more productive land; the more extensive grazings on poorer highland ground are often abandoned to rough grasses, bracken and wilderness. Large areas of hill land are particularly suitable for sheep rearing, and in many cases this is the only agricultural role of the uplands. The loss of such hill land to wilderness or tourism means that there is inevitably a greater pressure for grazing upon existing farmland, which is generally of better quality and more suitable for intensive forms of agriculture.

The Government views hill farming also as a significant contribution to the saving of imports and as a valuable reservoir of land. If hill farming continues to decline then progressively more capital investment will be required to bring the hills back into productive use in the future. Current priorities given to farming activities in the uplands by regional aid and the EEC's Common Agricultural Policy are difficult to justify without equivalent or greater social assistance. Without new employment whole regions may cease to be viable and the hills could become unpopulated in many of the more remote areas — a process that has been evident in Highland Scotland, mid-Wales and the moorlands and dales in central and northern England.

No single source of income from either agriculture, forestry or tourism can provide a prosperous and satisfactory future for residents of the hills. The possibilities of planned integration of a number of uses in the uplands enabling agriculture, forestry, wildlife conservation and water storage to co-exist side by side, have been considered. Such proposals have the advantage of drawing upon the potential of productive hill land and the more remote unproductive areas. Integrated land uses and new forms of employment may be able to break the vicious cycle of decline and depression which agriculture alone cannot alleviate. However, there is considerable evidence that integrated upland uses are economically unviable and are rarely a commercial proposition within any one of the individual uses.[9]

As a result of declining farming in the uplands and urban growth and increased leisure activity in the lowlands, lowland agriculture is caught in a series of pressures that reduce the effective area of high quality agricultural land use. Farmland lost to urban growth, leisure and tourism together with non-viable upland activities, are all leading to an increasingly centralised farming activity, focussed upon the fertile lowland areas and inevitably sharing the spotlight with competing urban develop-

Diminishing public expenditure and public transport facilities are emphasising the problems of remoteness and poor accessibility, not only in the uplands, but in a growing number of lowland areas. (Photograph: Gus Wylie)

ment. However, the working countryside does not end with the uplands. Wilderness, once regarded as a 'wasting asset' is now coveted as an area least affected by the hand of man, where flora and fauna co-exist in an almost natural state, rarely reached by pesticide or fertiliser, bulldozer or plough and frequently far enough away from urban centres to ensure that only the dedicated visitor breaks the peace and quiet of this truly rural landscape.

Wilderness in plenty?

As urban development has steadily polluted the habited countryside through more people, cars, chemicals, fumes, industry and all manner of buildings, so wilderness has achieved a value that is difficult to quantify, that is until threatened by change. In his eloquent Reith Lectures in 1969, Sir Fraser Darling observed:

'Natural wilderness is a factor for world stability, not some remote place inimical to the human being. It is strange that it has been so long a place of fear to many men and so something to hate and destroy. Wilderness is not remote or indifferent but an active agent in maintaining a habitable world, though the co-operation is unconscious. Only we are conscious of what we are doing and capable of forecasting the consequences.' [10]

Wilderness has not always escaped unchanged. In many areas it has fluctuated between the temporary grazing of hill farm and a vast wildlife habitat. Subjected to agricultural activities such as heather burning, it has developed a unique, often ecologically valuable semi-natural vegetation, providing a museum of the nearest thing we have in Britain to wild original plant and animal communities. Moorland areas in particular are now becoming the focus of increasing attention and conflict as Lord Porchester's 1977 study of Exmoor indicated:

'It seems inappropriate for a Government department to be dispensing grants to farmers to enable them to so improve moorland pasture that it loses its characteristics of wildness.'[11]

Fraser Darling also believes that wilderness exists as something unique. He emphasised in his Reith Lectures that its intrinsic value must be preserved at all costs for we need it more than we realise, as long as we have dense urban conurbations. This view is certainly supported by leading ecologists and ramblers who value the natural wildlife and landscape of these areas, from the towering cliffs of the Western Highlands, with golden eagle and osprey, to the wind-swept tangles of briar and gorse of the Dorset heaths. However there are those who consider that we cannot afford such luxury. It has been suggested that the hills provide an endless stock of land that could solve our forestry problems. Agriculture may be unsuccessful there, it is argued, but trees can be grown. It is true that this would help to reduce Britain's 92 per cent dependence upon imported timber and also relieve pressures upon marginal food-producing farmland for use as commercial forest. Mineral extractors and water undertakers remove land from wilderness areas from time to time. But development, no matter how small, changes the nature of wilderness and moorland, which then cannot be quickly replaced. The conflict between the value of wilderness for forestry, water storage or mineral extraction and its value for wild plants, animals and natural beauty, is an issue that will continue to absorb society in the future. Can we afford such areas devoted to non-economic activities; are they a luxury or a necessity? Wilderness may not be economically productive at the moment and is, in economic terms, a wasting resource — but despite present and future demands from forestry, agriculture and other users of land, wilderness provides at worst a strategic reserve against the inefficiency of official forecasting or the failure of foreign food markets, and at best a glorious bounty for man's enjoyment of nature. However, we may be unable to keep our options open for more than a short period of time. Demands for forestry are increasing and faced with an official policy for greater self-sufficiency in home timber production, forestry land will have to be found from somewhere. It seems likely that increasing areas of wilderness will become commercial forest.

Trees for the wood

The need to expand home production of timber relates to a long history of dependence upon imported wood. The first serious attempts to replenish timber stocks with plantations came in the 1700s, after centuries of deforestation and reduction of supplies. Lack of confidence and better returns from our investments such as railways and industry led to a decline in British forestry until by the First World War, Britain was importing 93 per cent of the nation's timber needs. Since the creation of the Forestry Commission in 1919, the Government has been encouraging expansion of forests and has offered tax incentives to private forestry.

Despite recent changes in taxation through capital transfer tax, forestry can still represent an attractive investment to those who would otherwise pay a high tax, and a number of forestry companies have been established which specialise in this form of investment. Tax changes, however, have had a greater effect on the small owner-occupier with cash flow problems and it is expected that future policies may try to assist development in this area. The original aim of the Foresty Commission was to achieve a target of 5 million acres of forest by the year 2,000. Planting and land acquisition rates of 96,000 acres per annum fell during the 1970s to 50,000 acres and it seems unlikely that the Commission will be able to reach its original target. A further complication lies in the rising demand for timber, which means that afforestation rates must double for Britain to remain at the same level of self-sufficiency by the end of the century. But difficulties in obtaining suitable land have lowered the rate of planting. It is also possible that rising land prices may make it uneconomic for land to be bought outright and new schemes may have to be devised. One possible solution may be to encourage wood leasing, by which the Forestry Commission could rent land for timber production, paying the landowner a regular income, rated to the eventual sale value of the crop.

At present over two-thirds of Britain's production is softwood, which meets barely 1½ per cent of the overall timber demand. Of the hardwood demand, 25 per cent comes from home supplies, while the loss of hedgerows has seriously affected home-production of low-grade hardwood. Most supplies of high quality hardwood for furniture or other special uses, come from imports, because the time scales involved in maturing hardwood (often over 120 years in Britain) are more favourable financially in countries such as France. However, hardwoods are rapidly being replaced in furniture manufacture by softwoods and imported composition boards.

Silhouetted against the snow – climbers descend the Cairngorms after having taken on one of Britain's toughest and most popular wilderness areas. (Photograph: John Cleare/Mountain Camera)

90

Expansion of British production is likely to be in coniferous softwood, which is particularly suitable for pulp composition panels and veneers. Increasing world demand for timber and rising prices of diminishing stocks meant that by the 1970s tropical forests were being felled at the rate of 75 acres a minute or 35 million acres a year. Under these circumstances dependence upon imports becomes more expensive and uncertain. The outlook may be further complicated if timber becomes a necessary replacement to exhausted oil and fuel sources.

It would be technically possible to double Britain's present forest areas from 8 per cent to 16 per cent of the land area by the year 2,025, if the Forestry Commission planted at the rate of 145,000 acres per year instead of the current 50,000 acres. This could then provide approximately 30 per cent of the nation's timber needs if it were undertaken in conjunction with a more economical use of timber in the future. Increased afforestation would be possible in the hills — it is estimated that 5 million acres of forest land could be made available at a loss of only 2 per cent of agricultural production. If forestry is going to use more land in the uplands, as seems increasingly likely, then closer integration with agriculture will be necessary. The use of mixed grazing and spaced planting could enable food and timber production to co-exist side by side.[12] Since its 1972 Consultative Document, the Forestry Commission has considered employment, recreation, amenity and landscaping as part of the role of its forests. Tax relief for private forestry is also only available if a certain level of recreational access is provided. The Forestry Commission has since been incorporating recreational facilities in many of its own forests. Woods and forests can absorb a surprisingly large number of people and cars and they would seem destined to play an important role in the future of recreation in the countryside.

The impact of leisure and recreation
The last 30 years in particular have seen a dramatic increase in the demand for outdoor recreation, focussed largely upon the countryside and coastal areas and brought about by increased leisure time, higher incomes and more personal mobility.

'If everyone in England and Wales went to the seaside at the same time each would get a strip of coast 3½" across.[13]

In 1978 the Countryside Commission estimated that the major impact comes from families with cars, professional and managerial groups being likely to make twice as many trips as skilled workers. Limited to day or weekend trips, other longer term trips are traditionally spent on home coasts or abroad. Pressure on the countryside from traffic and visitors has often led to trampling, trespass and damage to livestock. While farming areas can absorb a certain amount of people and traffic, the more intense farming systems are more economically sensitive to trampling feet and infected livestock. However many farmers are prepared to take the risk, by purposely encouraging tourists upon their land. In 1975 as many as 15,000 farmers received £15 million from farm-based recreation schemes. Loss of production in exchange for 'controlled' recreational facilities, it was argued, would reduce pressure upon other areas of farmland.

Official policy towards recreation and amenity has been to reduce conflict of land-use, whilst channelling recreational and tourist activities into specified areas. The

1949 National Parks and Access to the Countryside Act and the 1968 Countryside Act enable the Countryside Commission to promote the enhancement of the natural beauty of the countryside, whilst providing open-air facilities. By 1980 there were 10 National Parks, 33 Areas of Outstanding Natural Beauty (AONBs) and 33 Heritage Coasts all introduced by the Countryside Commission, (in the case of Heritage Coasts, jointly with the local authorities) and all covering more than 20 per cent of the land surface of England and Wales. The Countryside Commission for Scotland does not have the same powers to designate National Parks and other areas, mainly because the conflicts are less. A lower density of people (concentrated largely into the Central Belt containing Glasgow and Edinburgh) weather, terrain, remoteness, and vast tracts of open upland, all conspire to diminish the effects of tourism and recreation outside the Central Belt. The main impetus of the Countryside Commission throughout Britain has been to establish Country Parks that are readily accessible to towns located, for example, in the urban fringes in restored gravel pits, old railway land and reservoir lands. More than 130 Country Parks had been established in Britain by the end of the 1970s. In addition the Nature Conservancy Council Act 1973, set up to identify nature reserves and to provide educational facilities, has resulted in the designation of nearly 3,000 Nature Reserves and Sites of Special Scientific Interest (SSSIs) covering nearly 5 per cent of England and Wales.

National Parks cover more expansive areas of land than either Country Parks or AONBs. Extensive farming such as sheep rearing, undertaken in the ten English and Welsh National Parks, can maintain an open landscape for recreation and animal grazing, accommodating large numbers of visitors. Conflicts tend to arise when leisure activities interfere with food production, or when farmers wish to improve the quality of their agricultural land. In the Exmoor National Park during the 1970s farmers were enclosing and ploughing areas of scenically attractive moorland to prevent public access. The 1978 Countryside Bill recommended that moorland areas should be protected from such activities by Moorland Conservation Orders and farmers duly compensated for the loss of potential productivity. This action is seen to bring the principles of development control in National Parks a step further towards the original recommendation of the 1974 Sandford Committee Report which argued for changes in agriculture or forestry land uses in National Parks to be made subject to planning control in order that their effects upon existing landscapes (which the Parks were originally set up to conserve) could be gauged before permission was granted.[14] Current criticism of National Parks policy is that it gives priority to amenity and landscape factors, and does not always take into account the social and economic needs of the residents who gain their livelihood from the land or associated activities. By the end of the 1970s the Countryside Commission was involved in a series of upland management experiments that were placing increasing priority upon these social and economic issues.

Towards a working countryside
Since the first Enclosure Acts of the mid-18th century, management of the various conflicts in the countryside has been the subject of extensive legislation and amenity activities. The result, as we have seen, has been a multitude of individual actions and legislation that have led to an extremely sectarian and diffuse series of organisations all acting within the countryside. A tendency for these bodies to pursue their own

independent aims and ideals has frequently exaggerated the conflict. Agricultural policy since 1947 has been concerned with stability and efficiency in farming and this has been pursued by the introduction of price supports and grants for improvement of land. But these improvements have often had an unfavourable effect upon amenity, recreation and wildlife conservation. Agriculture, in addition to producing food, has also traditionally managed and planned the appearance of the countryside. Wildlife habitats have been destroyed as farmers have undertaken grant-aided improvements by ploughing old pastures, draining meadows and removing hedges. Fertilisers and pesticides have in many instances also affected these habitats, both on the farm and around the boundaries of the farm. The Nature Conservancy Council holds many of its Nature Reserves and Sites of Special Scientific Interest under management agreements. In fact only 30 out of 145 Reserves in Britain are owned outright; conservation often depends upon agreements with farmers and foresters who are not subject to outside planning control over the way in which they use their land. As a result many ecologically valuable sites are vulnerable to changes in agricultural practice and the position of nature conservation and the role of the Nature Conservancy Council is still extremely tentative.

Apart from the conflicts between agriculture and amenity, the pursuit of policies for recreation and landscape preservation in National Parks has often been at the expense of the local economy. The development of small industries by the Council for Small Industries in Rural Areas (CoSIRA), or the expansion of tourist facilities through the National Tourist Boards has often suffered in the interests of amenity and food production. However, the post-war legislation establishing new towns and Green Belts in order to contain urban development, has not only contributed towards the leap-frogging effect of people and activities discussed in the next chapter, but has also led to pressure for development on urban fringe farmland and the loss of productive agricultural output. Between 1964 and 1974, 2,500 acres or more of green belt farmland around London was lost to urban development despite Green Belt legislation. The planning of rural areas, as required under present 'structure' and 'development' plan policies, provided under the 1968 Town and Country Planning Act, has been criticised for its preoccupation with housing, transportation and industrial development, which has tended to place further restrictions on the use of adjacent land for food production.

Towards the end of the 1970s there was a growing belief that more positive policies concerned with developing and managing rural resources, rather than creating rural backwaters, would be more appropriate. If the policies of various land-use agencies continue to be pursued in isolation, it will be harder for any single interest to benefit at all and harder still for management schemes to encourage integrated land use as a solution to the conflicts arising from official policy. The expansion of agriculture, forestry and industrial development under Government assistance will continue and the most difficult task will lie in deciding priorities for rural land use. This task will continue to be difficult until there is a more accurate picture of the actual needs of rural areas.

By the end of this century an expected population of 59 million people could be 80 per cent self-sufficient. To achieve this level of sufficiency, forestry, recreation, wildlife conservation, urban development and the preservation of best quality agricultural land for continued food production, would all need to be accommodated

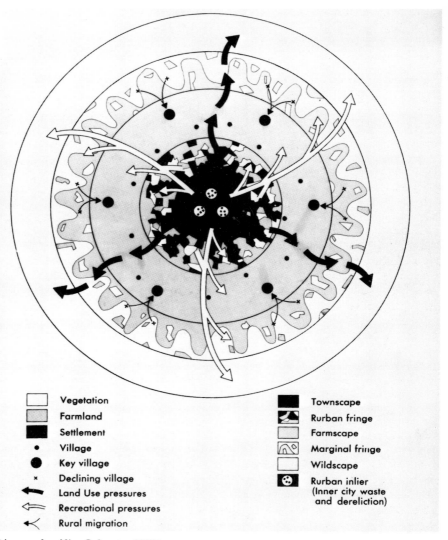

☐	Vegetation	■	Townscape
▨	Farmland	◪	Rurban fringe
■	Settlement	☐	Farmscape
•	Village	⬚	Marginal fringe
●	Key village	☐	Wildscape
×	Declining village	◉	Rurban inlier
⬅	Land Use pressures		(Inner city waste
⇐	Recreational pressures		and dereliction)
◄	Rural migration		

(Diagram by Alice Coleman, 1979)

under comprehensive decision-making and land-use management. However there is little indication that such a policy can be operated successfully when land ownership is in itself such a powerful planning tool. Changing ownership patterns of farmland have been affecting the appearance of the countryside, particularly since the beginning of the century. The proportion of owner-occupiers has risen from 12 per cent in 1911 to well over 50 per cent by 1977 and this has been paralleled more recently by an increasing ownership of farmland by institutional bodies such as insurance companies and pension funds. In 1979, Lord Northfield's Committee on

Between town and country lie areas of mixed activity. Here on the River Thames in mid-winter, wildlife, fishing, boating and industry achieve a balance. Summer brings a conflict of activities that fill the river banks with people, cars and boats, and pollute the water with rubbish, waste and myriad small craft. (Photograph: Popperfoto)

the Acquisition and Occupancy of Agricultural Land, reported that at the end of 1978 financial institutions owned a total of 530,000 acres of agricultural land (1.2 per cent of the total agricultural area of Britain). The Report forecast that at the then current rate of purchase, financial institutions might own 11 per cent of the. agricultural land area of Britain by the year 2,000. Lord Northfield concluded that whilst acquisition of farmland by these institutions needs to be carefully watched, there is no reason yet to introduce controls over non-agricultural ownership.[15]

Protection of farmland has been viewed traditionally in the context of the needs of recreation, amenity and urban development, and by the end of the 1970s there was a growing body of opinion calling for stronger controls over the transfer of farmland to non-agricultural uses and over the changing uses between agriculture, moorland and wilderness. In effect it was being suggested that all land use should be brought under development control procedures. However, in 1979 the Countryside Review Committee (established in 1974 to inquire into the problems of rural areas) warned against the introduction of such blanket controls, and in particular any interference with changing agricultural land uses.[16] Traditionally agricultural land has been kept in good heart (apart from periods of economic depression) largely because the farmer has been free to respond to changing market demands or government incentives, without being subjected to the kind of restrictions and delays brought about by

95

Conflicting land uses are at their most noticeable on the fringes of towns and cities where often large tracts of vacant, underused, derelict or rubbish-strewn land lie vulnerable to the march of development. (Photograph: Tony Ray-Jones)

control procedures operated on non-agricultural land use. Whatever the extent of the argument, it has become clear that stronger controls will be required over the transfer of agricultural land to urban development. Not surprisingly there was opposition from those who suggested that such action would not only be likely to place a premium upon green-field development sites, but would also inflate the value of agricultural land. As a consequence small farmers would be likely to be forced out and farming would be likely to be further concentrated into the hands of fewer, more affluent agricultural interests.

On the other side of the argument, there is concern that changing energy priorities and the increasing costs of oil-based farming will, in the long term, render capital- and machine-intensive farming less economic, making it feasible to increase employment opportunities in a number of machine-intensive, land-based industries. By the

96

end of the 1970s sophisticated microchip technology brought remote control operations to feeding programmes in intensive animal production and mobile farm machinery. The ability to plough a field by remote control, for example, using a driverless vehicle was just one of the many technological experiments being carried out within farming. The extent to which this kind of new technology grows and energy conservation policies affect, or are allowed to affect rural areas, will be likely to determine future patterns of agricultural land use and the well-being of our remaining agricultural communities. Although we may still have time to keep our options open over energy conservation, methods of farming and changing land ownership, it seems that we can no longer delay action over improved food production and the unnecessary loss of agricultural land to urban development.

Suburbia and the fragmented fringe

Loss of farmland to non-agricultural uses has always been at its keenest on the edges of cities, towns and villages. The continued erosion of farmland by urban creep is frequently the result of a commercial understanding between the urban developer with an eye for a bargain and the businessman farmer or landowner willing to part with peripheral or rundown areas of his land. Under these conditions the value of farmland may reflect a hope value providing considerably higher profits than would normally come from farmland sold at agricultural land values only. To this end, some farmers may welcome (perhaps even encourage) dereliction of their land — ploughing back their profits into further improvement of their existing holdings. Not surprisingly this is a view that the National Farmers Union does not altogether accept. To them the farmer is more often than not an innocent bystander earning his livelihood from land — unlikely and often unable to leave it fallow, or in a derelict state, without losing income from its productive potential:

'The farmer or grower on the urban fringe – though sometimes an ally or antagonist, is more often merely the bewildered proprietor of a battleground upon which competing claims of other land users – recreation, public utilities, housing and industry are fought out.[17]

Whatever the reasons for gradual transfer of farmland to urban use, early idealists like John Ruskin and later planners like Ebenezer Howard have striven to create a clean break between town and country in which the activities of town and the activities of the countryside are reconciled and where underuse of land, particularly farmland, is kept to a minimum. They have rarely been successful in their quest. As urban activities spill over into the countryside, farming, however well operated and however carefully coordinated, is constantly under pressure. The edges of towns and cities, have therefore been regarded by planners and developers as a transitional environment to be included sooner or later within a future urban area. Over the years as communications have improved and travel has become increasingly easy, urban development has eaten into the countryside, absorbing fields and farms, and destroying hedges and country lanes, woodland and wildlife.

Today the urban fringe is the edge of a continuously built up urban area frequently containing sprawling suburban development, industrial and housing estates. On the outer edges of cities and large towns, industry, employment and the rewards of town are not far distant in one direction; while fresh air, leisure pursuits and the amenity of open space and countryside lie in the opposite direction. The urban fringe is the closest countryside that urban residents have:

'To city dwellers the rural-urban fringe is often the nearest real countryside, the place to walk the dog, picnic, ramble, bird watch and do a host of other things. To the developer it offers potential for housing, industry, mineral extraction and leisure development. To the local authority it may be a green belt but also a place to locate sewage works, rubbish, bare fields, motorways, hospitals, prisons and other institutions, and many other services with which the city dwellers must be provided but are unsuitable within the city. Even central Government looks to this area for development of recreational facilities. It is not surprising therefore that the rural-urban fringe is seen both as a problem and an opportunity area.'[18]

Since the mid-1970s, the Countryside Commission has initiated long term experiments, in conjunction with other statutory bodies, into the maintenance and comprehensive management of fringe land an example of which is the Bollin Valley Land Management Experiment. The Bollin Valley lies to the south of the Manchester conurbation, and industrial development lines much of its northern edge.

With the growth of the Manchester suburbs, pressure for outings has increased, particularly from young people living within cycling or walking distance. Despite some formal legislative provision by private and public bodies, visitors still seek traditional sites in the meadows and valley sides where pastoral farming has remained largely unchanged. Many visitors come by car — almost 2 million people are within a 30 minute car journey. Three railway stations are about $\frac{1}{2}$ mile from the river. The town of Wilmslow lies on both sides of the river, while the suburbs of Hale and Bordon are on the Manchester side. The Valley provides an effective check to urban sprawl, but sustained and continual effort is necessary to safeguard its attractive character in the face of persistent and intrusive development.

In 1968 the Countryside Act introduced statutory powers of countryside conservation and maintenance that enabled local authorities to enter into agreements with landowners for specific types of shared use of their land so essential to its effective management. The Act formed the basis upon which the Countryside Commission is now drawing together the various land use interests within its urban fringe experiments in areas such as the Bollin Valley. The point at which a suburban housing estate ends and farmland begins so often marks the effective boundaries between the legal responsibilities of the Department of Environment and those of the Ministry of Agriculture, Fisheries and Food. Communication between these two government departments in particular has been poor. Consequently division between the two types of land use under their individual controls has grown increasingly untidy leaving marginal farmland and protective buffer land that is open to the encroachment of non-agricultural uses that frequently leave the landscape in a run-down and derelict condition and ready prey to urban development.

This type of land that has no dominant agricultural or urban use is known as 'white land', which, because of its ill-defined status, has contributed significantly over the years to the erosion of potential farmland by urban sprawl. Curiously, planning policies controlling the development of white land tend to have been at their strongest in areas of predominantly good farmland, often distant from metropolitan areas where the pressures for alternative uses are few. By comparison, controls over the development of white land have been at their most erratic and susceptible to development on the urban fringes and within green belt areas where pressures for alternative land uses are at their strongest. Although during the 1970s planning authorities tightened their control over the erosion of urban fringe land and the kind of haphazard sprawl that has been taking place, their involvement in the countryside today still remains a negative one of protection against urban encroachment rather than the more positive assignation of agricultural or potential agricultural white land (sufficiently large for efficient full or part-time farming) to agricultural or associated agricultural uses only.

The potential effect of urban sprawl is even greater than it seems, because many urban fringe areas consist of first-class agricultural land; also, an increasing amount of underused agricultural land is being purchased as a hedge against inflation by holding companies, who may manage the land through agents or tenants. Once agricultural land is purchased for speculative purposes, there is often less incentive to farm it well. This kind of 'farming-to-quit' attitude contributes to an unkempt and neglected landscape of overgrown fields, unmanaged hedges and woodlands and deteriorating farm equipment, buildings and fences.

99

Changing land ownership and agricultural activities have also contributed to the declining environment at the urban fringe. Growing numbers of suburban and urban fringe villages, for example, have either long since lost their manorial seats, or are in the final stages of change as the traditional manor and estate are sold for other uses, and as the squirearchy finally disappears. Today taxes and estate maintenance costs make it increasingly difficult for large estate owners to continue without putting their land to more commercial use, or selling it for the highest value by subdividing it into small parcels suitable for future urban development. In some estates around urban fringes which have not been sold off the landowner has introduced golf courses, vintage motor cars, rallies, zoos and wildlife parks. In areas of agricultural land estate owners have turned to intensive farming. Elsewhere manor houses on suitably sized pieces of land are being sold and the remaining land either leased or sold to neighbouring farmers for agricultural use, or to village residents anxious to protect their investment and their views of the countryside. Farmers readily admit that fragmentation of land in urban fringe areas is affecting the efficiency with which agricultural land is farmed and at the same time is opening up further chances of development in those rural areas where planning controls are weak:

'Farms are fragmented in such a way that the costs of agricultural production are increased and many holdings become either much too small for efficient land use, or large and monopolistic. This means that the most favourable part of the countryside, particularly those areas on the urban fringe, get too many urban and rural developments, while the remote or difficult areas are left to suffer the full rigours of selective rural migration.' [19]

As the process of division and subdivision of agricultural estates has occurred in urban fringe areas, particularly since the enclosure period, land has gradually changed in scale of ownership. It has become either more suitable for large-scale agricultural activities, or has been subdivided into smaller areas of land suited to the development of housing and industrial estates, individual houses or factories. This

TABLE 6   QUALITY OF FARMLAND LOST TO URBAN
DEVELOPMENT BETWEEEN 1933 AND 1963

Agricultural land grade	Percentage in urbanised area	Percentage in national area
First class	9·6	7·5
Good	43·5	37·6
Medium	37·4	36·5
Poor	9·5	18·4
Total	100·0	100·0

Sources: Second Land Utilisation Survey and *Land Use Perspectives*, Land Decade Educational Council, 1979

process has led to a conflict of use for land at the urban fringe, and to the gradual nibbling away of countryside that has already fallen idle or derelict because of its closeness to urban development. Agricultural buffer zones of idle or derelict farmland, set up informally to protect crops and livestock from nearby urban activities, have also acquired value for potential future development. However these areas of farmland, often characterised by grazing horses or rubbish dumping have, in a number of areas, reverted to agriculture in the form of part-time farming.

Conflict or conciliation

Improvement in communications and problems of theft have both contributed to the reduction in overall agricultural and market garden activities at the urban fringe. There is less need for agriculture to supply only nearby urban markets; produce is now easily transferable elsewhere. The attraction to landowners of releasing such land for urban development for a high price is a further problem facing planners. Around Edinburgh, for example, market gardens have gone — giving way in all cases to urban expansion. They have not been replaced and those that remain have done so not for economic reasons, but because of their long established reputation in the Edinburgh market. As in the case of many cities, Edinburgh has developed most of its available land within the green belt. Changes to the inner boundary of the city are now required if further development within the green belt or expansion of many of its suburban villages is to be made possible.[20]

Theft and damage to agricultural land is therefore a common problem facing most outer metropolitan authorities. Reconciling the needs of agriculture and the needs of urban expansion is being further hindered by the growing use of urban fringe areas for recreation and leisure. A survey of the Slough area in 1973 by the Ministry of Agriculture found that trespass affected 60 per cent of all farms, while crop damage, theft and dumping accounted for a third each.[21] In a similar survey of land around Cramlington New Town near Newcastle trespass affected 92 per cent of all farms with loss of land and fragmentation by new roads affecting 88 per cent.[22] In 1971 a survey by the National Farmers Union found that 78 per cent of all farmland adjoining suburban development underwent trespass in one way or another.[23] The same trend was noticeable for rubbish dumping and livestock worrying. In every case the urban fringe areas in the midlands of Britain would appear to have suffered the highest level of conflict between recreation and farming.

Although planning still strives to create a clean break between town and country, it is now generally accepted, particularly in the light of the experimental work of the Countryside Commission, that the activities of town and countryside can be reconciled and the underuse and misuse of land kept to a minimum. Land being worked by the hobby farmer and providing a modest secondary living is already showing signs of providing a better managed landscape. Traditional field patterns, hedges and ditches are being retained, while peripheral buffer land that would otherwise be lying waste is being kept in use and in good heart. Within the zone of transition containing high density urban development on the one hand and high density farming on the other, hobby farming may well assume an increasing importance in the search for conciliation between the two and management of the intervening landscape. Equally new woodlands, horticulture and parks provide a mixture of semi-commercial timber and food-growing activities based on small-scale ownerships often well suited to such a fragmented land use pattern. Each of these activities for example brings a more productive use of land and a more caring maintenance of the landscape without taking land out of farming. Such comprehensive approaches can only be successfully achieved by a greater knowledge and understanding of land use at the urban fringe and with the agreement of landowners and other land users. To this end the work of the Countryside Commission and other rural agencies will be vital to the better management of land and control of the conflicts created by urban pressures in the countryside. It is argued that some of these pressures could be eased by creating a network of small local parks throughout towns and cities upon some of the wasteland that is available. Not only would these parks help to relieve pressures upon the urban fringe, but they would also improve the quality of environment and life in the extensive areas of inner-city in particular, now one of Britain's most complex and pressing land use problems.

Notes·

1. *Agriculture into the 80s – Land Use, National Economic Development Office, 1977*
2. A. W. Rogers, *Urban Growth, Farmland Losses and Planning*, Rural Geography Study Group, 1978, p.13
3. Nan Fairbrother, *New Lives, New Landscapes*, Pelican, 1972, p.13
4. A Lincolnshire farmworker quoted in the series 'Who Owns the Land', *The Guardian*, September 1977
5. Anne Garvey, 'Fen Tigers', *New Society*, 1 September 1977
6. *Agriculture into the 80s – Land Use*, National Economic Development Office 1977
7. *The Development of Agriculture*, Government White Paper, 1967, p.4
8. Select Committee on Scottish Affairs, *Land Resources Use in Scotland*, Vol. 4, HMSO, 1972
9. Graham Moss, *Strath Gudie Integrated Upland Management Experiment, Scotland*, Edinburgh University Press, 1974
10. Sir Frank Fraser Darling, *Wilderness and Plenty*, Ballantyne, 1970, p.69
11. *A Study of Exmoor*, Report by Lord Porchester KBE, HMSO, 1977, p.5
12. Graham Moss, *op. cit*
13. Michael Dower, 'The Fourth Wave', *The Architects' Journal*, 1967
14. Report of the National Park Policies Review Committee, Department of the Environment, 1974
15. Report of the Committee of Inquiry into the Acquisition and Occupancy of Agricultural Land, Cmnd 7599, HMSO, 1979, p.16
16. Countryside Review Committee, *Conservation and the Countryside Heritage*, Topic Paper No. 4, HMSO, 1979, p.29
17. D. A. Hellard, 'Farmers and Landowners — Allies or Antagonists', National Farmers Union Countryside Recreation Research Advisory Group Conference, 1975
18. Countryside Commission, *The Bollin Valley – A Study of Land Management in the Urban Fringe*, HMSO, 1976
19. G. Wibberley and J. Davidson, *Planning and the Rural Environment*, Pergamon, 1977
20. A. J. Strachan, *The Rural Urban Fringe of Edinburgh*, undated paper presented to the

Royal Town Planning Institute Research Conference on Planning and the Changing Countryside

21. *Agriculture in the Urban Fringe: a Survey of the Slough/Hillingdon Area*, ADAS Technical Report 30, Ministry of Agriculture, Fisheries and Food, 1973
22. A. W. Tansley, *Farming in an Urban Fringe Area: a Pilot Study of Farms in a Parish on the Outskirts of Newcastle*, University of Newcastle-upon-Tyne, 1973
23. 'Results of a National Survey of the Effect on Agriculture of Non-Agricultural Development', National Farmers Union unpublished report, 1971

CHAPTER 7

The Declining Inner City

'There is a wide extent of vacant land in some inner areas, mainly in public ownership; and there is much under used land and property, with shops boarded up and sites and buildings neglected. The opportunities afforded by redevelopment to create publc open space have not been taken. This shabby environment, the lack of amenities, the high density remaining in some parts and the poor conditions of the older housing in the inner areas contrasts sharply with better conditions elsewhere. They combine together to make these areas unattractive, both to many of the people who live there and to new investment in business, industry and housing.'

Policy for the Inner Cities, *HMSO, 1977*

The extent of the problem

In 1977 the Civic Trust Report 'Urban Wasteland' estimated that there were at least 250,000 acres of dormant land lying in various stages of vacancy, temporary use or disuse. In some areas this dormant land is acquiring new and often novel uses — in others, land is left in a derelict and rubbish-strewn state. A regularly maintained community garden, or an ecological park, makes the best use of a bomb-site or land caught by planning blight; urban farms with all the excitement generated by animals and children enliven areas of empty dockland; blank end walls of buildings, exposed by the demolition of neighbouring properties or new roads, are given life and gaiety by the work of a growing band of energetic town artists; overgrown and vegetated areas of once thriving residential streets, cleared to make way for postponed redevelopment, are providing much needed playground facilities for children; derelict land and vacant old buildings have been restored to provide housing, small industries and a lifestyle not dissimilar to early industrial urban areas of Britain. But the future of the remaining wasteland is less assured. Unkempt, overgrown and rubbish-strewn, these areas of urban wasteland have now become a depressingly familiar characteristic of the inner-city. Offensive to the eye, dulling to the spirit and dangerous to all who stray within its boundaries, urban wasteland has an insidious and innate ability to spread. Frequently enclosed by graffiti-covered corrugated sheeting, or an array of wire fencing, garbage boarding and advertisers' hoardings, urban wasteland containing vacant buildings or the remnants of their foundations and fallen materials, invites further decay around.

The Civic Trust's estimate of a quarter of a million acres of wasteland is equivalent in area to the total amount of land required to build Britain's 34 new towns, designated between 1946 and 1968; or alternatively an area that could accommodate housing for 5 million people or produce food for a quarter of a million. Wasteland is

104

(Photograph: Architectural Press Ltd.)

most evident in the older industrial and heavily built-up areas. Weedy wastes not only lurk between buildings, but infiltrate the very buildings themselves as dandelions, nettles and rodents breed in the cracks of broken steps and punctured bricks. This kind of vegetated building is now a dominant part of the urban streetscape. An embarrassment to many local residents, such tumble-down areas instill little confidence within those who pass through their streets or among those organisations looking to invest in inner-urban areas. Why in the mid-1970s were the headquarters of Volkswagen and Coca-Cola lost to Milton Keynes New Town, despite all the political temptations that could be mustered to lead them to the inner-city? Why do so many housebuilders still seek green field sites when so much inner-city land is available? Why are so many people leaving inner cities? Depopulation and the inevitable rise in vacant land creates a self-perpetuating cycle of decline:

'Between 1966 and 1976, Glasgow lost 205,000 people (21 per cent), Liverpool lost 150,000 (22 per cent), Manchester 110,000 (18 per cent), Inner London 500,000 (16 per cent), Birmingham 85,000 (8 per cent).'[1]

As people and industry move away, the rate income is reduced and higher rate support grants become necessary. This situation frequently brings a severe decline in the provision of essential services such as education, health and welfare. Diminishing levels of maintenance and investment in existing building stock lead to further depopulation and a social, economic and physical environment that grows less attractive to existing and potential new residents and prospective investors. This in

105

turn leads to further depopulation, reduction in the rate income and fewer job opportunities and so on:

'Metropolitan life is breaking down, psychologically, economically and biologically. Millions of people have acknowledged this breakdown by voting with their feet, they have picked up their belongings and left. If they have not been able to sever their connections with the metropolis, at least they have tried. As a social symptom the effort is significant.'[2]

The character and speed of the present urban decline are new phenomena in Britain, and perhaps something that cannot readily be reversed. Such decline is after all the natural consequence of a 'de-industrialising' process that for the present may be too powerful to control, but which in the future will require heavy expenditure to clear away the mess and prepare for a new environment.

Causes of inner city decline

The 'inner-city problem' is a euphemistic heading for the process of change through which many of Britain's early industrial urban and rural centres are passing. This is most noticeable in city centres, where traditional industrial activities were at their most intense and are now either declining or have already grown redundant. Cynics suggest that the plight of the inner-city is further emphasised by the fact that extensive tracts of vacant and derelict land lie within a stone's throw of the seat of Government in Britain, in those areas immediately surrounding London's dockland. However, what is only now acknowledged as a problem in many of England's cities has been a world-renowned phenomenon in Glasgow for many decades. The inner-city problem therefore is a characteristic of many other areas that appear to suffer from four major misconceptions promoted largely by the media, political administrators and certain professions:

inner-metropolitan decline has not suddenly arisen as is sometimes suggested; it has been building up gradually over the decades as a result of earlier social and economic changes and more recently as a result of changing land-ownership patterns, land values and planning policies which have all compounded a generally deteriorating environment;

symptoms of decline and dereliction are not limited to inner-city locations, they are evident elsewhere in metropolitan and declining rural areas, although in many cities the symptoms tend to be at their most severe within the traditionally dense inner-areas;

the decline of the inner-city does not begin and end with decline and decay of land and buildings, but is a consequence of depopulation, industrial and economic decline and a weak development market for the re-use of land within traditional industrial areas of cities; and

the decline of the inner-city is not a direct cause or effect of the movement of people and industry to new towns. Evidence indicates that a small percentage of new-town residents originated from inner-city areas.

Depressing and untidy, urban wasteland has an innate ability to spread. (Photograph: Shelter)

The causes of inner-city decline are complex and long standing. During the 19th century, centralisation and concentration of activities brought compact, high-density growth, economies of scale and a level of activity that lead to a rapid turnover and re-use of urban land. Opportunities for land to lie vacant were extremely limited, as demand outstripped supply in the immediately accessible central areas. Every available area close enough to employment or to the market in proportion to the availability and type of transport, was built upon. Openness was limited to the inherited Royal Parks and consecrated ground; spaciousness of living was a privilege of rich merchants and entrepreneurs who built Victorian town houses or whole estates set in their own small parks or squares; and concentration and over-population were the lot of the poor labouring classes working in industry and living a cramped back-to-back life in the less desirable and frequently less accessible areas of the city, or within makeshift hovels scattered among the industrial activities themselves.

Concentration of activities was essential to daily life and communications between people at a time when transport was limited to the horse and carriage, bicycle and foot. With the advent of the motor vehicle, train, electricity and telephone, de-centralisation of industry and people became possible, enabling cities to spread within the limits of the new found mobility and communications. By the beginning of the 20th century, concentration was becoming less essential as wave after wave of extension to the urban fringe brought suburbia, the commuter and a seemingly endless and unco-ordinated mass of people and activities. Until the Second World War the vacancy rate of inner-metropolitan land was still low. Despite the declining condition of buildings, inner-city communities were active and content to be left alone. Re-use of buildings and land was rapid and there was continuing economic activity among industries. But after the Second World War the situation began to change. War damage, over-population, a rapidly deteriorating 19th-century stock of buildings and communications and changing industrial technology all combined to create increasingly unacceptable living and working conditions. This post-war convergence of a declining environment, of major industries reaching the end of their active life and of a planned policy of moving people out of cities meant that massive areas of 19th-century development gradually became obsolete and have, in many instances, remained so ever since. Only a limited re-use of land in the inner-city has brought expanding or new industries, newly rehabilitated buildings and shopping centres and the renewal of existing utilities.

In such an u ᵠ ⁾ertain situation, land values have tended to be held artificially high by landowners, whether local authorities or private individuals, so that the sale or re-use of land or buildings has not been easy. Many local authorities and private owners face heavy financial losses if they are forced to sell their investment for less than they paid for it, or in the case of a local authority, if they redevelop at greatly increased cost. Land, therefore, caught in the declining situation of the inner-city, is unlikely to be released rapidly and even less likely to be redeveloped in the short term. All the indications militate against an urban revival. At worst, it is argued, vacant urban land should be 'put out to grass' and those moving out should be allowed to settle elsewhere as they please. Others argue that because the inner-city has always been the inner-city, it should be retained for urban development only, with stringent controls over building on virgin land until the urban wastes are revived. Both arguments are equally unrealistic since land and people are rarely interchangeable.

The causes of land vacancy in inner areas can be summarised as follows:

changing industrial needs, productivity or methods of operating, requiring less land, or relocation closer to a primary resource, to better communications, to associated activities or to a more reliable employment potential;

decline in the structure and fabric of buildings making renovation or re-building in the same location an uneconomic exercise;

land in the process of change from one use to another and where redevelopment is in some way delayed;

land subject to planning policies that have demolished vast areas of buildings and have either changed programme or have become economically unviable;

land that is available for re-use, but is unattractive due to location, price or the uncertain future of surrounding land, buildings and activities;

land held speculatively as a hedge against inflation, or long-term investment; and

land surrounded by a poor quality environment, lacking good communications and essential services.

Whatever the causes of inner-city decline, and these are only a few of the most evident, extensive land vacancy in metropolitan areas, or in the many central areas of smaller towns and villages, is a reflection of the way in which urban land has been managed this century, particularly since the 1909 Town Planning Act and more seriously since the 1947 Planning Act:

'The existence of large areas of vacant urban land represents not only a misuse of valuable land resources and, in many areas, an unacceptable level of environmental degradation, but also it stands as a giant question mark to the effectiveness of land use control and to the credibility of a profession whose accepted role is to control land use and improve the environment.'[3]

While criticism of the planning profession may in certain instances be valid, there is little the planner can do without the goodwill of landowners and developers. Despite the wide powers of compulsory purchase introduced under the 1947 Planning Act, and the extensive areas of land bought compulsorily by local authorities since, much of this land in urban areas lies derelict — a testament to ideals and policies that could not be realised and the inability of many local authorities to assume the mantle of developer.

The ownership of vacant land

In a changing society the demands for houses and shops, factories and offices, roads and the provision of schools, doctors, hospitals and the many other services essential to community life, have also continually changed. More education facilities, improved housing more industry and additional playing fields are just some of the continuous requirements that urban society demands of land to varying degrees. Factors such as population numbers and social structure, regional and local economic fortunes, unemployment and prosperity levels and the general state and condition of building stock and infrastructure such as roads and sewers, have meant that land has to be readily available to meet these changing needs. Historically, private investment and speculation have provided industry and office building and to a lesser extent housing, entertainment and leisure provision; while public authorities and their statutory undertakers have provided welfare services that were considered too important to leave to the private sector, or which were unattractive to the private sector due to their low profitability. Low-cost housing, education, health and welfare, roads, essential services and open space provision are the main public services handled by local authorities and requiring land.

While the private sector has tended to be involved in projects that could be implemented rapidly, providing a quick and profitable return on investment, local authorities have rarely had the same commercial urgency. The result is that pockets of viable inner-city areas have often been developed or disposed of extremely rapidly by the private sector, while other land held by public authorities, difficult to develop for any number of reasons, has been put into a public land bank for future use. As this land bank has grown, so too have the environmental consequences of such land lying idle or derelict. It is suggested that many local authorities have exceeded their land acquisition requirements and have contributed seriously towards the decline of urban areas. Evidence indicates that the vacancy rate of public land is not only considerably higher than similar land held by the private sector, but is also considered to be far higher than is commensurate with good planning. Although at first sight the general ownership of vacant land appears evenly split between the public and private sectors, there is growing evidence that more than half of the private sector's share of vacant land is in fact held by statutory undertakers such as the British Railways Board, The National Gas Board, The National Coal Board and various Port authorities throughout the country. Further analysis suggests that private enterprise generally holds barely one-quarter of Britain's vacant land.

The Liverpool study[4] undertaken during the early 1970s by the Department of the Environment indicated that one half of all derelict land was owned by the city or county councils, most of which was acquired in the course of slum clearance activities. During the first 6 years the clearance programmes were successful, but although housing finance was often readily available, funds for highway construction and social provision were not. If housing provision was not to get seriously out of step with the provision of essential facilities like roads, schools and health centres, the new housing programme had to slow down or virtually stop after 1975. At this time land-use allocation and highway proposals in Liverpool were reviewed and a number of road proposals were rescinded. As a result by 1977 more than 11 per cent of the study area lay vacant and the report expected much of it to remain so in the immediate future. Housing policy since 1975 in inner Liverpool has placed greater emphasis upon rehabilitation and as a result a generally slower rate of renewal is likely to lead to increasing areas of vacancy over longer periods in land owned by local authorities. This is further proof that Britain's rebuilding and rehabilitation programmes of ageing buildings is not keeping pace with the rate of decline of building stock generally. There is little finance available to clean up or to landscape temporary areas awaiting re-use. In Liverpool, for example, only 6 per cent of all vacant land has received any kind of temporary landscape treatment.

A Civic Trust Survey in 1976[5] found that various organisations throughout Britain held 45 per cent of all derelict land and that private firms, individuals, churches, estates and trusts held 40 per cent. The British Railways Board has been singled out in a number of surveys as holding a high percentage of derelict land, particularly in urban areas, although the Board itself classifies all land that is not either awaiting sale or undergoing development as operational land. However, the Civic Trust indicated that British Rail held 13 per cent of all vacant or derelict urban land. Similarly Ports Authorities and Docklands Boards in London, Liverpool and Glasgow in particular, held a high proportion of vacant land. The joint Docklands Team in London suggested that the reluctance of statutory undertakers to release land was a major problem in their planning of London's docklands, of which the Gas Corporation alone held 700 acres in 1976. The Civic Trust's statistics also indicated that 54 per cent of all vacant land surveyed was completely unused, 10 per cent was in temporary use and 29 per cent was partly used and partly in temporary use. 27 per cent of all vacant land had planning permission for part or all of the site. The full extent of vacant land tends to be masked by temporary uses such as car parking, allotments, storage, market gardening, car breaking, prefabricated buildings and scrap yards. On paper, vacant and derelict land is often further hidden by its designation as operational, temporarily operational or as land awaiting disposal or re-use.

The generally high level of vacant land holdings by public bodies and statutory authorities is a result of a combination of the following factors:

historic ownership patterns of land by statutory authorities like Port and Docks Authorities, British Railways Board and other undertakers;

acquisition and ownership of land for planning purposes by public authorities

110

like housing departments, public works or recreation and open space departments, engineering and education departments;

ownership of land purchased for specific major public or joint public/private redevelopment projects relating to slum clearance and central area redevelopments;

increasing inability of public authorities to implement planning policies and development schemes, particularly since the economic decline of 1973; and

the duty of local authorities under recent planning legislation to realise and enhance the value of any land holdings or purchases made.

Increasingly large banks of inner-city land have been acquired by local authorities in line with specific planning policies. However, as these policies have changed, alternative uses for local authority holdings have not been forthcoming. Local authorities have often acquired land subject to vacancy, decay, or dereliction which has tended to be in unattractive locations and frequently totally uneconomic for private development.

The Civic Trust survey[6] indicated that more than 50 per cent of land currently vacant dates back to a period between 1964 and 1970 when the redevelopment and slum clearance programmes, which had reached a peak of activity by 1964, ran into the first economic decline of the late 1960s. In Liverpool, for example, three-quarters of vacant land had, until 1975, been designated for housing, highways, open space and schools. However, by 1976 over half of the vacant land had lain empty for two years or more, a situation that has been further compounded by the prolonged and worsening economic recession since the mid-1970s.

In 1979 the Conservative Government took steps to alleviate this situation by encouraging local authorities to sell off surplus vacant land holdings after having carefully considered their land requirements within future policies. In an effort to strengthen its powers against reluctant authorities, the Government introduced in 1980 District Registers of Vacant or Under-used Land (restricted to land held in public ownership). The purpose of the registers was to identify land that was being 'unnecessarily hoarded' and to enable the Department of the Environment to direct local authorities where appropriate to dispose of land either through sale or auction.

Housing degradation
Housing conditions tend to reflect the economic health of an area. When traditional industries gradually become redundant (as exemplified by inner urban areas dominated by traditional waterside, coal or iron industries), rising unemployment leads to the decline of housing and the local environment as houseowners no longer have the incentive or finance to maintain their properties. Similarly local authority housing falls into disrepair as decline brings a reduction in rate income and hence in expenditure on maintenance of housing and roads, and on public utilities and welfare services. Where housing needs were established in the 18th and 19th centuries, a continued level of local employment (or access to less local employment as transport improved) was necessary for housing to be well maintained. In the

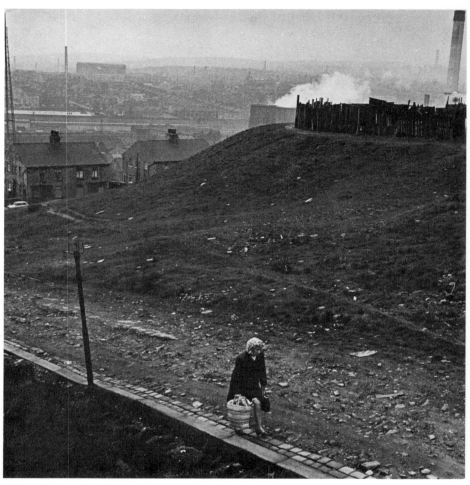

'The real tragedy of England, as I see it, is the tragedy of ugliness. The country is so lovely: the man-made England is so vile . . . a great scrabble of ugly pettiness over the face of the land. The English character has failed to develop the real urban side of man, the civic side . . . and it is partly due to his acceptance of hopeless paltriness in his surroundings.' D. H. Lawrence, extract from an article intended for the Architectural Review *in 1930, only part of which was actually printed in the* Architectural Review *issue 'SLOAP', October 1973. (Photograph: Shelter)*

scramble to be as close as possible to work, industrial centres became overcrowded and insanitary, with inadequate housing frequently rubbing shoulders with noisy and dirty industries. After a succession of local Housing Acts from 1846 aimed at setting better housing standards (including the Public Health Act of 1875) the first national Housing Act was approved in 1891, sponsored by Lord Shaftesbury. The improvement of living conditions included a higher level of open space and general spaciousness within and around housing. The Liverpool Improvement Act of 1886 incorporated the use of street widening and open space to reduce overcrowding, which at that time was estimated in some areas at well over 1,200 persons per acre.[7] As Victorian industries grew and expanded, people continued to flow into the city centres, living in cramped conditions of the kind found in Leeds in 1843:

'The Courts and cul-de-sacs exist everywhere. The building of houses back-to-back occasions this in great measure. In the cul-de-sac, in the town of Leeds, there are 34 houses and in ordinary times there dwell in these houses 340 persons or 10 persons to every house; but as these houses are many of them receiving houses for itinerant labourers, during the periods of haytime, at least twice that number are then here congregated.'[8]

The inner-city inheritance today is still based upon a predominance of old housing stock, which has not always been maintained and up-dated to meet changing needs and standards and is increasingly inappropriate to present industrial and residential needs. In 1953 William Ashworth suggested that:

'The general inadequacy of urban reform in the mid-Victorian period is perhaps to be attributed to two characteristics of the public at large: a zeal for economy in public administration and the somewhat narrow interpretation of what constituted economy; and secondly a persuasive apathy about the whole subject of sanitary improvement which seems to be of relatively minor importance, when set against the contemporary achievements of industry and planning.'[9]

This zeal for economy and apathy lingered well into the 1960s when decaying housing stock was joined by new high-rise inner-city homes, built to relieve the densities at ground level, whilst freeing the ground for open space. Had the inner Liverpool Study been undertaken in the early 1980s instead of the 1970s, it would doubtless have included mention of the demolition of not only buildings in slum clearance areas, but recently constructed tower blocks sometimes barely 10 years old — which had become the modern equivalent of the Victorian industrial ghetto and which was compounding the social problems of the city's housing stock. Three-quarters of the housing in inner Liverpool was still in private ownership in 1971, virtually all built before the First World War and much of it before 1891. Most private housing in the city is made up of 19th- and 20th-century terraces, small and lacking basic amenities. In 1977 it was estimated that 70,000 people — a quarter of the population of inner Liverpool — were living in substandard dwellings, in spite of the huge slum clearance programmes carried out in the city in the 1930s and after the Second War. There are still over a third of a million unfit houses in the worst category and slum clearance programmes are barely keeping pace with the growth of new slums. Further evidence from other cities shows that dilapidation of existing buildings, particularly housing, is far exceeding investment in maintenance and rebuilding programmes.[10]

The Liverpool study further indicated that 32,000 households lacked exclusive use of hot water (16 per cent of all households); 46,000 (23 per cent) lack exclusive use of a bath; and 58,000 (30 per cent) lacked exclusive use of an inside toilet. On Tyneside as many as 70 per cent of households lacked an inside toilet and bath.[11] The general extent of old housing stock is now of increasing concern — Liverpool contains 62,000 dwellings (almost 40 per cent of the total housing stock) composed mainly of large concentrations of Victorian properties. Such statistics become even more serious when this figure is seen to constitute three-quarters of all the properties which were

Much housing still lacks hot water, bathrooms and internal toilets – a severe criticism of past housing priorities. (Photograph: Shelter)

built pre-1900. In effect nearly one-fifth of all pre-First World War housing in Liverpool requires urgent attention. Within the inner area of Liverpool, more than 4,000 acres of land contain rapidly decaying housing stock which, if not treated and maintained speedily, will lead to further areas of decay, derelict land and buildings.

Housing throughout other similar inner urban areas of Britain is therefore likely to pose an ever increasing strain upon financial and human resources. There are seven basic problems contributing to the decline of housing and rapid depopulation:

large numbers of houses without basic amenities

deteriorating state of repair of homes

decline in supply of unfurnished rented accommodation

shortage of furnished rented accommodation, particularly for young single people and those in need of extra care

a congested and unattractive physical environment

a growing number of low income owner-occupiers experiencing difficulty in obtaining mortgages, and

lack of public and private investment in new housing or mortgage facilities in existing housing areas.[12]

There is every reason to be even more pessimistic about the future of housing in inner areas. Out of three-quarters of a million houses requiring improvement in inner-city areas of England in 1977, barely 60,000 were receiving treatment. With an estimated 100,000 empty dwellings in London alone, we do not appear to be tackling the worst consequences of social and industrial change.

Industrial decline and unemployment

Urban industries once relied upon shipping and railways as their main means of transport. They now use a far wider network of roads and motorways, airlines and highspeed railways. Freed from the necessity of being located near port or station, inner-city industry has either moved to outer metropolitan or green field sites, or has rationalised its activities and structure, now filling only part of its original land area, or closing down altogether. Industries like shipbuilding, coal, iron and steel and munitions have left behind acres of empty warehouses, port buildings, factories, out-of-date machinery and equipment.

'The bleakest planned bomb-site in Britain stretches for 3,500 acres along the River Clyde – the wasteland of the East End of Glasgow from Glasgow Green east to Shettleston, south to Dalmarnock and Auchenshuggle. This was once the powerhouse of Clydeside's heavy industry . . . Along the London Road or Tollcross Road, arteries through the area, façades of the late Victorian city shield, literally, miles of dereliction.' [13]

Three-quarters of the firms closing between 1970 and 1975 in south east London, for example, did so either because the goods that they produced were obsolete, or because their activities, such as shipbuilding, had grown uneconomic or less profitable than other similar industries, such as furniture and cabinet making. Some were short-term industries, trading in fashion and possibly occupying cheap, almost derelict premises; businesses like skateboards, mail order, women's dresses and shoes thrived for a short time only. Another cause is 'dis-investment', when insufficient profits are invested in keeping machinery and buildings up-to-date, so that the capital investment needed to make an industry more efficient and to provide better working conditions becomes too great. The industry runs down even more and finally closes.

As industries close down or move away, redundant employees are often unable to move elsewhere, and remain in the hope of better times; others move away to areas where there are similar jobs or better opportunities for alternative employment. In most cases, unemployment and depopulation are a direct consequence of industrial decline. For example, between 1961 and 1971 the city of Liverpool lost 28,000 jobs from port, railway, construction and utility activities; 21,000 jobs from retail and wholesale distribution and 31,000 from manufacturing. The loss of manufacturing jobs has accelerated since 1971 taking with it further service and retail jobs. In 1950 14 per cent of all Merseyside's employment was in the docks, with 21 per cent in related services and warehousing activities. However, since 1950, dock employment has fallen by almost two-thirds, whilst related activities have fallen by just less than half. The relationship therefore between the main heavy industries and associated industries and related services, is a chain where the closure of one main associated industry affects most of the others. This chain is not restricted to industry. Inner areas that have been closely knit and traditionally reliant upon industrial concentration have felt the effects of closure and unemployment upon their populations, housing, shopping and essential services. As people become unemployed and in

The stark emptiness of industrial decline and redundant land and buildings in dockland Liverpool. (Photograph: Richard Reid)

some cases move away, essential services are reduced and inner areas become poorly maintained. This effect leads to a cycle of decline which has many similarities, though on a different scale, with the decline of rural areas.

Declining urban services

The provision of essential services in declining urban areas is financed in theory by a combination of rate income from residents and businesses and the rate support grant provided by central government to supplement the shortfall between rate income and the actual cost of providing the services. Depopulation, decline of industry and building vacancy mean a lower rate income, with either greater reliance on the rate support grant or cuts in services like schools, hospitals, doctors, dentists, post offices and chemists; this is generally accompanied by poor maintenance of roads, footpaths, open spaces, sewers and piped services. As a result selected education and health facilities close down, or continue only within poorly maintained buildings; rubbish is cleared less frequently; roads and open spaces become littered with debris and the upkeep of buildings becomes seriously inadequate. The area becomes progressively more unattractive to the remaining residents, to potential newcomers and to businesses, leading to further industrial closures and more vacant land and buildings. This kind of environment is no place in which to raise children:

116

'His own children had grown up in dereliction and decay, and in his view the Corporation had waged a war of attrition against a whole neighbourhood, steadily depriving it of its amenities. Pubs and chip shops had closed, street lights were not maintained, the pavement was unsafe. Vandals and petty thieves were looting the adjoining houses and had frequently broken into his. His neighbours used to be his childhood friends. Now the only neighbours were rats, winos, vagrants and lead thieves.'[14]

The decline of inner-city services is both result and cause of industrial decline and depopulation. Yet if provision continues to be reduced, the chances of any revival are equally reduced. If they are maintained to a high level, then like declining rural communities they will require an equally high level of public investment from people throughout Britain, not necessarily living within inner-city or urban areas. The maintenance of services within derelict inner urban areas is therefore seen as wasted investment. The cost of maintaining basic standards for the people living there falls upon all of us. Studies in Liverpool indicate that the needs of a particular inner-city area tend to be met on a standard allocation basis rather than upon a local discretionary basis. Similar characteristics are found in declining rural areas, where the reduction of essential services tends to be in areas where reduction is least desirable. The reduction of inner-city services is worsened by the fact that they are frequently shared by non-residents who commute to work and use services which may already be inadequate for the local population:

'Outer London residents make extensive use of the inner-city facilities, for many women go to a clinic close to their place of work which is more convenient for them than the clinic close to their home address.'[15]

This trend is equally true of inner-city doctors, dentists, chemists, opticians and local shops.

Schools suffer from two associated factors as education budgets are reduced. The pupil-teacher ratio rises and school buildings are rarely adequately maintained — many retaining a murky Dickensian inheritance:

'. . . they are quite untypical of schools in the rest of the country . . . Tiny playgrounds; giant looking buildings; often poor decorative conditions inside; narrow passages; dark rooms; unheated and cramped cloakrooms; unroofed outside lavatories; tiny staff rooms; inadequate storage space with consequent restriction on teaching material and therefore methods; inadequate space for movement and P.T.; meals in classrooms; art on desks; music only to the discomfort of others in echoing buildings; non-sound-proof partitions between classes; lack of smaller rooms for group work and . . . all round the ingrained grime of generations.'[16]

Similar social and environmental degradation surrounds the character of many doctors and dentists surgeries, in poorly maintained old buildings, where disease looks more at home than hygiene. It now seems certain that the problems of inner-city medical facilities in Britain will follow the trends that are apparent in America, where the scarcity of doctors and the unhygienic conditions of their surgeries mean that patients have to undertake long and expensive journeys and, as a result, hospitals are used for the most minor of ailments.

The problem of access to essential services has parallels again with declining rural areas, where diminishing populations make public transport less viable, in turn

Empty streets amid derelict buildings inspire little confidence in the urban future. (Photograph: Bernard Humphries)

creating a greater reliance upon private transport. Cities which have an underground as well as a bus system have an advantage in this respect since car ownership in inner-city areas tends to be well below the national average. *Change or Decay*, the Department of Environment report on inner-Liverpool indicated that car ownership in declining urban areas was two-thirds that of the city, dropping to less than a quarter of the city average in the inner council estates.[17] Roads in inner-city housing areas and particularly in existing council estates are poorly maintained and the

118

mixture of broken pavements, cobblestone and patched-up tarmacadam can be dangerous and contributes further to the unkempt appearance of the area. Hidden public sewers and piped water services are falling into a state of disrepair, but many city authorities think there is little point in investing money in existing services within declining areas, and give them a low priority. Since 1978 underground sewers have begun collapsing in areas of Manchester and other cities, demanding immediate and expensive remedial work and drawing extensive public finance away from educational priority areas, housing action areas or general improvement areas. The economics of providing inner urban services is a finely balanced set of priorities caught between inadequate public funds and the increasing cost of maintaining existing facilities or providing new ones.

Inner-city land and planning

Vacant land is now likely to be a long term feature of inner-city areas, particularly as further areas of land and buildings fall vacant and derelict, with only a small proportion being redeveloped or re-used. It is becoming necessary to devise ways in which vacant land can be held in readiness for use without creating a derelict or declining environment:

'It attracts vandalism and contributes to an atmosphere of obsolescence, dilapidation and decay. It is not only that people living nearby have their home environment blighted, but that attempts at regeneration through attracting private investment are stultified whether it be in housing or jobs: and little private investment is likely to come to inner areas of its own volition.'[18]

Dreams of an economic miracle for the inner-city have gradually disappeared. The problem is not merely economic, nor is it merely social, nor merely a problem of land use or planning. Adequate jobs, homes, local shops, schools, doctors, a regular and rapid public transport system and an agreeable environment together form the ingredients of inner-city revival. Until these areas can compete with the amenities of suburbia, or the openness of the countryside, they will continue to decline. The single most serious mistake is that successive urban generations have failed to clear up the mess of redundant past activities, they have failed to renew housing and essential services and most of all they have created a stigma against the inner-city, which discourages those who might otherwise have settled or invested in the area. It has also bred a depressed mentality in those residents caught amid the decay that has no civic pride or respect for environment.

The problem of inner-cities has been laid at the door of the planner, as if by the use of some supernatural power he could order a revival. But the problems are too complex and the consequences of decline too ramifying. Land, people, investment, administration and building combine to form a complex of activity which it is almost impossible to control in a period of growth (as planners found during the economic euphoria of the 1950s and 1960s); in a period of decline it is equally impossible to handle. The re-use of derelict urban land and buildings will emerge from the revival of industry and job opportunities and the consequent need to provide accommodation. Since 1972 when Peter Walker, the then Secretary for the Environment, set up the Inner-City Studies, the problem has been besieged by endless reports and discussions from which it has been possible to define a number of major administrative factors that contribute to urban decline:

A mixture of urban renewal and housing improvement has proved popular with the local Byker community in Newcastle. (Photograph: Shelter)

poor location of local services

inadequate financial analyses of policy issues

over-rigid job specification in local administration

too many managers and too few operational staff

uncertainty over future schemes and planning policies

over-ambitious schemes incapable of implementation

over-rigid local plans, and

a slow and unresponsive planning system.

A number of the studies are agreed collectively upon certain actions that planners should take in assisting an inner-city revival:

a national vacant land survey should be established with specific reference to publicly-owned inner-city land

declining inner-city areas should be zoned as 'enterprise areas' within which planning legislation and taxation are eased to encourage the re-use of vacant or derelict land

co-ordination of inner-city areas by commercial agencies similar to new town corporations

vacant land should be regarded as a long-term feature of inner-city requiring temporary treatment and landscaping

vacant land should be eased of its restrictions to enable local communities to use space for recreation, allotments, small parks and general local initiatives

decision-making should become more localised, involving local people more readily than is possible under existing administrative systems.[19]

In 1980 the Conservative Government began to implement most of these recommendations, partly by streamlining the previous Labour Government's extensive urban programme of partnership areas and inner-city and derelict land grants; and partly by the forceful introduction of the Local Government, Planning and Land Bill.[20] The purpose of this document was to ease some of the over-complex and often stultifying planning procedures and legislation, while bringing three particular instruments to the statute books aimed at encouraging the re-use of urban wasteland and at the revival of local inner area economies:

Land Registers — public authorities in selected areas containing a high level of wasteland would be required to register land that is within their ownership and is unused or underused. The Secretary of State for the Environment would have the power to direct public bodies (such as local authorities, British Rail, local Water Boards, etc.) to dispose of sites on the Register by sale or auction. Two weaknesses of land registers are that they do not include privately owned land and that the release of publicly owned land to the private sector does not mean that vacant or derelict land will necessarily be reclaimed or developed.

Urban Development Corporations (UDCs) — these would be established within defined Urban Development Areas. By 1980 UDCs had been established for the London and Merseyside Docklands with chairmen from each brought in from the private sector. The powers and duties of the UDCs broadly match those of the New Town Development Corporations so that they can develop land in the same way as a private landowner, but with more assurance that the local authorities concerned will grant planning permission. UDCs have a single-minded purpose of stimulating urban development and the reuse of vacant or underused land. However, it is feared that such an aggressive approach to inner-city areas could create poor quality architecture and environments similar to much of the staid and insensitively built environments created within many of Britain's new towns.

Enterprise Zones — a number of experimental zones of approximately 500 acres would be established in which planning and taxation controls would be significantly eased, or removed altogether,[21] to enable the more desolate areas of vacant urban land to be brought back into use — particularly in areas where land and buildings are poorly maintained. The Royal Town Planning Institute raised serious doubts over the designation of such zones which in effect would mean a return to the pre-1947 Town and Country Planning Act days in which there would be few development controls and in which a developers' free-for-all could result in a low quality environment.

Although the Local Government Planning and Land Bill placed emphasis upon the re-use of wasteland by the private sector, substantial financial and administrative arrangements were made for public authorities to support private initiatives:

Derelict Land Clearance Grants — these were an extension of existing land clearance grants (up to 100 per cent in some areas) in which payment would be

Derelict Land Clearance Grants these were an extension of existing land clearance grants (up to 100 per cent in some areas) in which payment would be made directly to private individuals and organisations rather than to local authorities only. The grants would also be made available for all reclamation schemes (no longer restricted to approved schemes within Derelict Land Clearance Areas) and included, for the first time, grant-aid for the basic development of associated infrastructure such as sewers, roads, piped services and special foundations.

Partnership and Programme Areas — the new legislation brought an extension of existing partnerships between central and local government. Central government aid was also made available to programme authorities, through the urban programme, for projects such as the construction of small factories, the sale of public land for private housing, the creation of landscaped open space and land and building improvement initiatives contributed by voluntary organisations. In 1980 the Government White Paper *Expenditure Plans* emphasised that the partnership and programme authority arrangements introduced in England by the previous government would be strengthened, but would continue to offer a co-ordinated attack on inner area problems through special programmes.[22]

By 1980 it was being suggested by a number of professionals involved in inner city land use that the planning provisions made during the second half of the 1970s by successive governments were inadequate and merely tinkering with an existing system of land use management that required an overall review. The effectiveness of these changing inner-city policies will inevitably take time to emerge — longer certainly than the average life of a government:

'vacant land is not an insignificant and temporary feature of the environment or of the land economy. The spatial and temporal extent of land vacancy has grown too great to be regarded merely as elbow room for city development or as a necessary and temporary means towards some environmental end-state. This 'temporary environment' is all that many of those who live and work in the cause of great cities have ever seen and are likely to see for years into the future, unless it is realised that the vacancy period between the cessation of one use on a site and its redevelopment for another use, does exist and requires as much planning and attention as is given to the more established uses of city land. Recognition of the situation by everyone, such as becomes a political issue, is essential if effective action is to be taken.[23]

The inner-city will preoccupy administrators and decision-makers to the end of the century and well beyond. Although vacant land is only one aspect of the inner city problem its presence, unlike many of the less evident social and economic problems, is a constant reminder that urban society is now passing through one of the most radical technological changes since the Industrial Revolution. For this reason alone the recreation of inner city *as it was* is a foolish notion — its revival will rely more upon innovation and the unfamiliar.

Notes

1. *Policy for the Inner Cities*, White Paper, HMSO, 1977, p.70
2. Lewis Herber, *Our Synthetic Environment*, Jonathan Cape, 1963

3. John Burrows, 'Vacant Urban Land — a Continuing Crisis', *The Planner*, January 1978
4. Department of the Environment, 'Change or Decay', Final Report of the Liverpool Inner Area Study, HMSO, 1977
5. *Urban Wasteland*, Report on land lying dormant in cities, towns and villages in Britain, Civic Trust, 1977
6. *Urban Wasteland, op. cit.*
7. *Report of the Royal Commission on Housing of the Working Classes*, 1884
8. *Sanitary Conditions of the Labouring Population of Great Britain*, Poor Law Commissioners, 1843
9. William Ashworth, *The Genesis of Modern Town Planning*, Routledge and Kegan Paul, 1953
10. 'Change or Decay', *op. cit.* and Department of the Environment, *Inner Area Studies: Liverpool, Birmingham and Lambeth*, HMSO, 1977
11. P. J. Taylor, A. M. Kirby, K. J. Harrop and G. Gudgin, *Atlas of Tyne-Wear*, Newcastle University, 1976
12. *Housing Associations in the Inner City Housing Market*, Paper to the National Federation of Housing Associations Conference, 1977
13. Rosemary Righter, 'Glasgow Wakes to Wasteland', *Sunday Times*, 30 January 1977
14. Colin Ward, *The Child in the City*, Architectural Press, 1978, p. 34
15. D. G. Price and A. J. Cummings, *Family Planning Clinics in London*, Paper No. 21, Polytechnic of Central London, nd
16. Quoted by D. Herbert in D. Herbert and R. Johnston (eds), 'Urban education: problems and policies', *Social Areas in Cities*, Wiley, 1976
17. 'Change or Decay', *op. cit.*
18. Department of the Environment, *Liverpool Inner Area Study – Vacant Land*, Report by the Consultants, 1976
19. A summary of the main recommendations made by Graham Moss in his opening address to the Conference 'The Conservative Approach to Inner City Problems' and supported by Michael Heseltine MP in his closing speech to the same conference held in Birmingham on 17 July 1978
20. Local Government, Planning and Land Bill (No.2), HMSO, London, 1980
21. Sir Wilfred Burns, Deputy Secretary and Chief Planner of the Department of Environment speaking at the Conference on 'Urban Wasteland' organised by the Royal Society of Arts on 18 June 1980, defined the structure of Enterprise Zones:
    (a) they will be areas of significant size — perhaps 500 acres;
    (b) there will be 100 per cent capital allowances for industrial and commercial buildings;
    (c) full relief from DLT;
    (d) full derating of industrial and commercial property;
    (e) exemption from the scope of industrial training boards with consequent exemption from industrial training levies;
    (f) accelerated handling of applications for warehousing free of Customs duty;
    (g) a simplified planning control system with the Secretary of State agreeing with the LPA the broad planning proposals and policies for the area and the arrangements for ensuring quick decisions (for building regulation applications as well); detailed control is to be avoided;
    (h) abolition of IDCs;
    (j) minimal requests for statistical returns;
    (k) designation initially for a period of ten years
22. Cmnd 7841, 1980
23. John Burrows, 'How much vacant land?', *The Architects' Journal*, 18 May 1977

CHAPTER 8

Land and the Technological Fix

'Each person in an industrial society is dependent upon what amounts to a vast life support system in which he plays only a minute part. Where the members of a family could once clothe themselves in woollens and leather using their own raw materials, we are now dependent for clothing on oil-wells, oil tankers, refineries, the chemical industry, textile-machinery manufacturers, and the metal and power industries needed to back them up. The same goes for our food, heating, transport and almost every other item that we consume. The productive system depends increasingly upon . . . more fundamental and radical transformation processes, and the technology it needs becomes ever more sophisticated.'

Richard Wilkinson, 1973

More is less

The momentum of two centuries of industrial development has now carried western society into a position of deepening dependence upon a technology which demands more and more from the land. Our expectations as consumers have risen as an endless stream of scientific and technological innovation has pampered and eased us into an often unthinking complacency. We have committed ourselves totally to mechanisation: automation has taken the place of human labour; high speed transport has brought a highly mobile society; modern communications have brought instant contact between people over vast distances; new forms of energy have brought heat, light and sound to each of us at the flick of a switch or the push of a button; modern industrial farming techniques are bringing 'conveyor belt' food grown with the use of chemicals and artificial fertilisers; medicine is rearing progressively aseptic beings and a society reliant upon artificial aids and drugs, which like agricultural chemicals may be interfering with the biological activities of nature. This widespread dependence upon scientific advance has ensnared us in a 'technological fix' from which we are unable to free ourselves without determined and courageous decisions that would change the very philosophies and comforts that characterise our twentieth-century lives. We are caught in the clutches of advanced and often potentially lethal technological innovations employed to maintain the status quo and to delay the day of reckoning.

Where changing technologies once had the effect of freeing land for agriculture — as in developments which permitted the substitution of coal for firewood and mechanisation for animal power in mining and transport — the onset of what was called the 'new industrial revolution' has tended towards a large-scale and often permanent removal of land from agricultural and other biological uses. As urban society

(*Photograph: Architectural Press Ltd.*)

developed, rural society has inevitably given way to technological changes that have made life in the countryside easier, communications more certain and living standards more reliant upon modern invention. However with these benefits have come disadvantages. As technology has become more demanding and often dangerous, polluting, noisy, poisonous and obnoxious, society has tended to place a buffer between itself and the very activities upon which it relies, but which it cannot tolerate at close range. Whilst it may be possible to produce figures of land taken permanently out of the countryside and agriculture for developments such as motorways and major industrial installations, it is less easy to define the areas of often sterile buffer land around these developments. There are considerable official and unofficial restrictions on the potential use of land in the vicinity of motorways, nuclear power stations, airfields, mines, hazardous and toxic industries and pipe lines, and waste dumping grounds. These restrictions frequently force other urban developments into a wasteful, piecemeal encroachment on land: either threatening its potential productivity or more generally menacing human and wild life with pollution, noise, danger, smell or other intolerable environmental consequences. This is the price paid by a society that continues to rely upon the innovations of modern science and technology; a price that rises as traditional sources of energy and materials and methods of processing begin to fail.

When, in 1959 in *English Rural Life*, H. E. Bracey warned of the first stages of the 'new industrial revolution' making its incursions into the British countryside, he could not have foreseen that more than 20 years later Britain's land use planning system would still be operating on assumptions inherited from a time of plentiful agricultural land and technologies of lesser environmental impact. The proliferation of wasteful development and despoiled and sterilised land is the legacy of a developing society and a planning system that has lacked the collective imagination to understand and then to minimise the consequences upon land of such a high rate of technological change and resource depletion. It is also a reflection of a failure in values, through the inconsequential and prodigal manner in which we have inflicted irreversible changes on our precious and finite resources of land, mineral wealth, beauty and solitude. Each small incursion into any one of these precious resources leaves a little more damage and interference to the landscape:

'As users of land, we sometimes behave as though we inhabited the centre of a vast virgin continent instead of a relatively small island.'[1]

What has been the impact so far of modern science and technology upon Britain's land and natural resources?

An age of mobility
Late 20th-century society is characterised by the speed with which available methods of transportation have developed — methods that are extremely vulnerable to sudden and rapid change, as was emphasised during the 1970s when the Oil Producing and Exporting Countries (OPEC) showed how easily a world that had become accustomed to uninterrupted travel could be held to ransom. Britain is one of the most over-roaded countries in the world. There are 2.4 miles of road for every square mile of land. A cursory examination of airfield and railway closures since the last war might suggest that as much land had been released for other uses as had been taken for motorway construction or airport extensions — but this is not the case. New transport technologies exert increasingly restrictive influences on land use wherever they extend.

Roads
The most noticeable change in transportation since the War has been the switch from

(Photograph: The Guardian)

126

Since the last war the spread of roads and the development of vehicle technology have brought unlimited mobility and an uncompromising impact upon land and the living environment. Strathclyde, Scotland. (Photograph: The Scotsman Publications Ltd.)

rail to road of both goods and passengers. By 1975, 92 per cent of passenger traffic and 65 per cent of goods traffic in Great Britain were thundering along our highways, carrying nearly 18 million vehicles. Road transport has been dominant since the middle of the 1960s assisted on the one hand by railway line closures implemented under the Beeching Plan during the 1960s, together with a general reduction in local railway networks; and on the other hand by the enormous power wielded by the 'road lobby'. This has resulted in a drastic loss of land and in the declining

TABLE 7 CHANGES IN BASIC ROAD AND RAILWAY STATISTICS BETWEEN 1920 AND 1977

	ROADS				RAILWAYS		
	Length of all public roads (miles)	Length of motor-ways (miles)	Road vehicles in use (millions)	Road vehicles per mile of road	Length of track open to traffic (track miles)		
					Running lines	Sidings	Total
1920	n.a.	-	0·65	-	n.a.	n.a.	n.a.
1930	179,290	-	2·27	12·7	n.a.	n.a.	n.a.
1940	n.a.	-	2·32	-	n.a.	n.a.	n.a.
1950	183,820	-	4·41	23·9	36,250	15,750	52,000
1960	194,180	95	9·44	48·6	34,500	14,380	49,180
1970	200,390	655	14·95	74·6	23,730	7,550	31,280
1975	208,280	1,420	17·70	85·5	22,230	6,350	28,580

Source: Annual Abstracts of Statistics

Railways have brought access to the most remote areas of Britain. (Photograph: Impact Press Pictures)

environmental conditions of so many areas through which new roads and motorways have been built, even after early warnings from OPEC in 1973. The imbalance between the extensive and penetrating road networks and the relatively limited railway networks is reflected in the mileages of both, shown in Table 7. In 1977 the railways had over 22,000 miles of running lines and 6,000 miles of sidings; by comparison Britain's public roads extended for more than 210,000 miles, of which 1,500 were motorways.

Given the prodigious increase in car ownership in Britain, particularly since 1960, it might seem that an increase of only 16 per cent in the mileage of public roads over the last half century constitutes an under-provision. In fact land take for each road mile appears to have increased significantly. In 1949 government estimates for land take for the proposed motorway programme were set at 12-20 acres for each motorway mile. In 1979 the government estimated that 38,000 acres of land had been taken for the construction of motorways.[2] However a detailed article in the *Journal of the Town and Country Planning Association* in 1978 based upon a survey of land take for new roads estimated that the government's motorway figure was more likely to be 50,000 acres and that the estimate of land take for each motorway mile would be double the government's original estimate.[3]

Motorways and other major roads do not merely serve as a focus for new development; they also repel it along their borders, so that long strips of land are left sterilised because of traffic noise and fumes, unfit for any kind of urban use other than waste dumping and gipsy encampments. This situation has come about as a result of government guidelines laid down for planning authorities in 1973, when the Department of Environment advised strongly against residential development in areas subject (or likely to become so within 15 years) to specific noise levels on an officially adopted scale.[4] Although the use of noise insulation allows this buffer zone around roads to be narrowed, the extra building costs incurred tend to discourage new construction near major roads, except in localities where building land is in short supply. The interchangeability of land and insulation, and the variation in standards adopted by planning authorities, make any calculation of the area of land left sterilised and wasted extremely uncertain.

Railways
Almost as difficult to calculate is the area of land lying derelict and unused as a result of railway closures. British Rail claims that it is under statutory obligation to act commercially in all its land transactions, although, like all other nationalised industries, it is obliged also to take into account the public interest when disposing of land. The slowness with which idle railway land has been converted to other uses must also be attributed to the failure of statutory authorities to take advantage of the procedure whereby they are allowed up to twelve months to prepare plans for the after-use of disused railway lines in the countryside.[5] Local authorities do not always appreciate the possibilities of re-using disused railways for footpaths and bridleways, or even future re-use as railways, by-passes and slip roads. The sale of small portions of such land can destroy the possibility of using its potential to the full.

Although much abandoned railway land still lies idle, there has been a technical improvement since 1968, when only just over one-third of the railway lines closed in Britain since nationalisation had been sold.[6] By the end of 1978 a higher proportion

The closure of railway lines leaves extensive arteries of land that could be held in readiness for future communication needs while offering a variety of leisure and recreational uses in the meantime. The sale of even the smallest strip of land can interrupt its future communications potential. Accrington, Lancashire. (Photograph: Civic Trust)

Redundant railway structures offer a range of possible alternative uses. Keswick, Cumbria. (Photograph: Civic Trust)

130

of railway land subject to closure had been sold, leaving a balance of approximately 31,000 acres of land regarded by British Rail as 'non-operational'.[7] Land sale does not, however, guarantee that such land is put to use. The derelict land surveys of England (1974) and Wales (1972),[8] which included railway land lying derelict irrespective of ownership, showed that there were at least 28,500 acres of derelict railways; it is possible that further areas were not recorded, simply because they had passed out of British Rail ownership, or because they were not readily classifiable as 'abandoned'. Although lack of statistical information makes estimates extremely tentative, it seems likely that from various statistics there may have been more than 45,000 acres of derelict railway land at the end of the 1970s in Britain.

Airfields
The impact of transport upon land is not limited to road and rail; civil airfields have also expanded since the last War. They have increased in number from 90 in 1935 to 125 in 1980, and the need to accommodate more and larger aircraft has brought a sharp increase in land used for airfields, from 12,000 to 45,000 acres over this period.[9] The impact of this expansion in air traffic has been felt most strongly on land surrounding major commercial airfields, in two particular ways:

1   Local authorities have been required to establish Public Safety Zones at each end of any runway having 1,500 actual or 2,500 potential air transport movements in any one month. Development controls are then exercised to ensure that there is no significant increase in number of people living, working, or congregating within the Zones. Each Zone covers on average more than 200 acres; observance of development controls, which are monitored by the Department of Trade, can define an area up to 6,000 acres within which virtually all new development is precluded.[10] In addition local authorities' controls can add to the extent of land that is 'blighted'. However these central and local government controls rarely affect the use of land for agriculture.

2   Development controls covering aircraft noise extend over a much wider area than Public Safety Zones, and were suggested originally in 1973 by the Department of Environment, which set out broadly the controls established independently in 1967 by Surrey County Council for land around Gatwick Airport.[11]

The standards are expected to be adhered to unless development 'need' is overriding and clearly cannot be met on alternative, less noisy sites. An examination of the noise contour map published by the Department of Trade[12] shows on measurement that approximately 300,000 to 400,000 acres of land fall within a noise contour 35 (referred to as Noise and Number Index, or NNI, 35) within which planning applications may be refused when considerations of aircraft noise are taken into account; and that over 50,000 acres around the main British airports fall within the 50 NNI limits in which most physical development is unlikely to be allowed. Although these airport buffer zones are likely to contract as larger, quieter aircraft are introduced, it is nevertheless evident that as air transport has grown in intensity, large tracts of land have been left sterilised, in the interests of health and safety, and are now incapable of normal development. As with other buffer zones, those around

(*Photograph: Architectural Press Ltd.*)

airfields have encouraged wasteful fragmentation of urban development and a costly encroachment onto agricultural land elsewhere. The apparent inability on the part of Britain's planning and legislative system to minimise the impact of changing technological innovation is not limited to transport — it has also become progressively evident around industrial activities.

The demands of modern technology

As our society has become more dependent upon technology, and the gap between the production of raw materials and their final consumption has widened with the proliferation of complex manufacturing processes — so too have these new technologies generated powerful and intractable needs of their own. The 'technological imperative' (though vociferously challenged by conservation groups and exponents of alternative technology) has extended to the creation of highly specific demands upon land. Only 40 to 50 per cent of land in urban use is taken up by residential development; much of the remainder falls under uses of high technological intensity which are considered to be: 'Very much more difficult for planners to control because they tend to be generated by powerful national bodies who are rather inflexible in their siting requirements'.[13] In addition to their specific siting requirements, modern industrial and power-generating technologies have often created a multiplicity of actual or potential hazards to health or life. These dangers have given rise to widespread restrictions on the uses of nearby land, which usually far exceed in area the land taken for the installations themselves.

Not all industrial installations pose planning problems of equal magnitude. Secondary processing and manufacturing installations tend to be much more flexible in their siting requirements and tend to contain facilities which can be more readily converted to other uses. Nevertheless the requirements for raw materials, fuel and water are potent contributors to any consideration of major land use changes. The demands of modern industry for process cooling water, for example, have contributed to the shift of reservoir construction away from Britain's uplands into valuable agricultural areas nearer to concentrations of industry and populations.

Electricity

By comparison with industrial processes, the demands of electricity generating stations for water are phenomenal. A 660 megawatt station requires an average of 13 million gallons of cooling water per hour. However there are other fastidious requirements that have a bearing on site quality and location, including:

large areas of flat land with high load-bearing capacity

close proximity to major coalfields for coal-fired stations, and access to deep water or oil refineries for many oil-fired stations; and

remoteness from centres of population in the case of nuclear power stations and related facilities.

The electricity generating industry has been a major force in the spread of obtrusive installations throughout Britain's river valleys and along her coastlines.

133

Electricity power stations are making increasing demands upon Britain's coastal and estuarine land. Design and landscaping have not always been given priority. Wylfa Nuclear Power Station, Gwynedd, North Wales. (Photograph: Aerfoto (London) Ltd.)

Although power stations are perhaps unique among major installations in their capacity to give weight and form to landscape (which may otherwise remain indeterminate), their visual intrusion in the more sensitive areas of outstanding natural landscape has commonly given rise to local public opposition. A new 3,000 megawatt coal-fired station might have boiler, turbine houses and ancillary plant of up to 1,000 feet in length and nearly 250 feet in height, with associated clusters of cooling towers more than 300 feet high, all given dominance in the landscape by a chimney stack of over 650 feet.

The shift in the location of electricity generating stations away from urban centres over the last two decades, under the impact of changing economies in fuel supply and technical developments in transmission, has brought a major impact upon the landscape beyond that associated with the power stations alone.

By 1975 the super-grid consisted of 2,900 miles of 400 kv and 1,300 miles of 275 kv transmission lines, none of which had been in existence two decades previously. The 400 kv network alone will have taken over 400 acres of land for its five pylons a mile. Beyond this, every new tentacle of overhead line requires electricity sub-stations for its intermittent joints, each taking upwards of 25 acres, and rising to a height of 60-70 feet. Although the recent high rate of extensions of the super-grid is likely to fall somewhat in the 1980s large scale development of alternative energy sources such as wind-power may create 'wirescapes' in hitherto untouched areas, as will the continuation of coastal siting of major industrial facilities such as oil and gas processing plants and nuclear installations.

134

TABLE 8 LAND AND SITING REQUIREMENTS OF OIL- AND GAS-RELATED INSTALLATIONS

Installation	Land take (acres)	Example	Site requirements (see note)
Gas			
North Sea gas terminal	170-200	Bacton	INFL
Gas terminal and separation plant	500	St. Fergus	FL
Natural gas liquids plant	200	-	
High pressure methane pipeline	-	Gas council grid	Wayleaves: no development on 9·5 acres/mile Restricted development on a further 50 acres/mile
Gas pipeline compressor stations	60	-	Every 40-50 miles; FL
Oil and petrochemicals			
Production platform construction:			
concrete	20-100	Loch Kishorn	V.INFL
steel	70-170	Graythorpe	INFL
Oil pipeline landfall and pumping station	20	Cruden Bay	INFL
Oil terminal and related plant	150-850	Milford Haven	V. INFL
Oil refinery	250-1100	Fawley (1000 acres)	INFL
Tank farm	350	Llandarcy	FL
Petrochemicals:			
ethylene cracker	200	Baglan Bay	INFL
olefin production	250-2000	Teeside	INFL
High pressure ethylene pipeline	-	Grangemouth to Teeside	Wayleave: no development on 2·4 acres/mile

Note: V. INFL — very inflexible; INFL — inflexible; FL — flexible. Where a range of figures is given, the higher figure reflects groupings of associated processes and land acquired for further development or protective zoning.

Sources: Scottish Development Department, *Land Use Summary Sheet No 6 Oil, Gas and Petrochemicals* 1977; A. Hutcheson and A. Hogg, *Scotland and Oil*, 1975; J. Blunden, *Energy Development and Land Use in the UK*, 1979 and J. Blunden, *The Mineral Resources of Great Britain*, 1975.

Oil and gas processing installations

Developments associated with the production and primary processing of oil and gas can create planning difficulties because of the inflexibility of their siting requirements alone, even where landtakes are small (see Table 8). Perhaps the outstanding examples in this respect are sites for concrete oil-production platforms. Although these only require around 20-100 acres of land, the completion of platform construction needs nearby sheltered waters approaching depths of 700 feet, and then towing

135

Electricity supply lines can affect the efficient use of farmland and are not always a welcome feature in the landscape. (Photograph: Architectural Press Ltd.)

channels of up to 130 feet in depth. These needs can often be met only in remote coastal areas, which tend also to be highly valued for their landscape beauty. It was the resistance of the local planning authority to just such a proposed site on Loch Carron that, in 1974, forced the Conservative Government to introduce new legislation to circumvent the normal planning processes, allowing the compulsory purchase of sites proposed for oil-related development. Although the Bill was shelved by the incoming Labour Government, continuing pressure to maximise both the extraction of oil and Britain's involvement in the manufacture and provision of technological hardware for the North Sea had not eased the difficulties faced by local communities in absorbing large-scale and often short-term development.

Over the last 15 years, gas processing and distribution has, like electricity generation and transmission, become predominantly rural-based where previously it was almost exclusively town-based. Prime agricultural land has often been built over, as happened at Bacton where the North Sea gas terminal took 200 acres of valuable land against the wishes of Norfolk County Council. A less visible, but nevertheless extensive, impact of the development of North Sea gas has been the construction, since the mid-1960s, of a nationwide gas grid extending over 3,000 miles. Although agriculture can proceed normally once the pipelines have been laid, 'wayleave' requirements for maintenance access are such that 9.5 acres per mile of pipeline must normally be kept free from all physical development, and a further 50 acres per mile or more of development is severely restricted. Similarly, although the 25 or so pipeline compressor stations built for the new grid each cover only 10 acres of land, soundproofing and screening requirements increase the enclosed area to 60 acres.

Nuclear installations

Like oil-processing industries, the nuclear industry has stringent requirements not only for land required for buildings, but also for buffer land between itself and other activities. While a nuclear power station, for example, may physically occupy an area of 80-130 acres, provision for the construction of further reactors to replace old ones at the end of their relatively short working life may inflate this figure considerably.

Until 1968 sites for nuclear installations were selected according to population levels within a 5 mile radius of those locations which met the other requirements of nuclear technology. All subsequent development was then restricted so that emergency plans for dealing with accidents would not be hindered and so that the number of people at risk in the event of an accident was kept to a minimum. Since 1968 Britain's expanding nuclear programme, prompted latterly by a growing energy crisis, has of necessity increased official confidence in the safety of reactors and strong competition with other uses for a limited number of potential sites has brought a relaxation in the siting requirements for proven designs being built at the end of the 1970s — for example, those near Heysham and Hartlepool. Development controls are still retained and all proposals that may involve an increase in population within a zone of two-thirds of a mile, or developments providing accommodation for 50 people or more on land between two-thirds and two miles of a nuclear plant, must be referred to the Secretary of State for Energy, who will allow such development only under exceptional circumstances. These two zones constitute areas of nearly 900 acres and over 8,000 acres, respectively. More relaxed controls are also operated over wider radii; at Bradwell and the Winfrith Heath reactor research station in Dorset, for example, controlled zones extend for a radius of 5 miles, covering over 50,000 acres of surrounding land.[14] Around the 19 major nuclear sites in Britain at the end of the 1970s there were approximately 165,000 acres of land upon which development was severely restricted.

In 1974 an explosion occurred in a plant processing raw material for the manufacture of nylon, built on 60 acres of land just outside Flixborough Village in Humberside; 28 people were killed, 36 were seriously injured and within a 3-mile radius 1,575 houses were damaged. So powerful was the explosion that 90 per cent of

All too frequently petrochemical industries have been allowed to scar the landscape and pollute the surrounding environment with smoke, solid and liquid waste. The demand for cleaner industrial processes grew during the 1970s. (Photograph: Architectural Press Ltd.)

The advent of nuclear power has brought a new threat of irreversible contamination to surrounding land and is a potential danger to nearby communities in the event of accident. Buffer land surrounding such hazardous installations is subject to planning restrictions that can bring an underuse of land – often good farmland. Wylfa Nuclear Power Station, Gwynedd, North Wales. (Photograph: Central Electricity Generating Board)

138

all buildings within a 2-mile radius were damaged. In the aftermath of the disaster the Health and Safety Executive set up an Advisory Committee on Major Hazards, whose terms of reference included an assessment of the planning system as applied to the control of major industrial installations. Since 1976 the Committee has been preparing siting guidelines and hazardous substance regulations. However, by the end of the 1970s the Health and Safety Executive was still a non-statutory advisory body to whom local authorities could refer major industrial planning applications for risk appraisal. By 1979 the Health and Safety Executive had adopted a standard radius of two kilometres for this safety appraisal zone. Planning authorities were also advised to minimise hazards arising from new industrial development by careful siting. By the end of the 1970s there were more than 500 major installations that constituted health and safety risks.

The potential hazards, and the peculiar demands which modern industrial methods make on land, have effectively encouraged a division of responsibility at central Government level with regard to land-use planning. As a result land-use planning has suffered both in coherence and in achievement. This division of responsibility is nowhere more keenly demonstrated than between the Department of Environment and the Ministry of Agriculture, Fisheries and Food. However, although agriculture has repeatedly been the loser in any land-use conflict, technology has again stepped in to appease the situation.

The future of modern agriculture

A remarkable feature of Britain's industrial progress this century has been the extent to which productivity improvements in industry have been consistently outstripped by those in the supposedly conservative agricultural sector. Output per acre of most crops has increased by $1\frac{1}{2}$ to 2 times the levels attained in 1900; similar increases have been registered in animal husbandry, for example in milk and egg yields per animal.[15]

This progress has largely been achieved through a wide range of innovation in agricultural machinery, fertilisers, pesticides and herbicides and in the breeding of special crop and animal strains, as well as the rationalisation of farms into fewer, larger units of land better capable of physically and economically accommodating these innovations. The extension of a technologically controlled environment over an area of crops and grass, which has diminished by $4\frac{1}{2}$ million acres during this century, has meant that domestic food production has increased at a faster rate than Britain's population.

The critical factor for justifying concern over the diminishing stock of Britain's agricultural land is the increasing costliness of fuel and the crisis that has developed over oil-based technology since the end of the 1970s. Although the direct use of fuel in agriculture amounts to only 1 per cent of total primary fuel consumption in Britain, the dependence of farming on oil-based products including fertilisers, chemicals and machinery takes this figure up to 4 per cent. In the past half century, farmers (like industrial and domestic consumers) have based their use of fuel on the assumption that fuel supplies will remain plentiful and cheap indefinitely. Despite the prospect of a temporary abundance of North Sea Oil, it is certain that fuel will now become more expensive and more scarce, as will fertilisers and agricultural chemicals manufactured from petrochemical processes.

TABLE 9   USE OF ENERGY IN THE UK

	% of primary fuel	% increase in consumption per year
Agriculture	1·0	+ 4·1
Iron and steel	7·4	- 1·5
Other industry	21·8	+ 2·7
Railways	0·6	- 7·0
Road transport	11·3	+ 6·6
Shipping	0·5	- 2·7
Air transport	2·2	+ 9·7
Domestic	16·9	+ 0·3
Public services	4·0	+ 3·4
Miscellaneous	3·4	+ 0·1
General losses	30·9	
	100·0 .	

Source: Sir Kenneth Baxter, 'When the Oil runs out...', *Farmers' Weekly*, January 20, 1978, pages 83-87, Table 5.

TABLE 10   ENERGY INPUTS INTO UK AGRICULTURE

	% of total
Direct fuel	38
Fertilisers, lime and agrochemicals	41
Machinery, repairs and barn machinery	16
Transport to and from the farm	5
	100

Source: Sir Kenneth Baxter, 'When the Oil runs out...', *Farmers' Weekly*, January 20, 1978, pages 83-87, Table 6.

It is a reasonable assumption that energy-saving innovations will become available to agriculture in the near future; the development of a nitrogen-fixing capacity in crop plants and the extension of biological controls of pests in place of pesticides are only two of many possibilities. Equally, economy in the use of direct energy on the farm, changes in dietary habits, and energy-saving through regional and national crop specialisation are likely to ease the transition from an era of cheap fuel into a period of scarce and expensive energy. Nevertheless, it remains true that the age in

Transporting and burying nuclear waste has become the single most terrifying land use activity. Railyard, Southminster, Essex. (Photograph: Patrick Kinnersley)

which more energy can be freely substituted for less agricultural land is drawing to a close. While it may no longer be possible to maintain or increase Britain's food production by cropping more acres, the continuing and unprecedented loss of agricultural land to other uses will have to be quickly reduced if we are to retain an option of falling back on agricultural land which may otherwise be taken out of farming by a single-minded belief in technology.

Landscapes of defence

Wherever modern technology has been brought into use on a large scale it has generated buffer zoning of a hitherto unprecedented nature on a similarly unprecedented scale, and this at a time when the competing demands for scarce land have also reached new levels. Land used for military purposes is no exception. Pre-war land in use by the Services constituted an area of 252,000 acres. By 1973, when Britain's world military role and the numbers of men in the armed forces had both diminished substantially, the Services used a total of 750,000 acres. Although this area represents a very considerable reduction over the wartime figure of 11.5 million acres, it nevertheless indicates a trebling of land holdings over immediate pre-war levels as a result of modern technology. Such an extensive ownership of land by the armed forces may have some justification when viewed in the national interests of defence, but land covered by an unsightly assortment of barracks and gun emplacements, trails of rusting barbed wire and patchworks of concrete is difficult to justify, and is a dismal legacy of military ownership.

141

Caught in the technological fix, modern farming has become heavily reliant upon the oil, chemical and machine industries. Traditional field patterns have changed to accommodate new machinery and industrialised farm buildings that produce food more efficiently – but which barely compensate for the loss of agricultural land. Spratton, Northamptonshire. (Photograph: Farmers' Weekly)

Prior to 1974 no official survey of dereliction had included figures on that caused by the Services, on the grounds that all land held by them was, like the British Railways Board definition, operational land, and was still in use for defence purposes, whereas all land released could not be classified as derelict because compensation had been paid for reclamation. In 1974, however, over 9,300 acres were recorded under 'military and other service dereliction' by the Department of the Environment survey.[16] This innovation may be progressive in the sense that at least there is now official recognition of the problem. But other sources suggest that the extent of the problem is considerably understated by this figure.[17]

Acres of attrition

Table 11 indicates that by the end of the 1970s there could have been 1.2 million acres of buffer land affected by or likely to be affected by industrial pollution or environmental damage of some kind. A large proportion of this land is agricultural or potentially agricultural and is being farmed or used with various degrees of efficiency depending upon the damage, restrictions or limitations placed upon it by neighbouring incompatible activities. If urban wasteland, despoiled or derelict mineral land and potentially despoiled and derelict land is added to this figure then it is quite possible that at the end of the 1970s as many as 2.5 million acres of land in Britain were lying derelict, despoiled, underused or idle or potentially so — an area equivalent to 4.5 per cent of the land surface.

If these figures prove accurate, and from the extremely fragmented information

TABLE 11   SUMMARY OF ESTIMATED AREAS
OF MAIN BUFFER LAND IN BRITAIN IN 1980

Category	Extent (acres)
Nuclear installations	150,000
Hazardous industrial installations	200,000-600,000
Pipelines (wayleave of natural gas, BNOC and commercial pipes)	190,000
Roadside verges and wasteland	170,000-200,000
Airfields: public safety zones	6,000
noise zones	50,000
Approximate total range	766,000-1,196,000

Note: Not all of this land is vacant or underused and it is often still being used for agricultural or associated agricultural purposes, with certain restrictions and limited interruptions to normal operations.

Lagoons of liquid toxic waste at Pitsea in Essex. Can such land ever recover its biological potential for agriculture or will it automatically be designated for further urban expansion? (Photograph: Southend Air Photography Ltd.)

143

TABLE 12 SUMMARY OF BRITAIN'S WASTELAND OR POTENTIAL WASTELAND

Category	Definition	Source	Extent – Annual (acres)	Extent – Total (acres)
Farmland				
Official annual loss to urban use (annual average based on six-year period 1970–1975)	Farmland released to urban industrial and recreational development (England, Wales and Scotland)	Ministry of Agriculture, Fisheries & Food (England & Wales), 1978 Department of Agriculture (Scotland), 1978	37,800 2,500	- -
Official annual loss to other non-urban uses (annual average based on six-year period 1970–1975)	Farmland released to forestry, open space, military activities, leisure and recreation, reservoirs, etc. (England, Wales and Scotland)	Ministry of Agriculture, Fisheries & Food (England & Wales), 1978 Department of Agriculture (Scotland), 1978	38,300 50,000	- -
Total annual loss of agricultural land to non-agricultural uses in England, Wales and Scotland			128,600	-
Mineral wasteland				
Official derelict and despoiled land	Official definition includes operational land and abandoned spoil heaps, excavations and other land associated with these types of activity and including land so damaged by industrial or other development that it is incapable of beneficial use without treatment (England, Wales and Scotland)	Progress in Pollution Control, Pollution Paper No. 16, 'The UK Environment', HMSO, 1979 Department of the Environment The Welsh Office The Scottish Office	-	350,000
Unofficial estimate	Local authorities and other experts consider that the official definition is not comprehensive and is an underestimate of the true amount. Mineral land holding planning permissions or existing use rights is also at risk and considered potentially despoiled or derelict land (England, Wales and Scotland)	Survey in 1979 of county, regional and district authorities by author and other independent specialists indicated that derelict and despoiled and potentially derelict and despoiled land could be more than twice the official estimates	-	700,000+

	Land description		Source	Figure
Urban wasteland				
Unofficial estimate	Civic Trust definition of land lying vacant or in temporary use which could be brought into permanent use without major works of reclamation	–	Civic Trust report *Urban Wasteland*, 1977, based on sample returns from local societies in England, Wales and Scotland	250,000
Unofficial estimate	Wasteland and scrub found in the Second Land Utilisation Survey's definition of rurban land	–	Second Land Utilisation Survey England and Wales 1963 (excluding Scotland)	(346,000)*
			Forecast for 1977 (excluding Scotland)	(700,000)
General buffer land				
Unofficial estimate	Land in England and Wales that is underused or has ceased to be used for any specific purpose. Much of the land identified includes land uses covered by the author's figure below	–	Clifford Tandy in a paper given at the second Countryside in the '70s Conference in 1965, entitled 'Technology in Conservation'	(900,000)
Unofficial estimate	Land in England, Wales and Scotland either underused, vacant or otherwise blighted because of aircraft and traffic noise and fumes or toxic waste from industry; derelict land and land lying generally around industries, dangerous or otherwise incompatible technological installations and activities. Also includes large areas of land being farmed with only limited operational restrictions or interruptions	–	Sample survey in 1979 by the author covering major hazardous installations, nuclear developments, pipelines, road-side verges and wasteland, and airfields	Between 766,000 and 1,196,000
Military buffer land				
Unofficial estimate	Derelict military land in England and Wales	–	Estimated in 1978 by R. N. E. Blake in Trent Paper in Planning No. 78/8	20,000
Official estimate	**Derelict military land in England defined by the Department of the Environment**	–	Department of Environment, *Derelict and Despoiled Land in England 1974*	9,3000

* Figures in brackets are included, either in part or fully, in other figures for the same category.

available they could be an underestimate, then Britain's land use problems could be reaching crisis level — a crisis which will require at the very least a national land use survey to determine the ways in which Britain's land is used and could be used more rationally and a register of derelict land to enable local authorities to establish reclamation programmes. Despite our efforts now it will be future generations who will be forced to meet the cost of reinstating these landscapes. The last part of the book therefore looks at what we are doing and what we could be doing to prepare future generations for their responsibilities towards land.

Notes

1. A. Coleman, J. Weller and G. Moss, *Land-Use Perspectives*, Land Decade Educational Council, 1979, p.6
2. Hansard, 12 June 1979, HMSO
3. M. Bell, A. Hearne and D. Van Rest, 'Agricultural Landtake for New Roads', *Journal of Town and Country Planning*, March 1978, Vol. 46, No. 3, pp.164-7
4. Department of the Environment Circular 10/73, Planning and Noise, in which traffic noise levels are expressed in the so-called L10 (18 hr) scale; the area of land falling within the 70dB (A) level will vary considerably according to local topography, traffic flow, road gradient, etc.
5. Department of the Environment Circular 72/71, Disused Railway Lines in the Countryside
6. See J. Appleton, *Disused Railways in the Countryside of England and Wales*, 1970 and E. Parham, *Disused Railway Lines in Scotland* — A Strategic Appraisal, 1972, both prepared for the Countryside Commission
7. The Annual Abstracts of Statistics for 1978 indicate that over 8,500 miles of railway had been closed to traffic since 1948, suggesting that at least a further 7,000 acres could be realistically added to this figure
8. Department of the Environment, *Survey of Derelict and Despoiled Land in England*, HMSO, 1974 and Welsh Office, *Derelict Land Survey of Wales 1971-1972*, HMSO, 1975
9. R. N. E. Blake, 'The Impact of Airfields on the British Landscape', Geography Journal, 1969, Vol. 135, pp.508-28
10. Department of the Environment, Circular 96/72, Aerodrome Safeguarding, Town and Country Planning (Aerodromes)
11. E. Sibert, 'Aircraft noise and development control — the policy for Gatwick Airport', *Journal of the Town Planning Institute*, April 1969, pp.149-52 The Gatwick Scheme was based on the conclusions of the Wilson Committee Report *Noise*, Cmnd 2056, HMSO, 1963
12. Department of Trade, *Airport Strategy for Great Britain*, Vols. 1 and 2, 1975 and 1976
13. Alice Coleman, 'Is Planning Really Necessary?', *Geographical Journal*, 1976
14. H. E. Bracey, *Industry and the Countryside*, 1963
15. E. A. G. Robinson noted in 1967 that since 1900 'productivity per head in agriculture has risen by four-thirds, of the increase in productivity per head in industry. Over the period

from 1936 to 1938 output per worker in agriculture has risen $1\frac{1}{2}$ times as fast as output per worker in industry.'

16. Department of the Environment, *Survey of Derelict and Despoiled Land in England*, HMSO, 1974
17. R. N. E. Blake has estimated, after long acquaintance with the planning issues arising from the release of surplus military airfields, that the area of dereliction around these facilities alone constitutes about 20,000 acres. R. N. E. Blake, *Disused Airfields as a Planning Resource*, Trent Papers in Planning, No. 78/8, July 1978

PART 3

A TIME FOR CARING

'*That land is a community is the basic concept of ecology, but that land is to be loved and respected is an extension of ethics . . . We abuse land because we regard it as a commodity belonging to us. When we see land as a community to which we belong, we may begin to use it with love and respect.*'

Aldo Leopold, Sand County Almanac, *1949*

(Photograph: Graham Moss)

CHAPTER 9

Concern for the Environment

'men must still need to live in some derelict and creative relationship with the land from which they have come. they cannot fail to be the poorer for its impoverishment, to be scarred by its mutilation. People of this Island should put their hearts, their hands, and all their spare energy, which science has given them, into the restoration of their country. At the beginning of the Industrial Revolution gangs of navvies moved about like shock troops embanking, tunnelling, bridge building. Now such forces could be mustered to clear the filthy litter which the revolution has left in its wake. Instead, wealth is spent on patching minds and bodies damaged by "dirt, stink and noise", and in attempting to educate children who are condemned to live in surroundings which would make the educated profoundly unhappy.

Jacquetta Hawkes, A Land, 1978

A growing awareness

As society has leaned more and more heavily on technology, it has set itself on a plane above nature that has wrought destruction and havoc: permanently damaging land, destroying wildlife and creating artificial environments that are often alien to the needs and hopes of human beings. These activities have brought frequent gasps of horror and outrage from paternal conservationists of earlier generations like the Earl of Shaftesbury, who in 1909 exclaimed:

'I shall no longer resist the passion growing in me for things of a "natural" kind; where neither "Art" nor the "Conceit" or "Caprice" of man have spoiled their "genuine Order" by breaking in upon the "Primitive State".'

Such concern has multiplied during the 20th century as rising numbers of organisations and individuals, vociferous in proportion to their concern, have committed themselves to those ideals surrounding the ethics of land use and to appealing to the goodwill of society generally to spare the environment any further unnecessary battering from modern science and technology; 'Harmony between man and nature is no longer a mystical and abstract but a practical and pressing matter'.[1]

Concern over society's abuse of land and natural resources has brought a growing public awareness of environmental problems. By the end of the 1970s the reuse of existing buildings and materials, the conservation of land and natural resources and the safeguarding of wildlife and ecological processes were all related issues that were

(Photograph: Shelter)

assuming importance internationally. In 1980 the United Nations and World Wildlife Fund produced a 'World Conservation Strategy' that was a most important international statement about the conservation of land and natural resources: 'Earth is the only place in the universe known to sustain life. Yet human activities are progressively reducing the planet's life-supporting capacity at a time when rising human numbers and consumption are making increasingly heavy demands on it.'[2]

Referred to in 1979 as the 'greening of politics'[3] the ecological or 'green' movement came of age in France during the mid-1970s and became a powerful minority voice in the 1977 French elections, having captured as its political ally none other than the Mayor of Paris — a self-styled successor to the French President. Although the 'Green Movement' remains a minority voice, it has spread throughout Europe with remarkable speed and with an even more remarkable following. Britain's Ecology Party emerged in Britain during this period and by the 1979 general election was able to present candidates to contest most parliamentary constituencies throughout the country. Although the Ecology Party did not gain any Parliamentary seats, it had become, almost overnight, the most consistently successful new environmental movement, asserting its political strength and offering increasing hope for conservationists in the 1980s. For the first time in Britain, environmental concern was regularly reaching political ears, with a monotony of the kind that imprints itself on the subconscious. The European elections held in 1979 provided a powerful environmental platform that called for a 'Green Europe':

'Industrial growth, as we know it, involves the destruction of natural systems, the waste of resources and the pollution of the environment. It destroys human relations and aggravates social violence. It is a threat to future generations....'[4]

This quotation was the basic position of the candidates put forward for election by the group for European Ecological Action (Ecologica Europa) in 1979. It had the support of conservation groups throughout all European member countries. It had also stimulated the emergence of Britain's own 'Green Alliance' which brought together prominent people of diverse parties and backgrounds dedicated to a programme of ensuring that political priorities were viewed within ecological perspectives. By reshaping the decision-making framework, it was argued that the Alliance — whose diverse membership included the environmental writer Lord Ritchie Calder and the Dean of Westminster — hoped to set an example that would radically change the face of national planning by following a specific ten-point programme:

1 Investment in measures to use energy more efficiently, thus reducing the need to construct further environmentally damaging power stations particularly nuclear power stations

2 A transport policy which treats movement as a cost not a benefit, which seeks to reduce the distance between people and goods and services they require and which, by also shifting necessary freight to rail and waterways, curtails road and motorway construction

152

3   Measures to promote increased access by individuals, small farmers and community groups to land upon which they grow food

4   Allocation of public funds to a new labour-intensive programme of environmental and energy conservation

5   The introduction of environmental impact assessment for all projects, policies and programmes in the public sector

6   A programme of urban renewal based on the encouragement of small enterprises and the development of a humane urban environment

7   The preservation of wildlife by all measures necessary to protect endangered species including a moratorium on whaling, a ban on the import of sperm oil, and action against over-fishing

8   The reduction of all forms of pollution including lead traces in petrol

9   Long-term assistance to developing countries with emphasis on steps to improve trading terms in their favour, and

10 Measures to facilitate genuine democratic participation in decisions on all matters affecting the environment.

At about the same time the Land Decade Educational Council was constituted by a group of environmentalists from diverse backgrounds and sharing a mutual concern over the use of land. The Council, including such members as Lord Hunt, the first conqueror of Mount Everest, and Lord Dulverton, Chairman of the Forestry Commission of Great Britain, worked towards the designation of a Land Decade 1980-90 during which a better understanding and use of land would be encouraged throughout Britain. The programme for the Decade has the primary aim of establishing an official comprehensive national land-use survey and the gathering and disseminating of information through research and publications, conferences, informative and educational coverage by the press and television, formal environmental studies, beginning in primary schools, and community activities. Awards and incentives are offered for work that contributes to the improvement or careful maintenance of land generally. 1979 also saw the emergence of the Land Trusts Association, whose membership included Lord Arbuthnott, a Scottish landowner and environmentalist, and agriculturalist Sir Ralph Verney, and whose aims are to provide an alternative to public and private land ownership. Small estates, farms and villages would be protected by the management of land resources within a specially designed Land Trust.

By the end of the 1970s land and its use had become an issue of the deepest concern to a growing number of influential individuals and organisations and the course was

The effects of pollution upon the environment and damage to land lie at the heart of the conservation and ecology movements that are emerging throughout Europe. . . (Photograph: Architectural Press Ltd.)

set fair in Britain for the 1980s to herald new land-use concepts and to rethink the traditional ways in which planning and politics viewed land priorities and the allocation of resources. This collective concern was the culmination of and a tribute to the work of those earlier environmentalists who fought for generations for a more appropriate and caring use of Britain's land, but who have been unable to steer society clear of the technological fix.

The gathering grounds

The 19th century saw Charles Darwin's powerful and influential research on the origin of species. He opened up a debate upon the hitherto accepted methods by which Industrial Britain had, until that time, been developing. His ideas have continued to influence critics of the 'new technology' and conservationists everywhere. The threat of dereliction and waste and the evils of what was referred to as the 'industrial disease' brought conservation to the forefront of early legislation and encouraged the growth of organisations like the Commons and Open Spaces and Footpaths Preservation Society in 1865; the National Trust for Places of Historic Interest or Natural Beauty in 1895; the Royal Society for the Protection of Birds in 1889; the Society for the Preservation of Fauna of the Empire in 1903; the British Ecological Society in 1913; the Council for the Protection of Rural England in 1926 and Wales in 1928; and the National Trust for Scotland in 1931 (see Table 14 at the end of this chapter). By the mid-1930s, society had assembled an array of conservation groups, as land and nature began to show even more severe marks from industrial technology, the agricultural depression and the rapid and uncontrolled growth of towns and cities.

Ruskin and Howard were among the earliest opponents of urban sprawl. By the end of the 1930s their misgivings had come true. The results were there for all to see. Vast tracts of land had been swallowed up for buildings, roads and railways and for excavations for materials and energy. Individual voices began to express more forcibly than ever their anxiety over what they considered to be a waste of land and natural resources and its consequences upon the environment generally. The 1930s became the early gathering ground of an environmental lobby which grew in fits and starts. The seeds were sown in 1937 by a number of leading environmental practitioners and commentators who published *Britain and the Beast*, a series of emotive essays that warned against the deteriorating and wasteful state of Britain's land. In one essay, Clough Williams-Ellis, originator of Portmerion, the now famous planned italianate Welsh village, asked rhetorically: 'What are we doing with our inheritance?'; as if in reply E. M. Forster, a noted commentator of the time, proclaimed: 'We are making a screaming mess of England'.

Sir Dudley Stamp's Land Utilisation Survey, undertaken during the 1930s, gave added credence to these voices of doom, by charting the land use problems that had emerged since the First World War. In 1936 Stamp prophesied a gloomy future for land, with increased conflict, and a growing mixture of wasteful sprawl and dereliction. Twenty-five years later, in 1961, he had cause to write: 'It is of no little interest to note how we seem to be moving towards my prophetic future'.[5] In his now classic book published in 1948, *The Land of Britain – Its Use and Misuse*, Dudley Stamp produced, for the first time, a picture of 20th-century man's impact upon land. Much of his work and the statistical evidence collected by the many willing

Britain's most endearing environments have been fashioned by a joint partnership between nature and man. River Derwent, Cumbria. (Photograph: John Topham Picture Library)

156

... *Portmerion, North Wales. (Photograph: Sam Lambert)*

... *Japanese Garden, Covent Garden, 1978. (Photograph: Civic Trust)*

volunteers and collated on a shoe-string budget, was made available to the 1942 Scott Committee on Land Use in Rural Areas. Stamp was vice-chairman of the Committee and his evidence, both during and after the War, made a major contribution to the emergence of the 1947 Town and Country Planning Act, which brought the private activities of landowners and developers under public control — a control considered at the time to be an interference with liberty. Ten years earlier a perceptive contribution to *Britain and the Beast* had forecast this alternative to a free and uncontrolled land market: 'Part of the price for a saner and more orderly England must be paid for in liberty — not omitting that most cherished and private right to do public wrong'.[6].

The mere fact that the 1947 Town and Country Planning Act had reached the statute book was evidence in itself of the depth of concern felt not only by the public, but by politicians who had used the war years to review the social and economic state of Britain. The three major studies commissioned at the beginning of the War were equally indicative of the concern felt by the Government over the social and economic state of land use and human settlement. The 1940 Barlow Commission on the distribution of industrial population: the 1942 Scott Committee on Rural Land, and the Beveridge Committee on Social Insurance and Allied Services in the same year, all summed up the spirit of the times and were to become the basis of post-war economic, land-use and social philosophies. Encapsulating the three basic ideologies of the Reports, the 1944 White Paper on the Control of Land Use caught the general mood of concern and reflected the 'new spirit' — referred to in Chapter 3 — which became so strong a part of the post-war years:

'it is essential that the various claims on land should be so harmonised as to ensure for the people of this country the greatest possible measure of individual well-being and national prosperity.'

The introduction of town and country planning appeased public disquiet for the time being and with the introduction of new and expanded town policies to ease Metropolitan congestion, and green belts to stop the outward spread of towns and cities, a sense of calm fell upon the environmental critics and a complacent confidence upon society. Dudley Stamp continued to uncover land misuse through his land survey work and his last publication in 1962 left no doubt as to the poor state of Britain's land in spite of an increasing variety of planning controls.

Environmentalists were again stirred. They found voice in the mid-1960s — this time under the articulate guise of the Civic Trust, set up by Sir Duncan Sandys (now Lord Duncan-Sandys) in 1957 'to stimulate voluntary action and to remove eyesores which mar town and country'. In 1964 the Civic Trust's publication Derelict Land drew attention to the growth of dereliction caused by mineral workings, estimated to be growing at the rate of 3,500 acres per year; and to the 1 million lowland acres of derelict pasture and woodland and to the half a million acres of saltings that could be brought into profitable farming use:

'The devastation that is going on, at a rapid and accelerating pace, presents a different kind of problem. The damage our grandfathers did cannot now be undone; it can only be repaired. The damage we are doing now is within our own control.'[7]

At the same time, work by the land-use staticians Best and Coppock showed wide discrepancies between the work of Stamp and that of other organisations — particularly the Ministry of Agriculture — in relation to agricultural and urban land uses.[8] The discrepancies arose initially from the records of land in more than one use being made more than once, and were a serious reflection on the inadequate techniques and information held generally on land use. In 1969, in a series entitled 'Are We Wasting Britain's Land', the *Farmers' Weekly* pointed out that in the whole of Britain, nearly 40 per cent of the total agricultural area was rough grazing, producing only 5 per cent of the country's agricultural output. The series also drew attention to the 90,000 acres of coastal reclamation, which, if undertaken, could have transformed many acres into productive use.

In 1958 the Council for Nature was established to co-ordinate the work of, and provide information for, the many bodies concerned with the effects upon nature of changing industrial and agricultural practices. During the post-war reconstruction years a report by the Nature Reserves Investigation Committee, produced at the request of the Ministry of Reconstruction, confirmed that 'the Government should take formal responsibility for the conservation of native wildlife, both plant and animal, within the context of specifically established nature reserves'. In 1949 the Nature Conservancy was established. Its success was outstanding and in 1973 it became known as the Nature Conservancy Council, financed by the Department of the Environment and used as the Government's official adviser on nature conservation. Today the Council holds 135 National Nature Reserves covering more than a third of a million acres and in addition holds over 3,000 Sites of Specific Scientific Interest.

The quiet revolution

National organisations like the Civic Trust, the Councils for the Protection of Rural England, Wales and Scotland, the National Trust and Nature Conservancy Council found ever-increasing popular support during the 1970s and indulged in strong campaigning and publicity over land use and environmental problems. The 'Countryside in 70' conferences originated and presided over by Prince Philip set a pattern for the new decade. European Environmental Conservation Year in 1970, European Architectural Heritage Year in 1975, European Urban Renaissance Year in 1981 and Land Decade 1980-90 all emerged from a concern for the environment and were initiatives taken during little more than a single decade. Nor has initiative been limited to the national level only. A multitude of both official and unofficial local amenity and action groups has grown up, all committed to the problems of a particular aspect of their local area. Development versus conservation has been the underlying *raison d'être* of so much local and national action, and there has been a growing awareness among local communities and national amenity groups that something more than public participation, as conceived under the 1968 Town and Country Planning Act, is needed in the coming years. A closer permanent working relationship and open communication between decision-makers and the public is considered essential.

In 1976, at a Royal Geographical Society lecture, Miss Alice Coleman, Director of the Second Land Utilisation Survey of Great Britain, following the earlier work of Sir Dudley Stamp, reported that a comparison of her survey figures with Stamp's earlier figures, indicated that agricultural land was diminishing at an alarming rate

The 1970s saw the emergence of increasingly active public participation and community action. (Photograph: The Architectural Press Ltd.)

160

and that the general picture of land misuse was perhaps similar to that of the pre-planning period. In a major feature in the *Architects' Journal* in 1977, 'Land Use Planning — Success or Failure?', Coleman suggested that planners were to blame for the misuse of land, and that as a result planning had been a failure. Public opinion was excited, planners grew defensive and politicians became alarmed when she posed the question: 'Can we afford the vast expense of planning establishments when free enterprise will do the same job free?'[9]

The Civic Trust, having emerged from its highly successful European Architectural Heritage Year of 1975, drew a little upon Coleman's statistics in producing its *Urban Wasteland* report in 1977, which linked the agricultural land-loss problem with the vast acres of idle and derelict urban land lying throughout Britain's cities, towns and villages — enough, it was argued, to house 5 million people. Environmentalists duly took note. A host of semi-official reports all focussed upon land use, and were not slow in taking up the challenge. The end of the 1970s saw a flurry of activity. A National Wasteland Forum was established: the Town and Country Planning Association and Friends of the Earth, the world-wide environmental pressure group, took up the anti-nuclear cause; the National Trust highlighted the poor state and frequently derelict condition of many of Britain's country houses; John Tyme, a voluble environmentalist, launched attack after attack on the motorway lobby, halting almost single-handed much of Britain's road-building programme. By the end of the 1970s public enquiries had grown noisier, more militant and rebellious. They were described by critics of the system like Tyme as 'political charades' as local amenity groups and national organisations attempted to exert their power over decision-makers. Although local authorities were being put to the test as development proposals and land use came under increasing scrutiny from local community groups, there appeared too few occasions when public representation had any influence upon the final decision. Towards the end of 1979 a report by the Association of Metropolitan Authorities emphasised that local authorities also wanted action against the misuse of Britain's land. The Association, normally restrained in its comments, put the official view of its members in a forceful and constructive way:

'*The Government, local authorities and voluntary organisations should make more determined efforts to bring into effective use the numerous areas of neglected land in towns and villages, thereby eliminating waste and ugliness.*'[10]

However, of all the public discussions over wasteland, the Civic Trust's publication *Urban Wasteland* brought the most clarity to the problem of vacant and derelict land, not only in urban areas but in the countryside also. The Trust was concerned that planning was too flexible and in conjunction with statutory landowners was responsible for many of the land use and environmental problems. The Trust put forward a number of relevant recommendations that attacked some of the causes and effects of wasteland:

Wasteland surveys District councils should be required to carry out regular surveys of cities, towns and villages and to publish schedules of land which is lying idle or in temporary use

161

Guide development Local authorities should use their planning and community land powers for development of wasteland rather than green-field sites[11]

Protection of farmland Agricultural land should not be diverted for any other purpose unless it can be shown that the new use is more important and that no alternative site is available

Control of demolition In order to prevent the creation of vacant sites, the Town and Country Planning Act should be amended to require consent for demolition, which should not normally be granted in the absence of planning permission for the reuse of the site

Rating of vacant land Rates should be levied on vacant land and should be progressively increased

Publicly-owned land Nationalised industries and local authorities should be required to review their land holdings at regular intervals of not more than 5 years in the light of changing policies and available resources

Adjacent land To minimise the creation of small or awkward areas of wasteland, local authorities should anticipate the effect of proposed development on adjacent land and where necessary secure modifications or impose planning conditions

Building regulations To facilitate the development of wasteland, especially small sites, local authorities ought to be prepared to consider some relaxation of planning requirements and building regulations

Tax relief The cost of landscaping or other enhancement of land should be encouraged by appropriate tax reliefs

Rubbish Local authorities should in appropriate cases exercise their existing powers to require owners to clear unsightly rubbish on neglected land

Advertisements The practice of displaying advertisements on vacant sites or sites on which building work is proceeding should be discouraged

Encouraging voluntary work Local authorities should encourage voluntary initiatives for the enhancement or temporary use of idle land by offering financial and other assistance

Licences for temporary use Local authorities should grant licences for short periods for the temporary use of vacant sites in their ownership

Vacant council sites Vacant sites owned by a local authority on which no development is planned within 2 years should be given some temporary use or landscape treatment.

Knowledge and responsibility

From all this environmental discussion and bustle of activity over land use, there emerged the kind of issues raised by the Association of District Councils, calling for changes or improvements to existing decision-making procedures and for the reconsideration of traditional environmental priorities. There appeared to be a growing distrust by the public and non-planning professionals of the information and forecasting systems used by land-use planners. Local civic and amenity societies were stirred into action by the frequently dismal effects of planning upon the built environment and the generally low standard of architectural design. Questions as to who is finally responsible for land and its use were emerging; landowner, planner and architect rarely escaped criticism. Planning by itself can only achieve so much — the independent activities and decisions of landowners, professionals and politicians tend to determine ultimately the use of land and the quality of the environment. By the end of the 1970s, doubt was being cast over the accuracy of our knowledge about land and the quality of the decisions being taken over its use.

TABLE 13   LAND USE CHANGES IN ENGLAND AND WALES

Category of use	1933	1963	Change (acres)	% change
Tended open space	266,582	461,834	192,252	+ 73
Airfields	20,755	108,478	77,723	+ 253
Other settlement	2,399,235	3,452,263	1,053,028	+ 44
Total settlement	2,696,572	4,022,575	1,326,003	+ 49
Permanent pasture	16,463,606	10,919,028	- 5,544,578	- 34
Leys*	2,243,345	4,784,556	2,541,211	+ 113
Arable land	7,352,671	9,116,909	1,764,238	+ 24
Orchards	259,719	274,283	14,564	+ 6
Allotments	60,812	48,849	- 11,963	- 20
Total improved farmland	26,380,153	25,143,625	- 1,236,528	- 5
Wasteland	2,115,464	2,993,889	878,425	+ 42
Other cover types	5,825,761	4,787,850	- 1,037,911	- 18
Water	321,359	394,375	73,016	+ 23
Total cover types	8,262,584	8,176,114	- 86,470	- 1
Total area	37,339,309	37,342,114	+ 3,005	

*   Land areas temporarily under grass.

Sources: Second Land Utilisation Survey of England and Wales; 'Land Use Planning — Success or Failure', *Architects' Journal*, special issue, January 1977.

It was suggested at the Land Decade 1980-90 inaugural conference in 1979 that the only way to develop a better understanding and use of land would be through an official decennial land use survey to coincide with the population census. Unofficial surveys such as the First and Second Land Utilisation Surveys have provided comparative information on the changing state of Britain's land and have revealed among other things the extent of agricultural land lost annually to urban development, the growth of land misuse at the urban fringes and the accumulation of urban wasteland. The surveys have, in their unofficial capacities, alerted us to wasteful trends in land use that we have not been able to see cumulatively before. As a result of the Second Land Utilisation Survey maps, more detailed surveys have been undertaken by individual counties or inner-urban boroughs to assess the extent of local land use changes and to define the action that should be taken for example to stem the loss of agricultural land to urban uses or to reinstate and reuse urban wasteland. For forty years the work of Stamp, and more recently Coleman, has made a consistant and articulate case for a better official understanding and use of Britain's land. Their work has demonstrated that there is no substitute for a single official national land use survey, updated on a regular basis, and although Government repeatedly insists that it holds all the informtion necessary it is noticeable that the early warning signs over land misuse have been provided, over the years, by environmental organisations like the Civic Trust and individuals like Oxenham and Coleman assembling their own information.

Many environmental organisations are suggesting that the involvement of young people from an early age in studying land use and local environmental issues that affect them directly, both at school and within the community, and the formation of environmental community groups, lead to a better public understanding, among future generations, of the problems of land use. Such a learning process would, it is argued, bring about a more caring approach towards the environment and might even reduce vandalism and damage to land and buildings. In an effort to stimulate public interest in environmental matters, the Civic Trust established a Heritage Education Group in 1976 aimed at all levels of education, but specifically at young people, and bringing together environmental specialists to achieve this aim. It is hoped that future generations will learn from an early age their responsibilities towards land and the environment. Care and attention is a way of life among members of the public in countries such as Holland and Scandinavia, where habitable land is a precious and valued resource. Knowledge and responsibility could be a powerful force in the revival and reclamation of so many of Britain's wasting and derelict acres, and in producing better maintained environments in both town and country.

TABLE 14   MAIN ACTIVITIES AND LEGISLATION AFFECTING LAND USE AND NATURAL RESOURCES

1791	Ordnance Survey	1865	Commons, Open Spaces and Foot-paths Preservation Society
1750-1850	Enclosure Acts of Parliament in England and Lowland Scotland	1877	Society for the Protection of Ancient Buildings
1750-1850	Private Clearance Acts in Scotland		
1828-1960	Game Acts	1882	Royal Forestry Society of England

1889	Royal Society for the Protection of Birds	1947	Wildlife Conservation Special Committee
1895	National Trust for Places of Historic Interest or Natural Beauty	1949	Nature Conservancy
1903	The Society for the Preservation of Fauna of the Empire	1949	Coast Protection Act
		1949	National Parks and Access to the Countryside Act
1907-1953	National Trust Acts	1949	National Parks and Conservation of Nature in Scotland
1912	Society for the Promotion of Nature Reserves	1957	Civic Trust
1913	The British Ecological Society	1958	Council for Nature
1914	Town Planning Institute	1958	Opencast Coal Act
1919	Ministry of Agriculture and Fisheries	1962	Pipelines Act
		1963	Water Resources Act
1919	Forestry Commission	1965	National Environmental Research Council
1921	Rural Industries Bureau		
1923	Men of Trees	1967	Forestry Act
1925	Road Improvement Act	1967	Countryside (Scotland) Act
1926	Norfolk Naturalists' Trust (first of several county trusts)	1968	Town and Country Planning Act (Public Participation)
1926	Council for the Protection of Rural England (Wales 1928)	1968	Countryside Commission
		1969	Countryside (England and Wales) Act
1928	Roads Beautifying Association		
1929	Institute of Landscape Architects	1969	Friends of the Earth
1931	Agricultural Research Council	1970	Department of the Environment
1931	Census (showing conurbation growth)	1970	European Environmental Conservation Year
1931	National Trust for Scotland	1971	Town and Country Planning Act
1932	Town and Country Planning Act	1972	Field Monument Act
1933	Local Government Act (protection of wild plants)	1973	Water Resources Act
		1973	Nature Conservancy Council
1935	Restriction of Ribbon Development Act	1973	Institute of Terrestrial Ecology
		1973	Tree Council
1937	Trunk Roads Act	1974	Town and Country Amenities Act
1937	Royal Commission on Geographical Distribution of the Industrial Population (Sir Montague Barlow)	1974	Control of Pollution Act
		1975	European Architectural Heritage Year
1940	Barlow Commission on the Distribution of Population and Industrial Land	1975	Community Land Act
		1976	Environment Heritage Group
		1977	Food from Our Own Resources
1942	Scott Committee Report (Land Utilization in Rural Areas)	1977	Policy for the Inner Cities
		1977	Inner-Urban Areas Act
1944	Control of Land Use (Government White Paper)	1978	Land Council
		1979	Countryside Bill
1945	Dower Report — National Parks in England and Wales	1979	Land Trusts Association
		1979	Farming and the Nation
1947	Hobhouse Committee — Report of the National Parks Committee	1980-1990	Land Decade
		1980	Local Government, Planning and Land Act
1947	Town and Country Planning Act		
1947	Agriculture Act	1981	European Urban Renaissance Year

Source: Adapted and extended from John Weller, *Modern Agriculture and Rural Planning*, Architectural Press, 1967

Involvement at an early age. A group of 9-13 year olds from Kingsdale School, Alleyn Park, London, at work on a housing project exploring the life of seven fictional families – neighbours in a road threatened by plans for redevelopment. The educational material includes a well illustrated and simply presented study pack. Environmental education is vital to a better understanding and use of land and the living environment. (Photograph: Shelter)

Notes

1. Max Nicholson, *The Environmental Revolution*, Hodder and Stoughton, 1970, p.14
2. 'World Conservation Strategy — Living Resource Conservation for Sustainable Development', United Nations and World Wildlife Fund, 1980
3. 'The Greening of Politics', *Journal of the Town and Country Planning Association*, May 1979, Vol. 48, No. 2, p.42
4. Manifesto of the candidates put forward for election to the European Parliament by the Group for European Ecological Action, 1979
5. L. Dudley Stamp, *The Land of Britain – Its Use and Mis-use*, Longman, 1962, p.487
6. H. Marshall, 'Rakes Progress' in Clough Williams-Ellis (ed), *Britain and the Beast*, Dent, 1957, p.164
7. The Civic Trust, *Derelict Land*, 1964, p.64
8. R. H. Best and J. T. Coppock, *Changing Use of Land in Britain*, Faber & Faber, 1962
9. Alice Coleman, 'Is Planning Really Necessary?', Royal Geographical Society, May 1976
10. Association of Metropolitan Authorities, *Development of Publicly-Owned Urban Land*, 1979
11. The 1975 Community Land Act was repealed by the Conservative Government in 1980

CHAPTER 10

Waste Not, Want Not

'Ripped paper bags and
smelly old rags,
Bent tin cans and rusty pots and pans
Cardboard boxes and ornaments of foxes
A broken down hut and bits of nuts.
People are mad because they make it look so sad
So many things are in our brook
No body smiles when they stop to look.

No more paper bags and
dusty old rags
No more engine oil or silver foil
Not a teapot nor a pan
The brook is clear and spick and span
Tadpoles and frogs, fishes and snails,
With their houses on their tails,
People now smile as they stop and look awhile.'

A cause for optimism

The 'Before and after' poem above, written by one of the children involved in the Civic Trust's Avon Schools Environmental Project in 1977, is a celebration of the perception of children and of the hope they bring for the future of the environment everywhere. The sublime optimism of the poem and the belief that children are through education, beginning to care enough about their environment and therefore about the land, give us hope that they will clear away the careless debris and waste that their parents have created. Waste not, want not is a photographic essay that illustrates what can be achieved with a little care and attention in areas of waste and derelict urban land, despoiled and damaged industrial land, run-down or decaying land and buildings or land that is temporarily out of use and awaiting re-use. It translates hope into reality by drawing upon a selected few of the successes to date.

(Photograph: Shelter)

Why should vacant land so often be uncared for when... (Photograph: Civic Trust)

... the enthusiasm of youth can keep land free from rubbish and dereliction in readiness for a game of football? Lace Market, Nottingham. (Photograph: Civic Trust)

170

Even the most unpleasant vacant corners can be brought to life and be given a positive use. Open-air Chess Garden, Covent Garden, London. (Photograph: Civic Trust)

Land can capture the imagination of the young and engender a creative spirit within the community... Rochdale Improvement Area. (Photograph: Architectural Press Ltd.)

... as an ecological park on once derelict land near Tower Bridge, London... William Curtis Ecological Park. (Photograph: Civic Trust)

172

. . . as an inner city farm, on derelict dockland. . . Surrey Docks Farm, London. (Photograph: Civic Trust)

. . . or as a simple food-producing allotment. By the end of the 1970s, there was a waiting list for allotments of more than 100,000 throughout Britain. (Photograph: Civic Trust)

Local authority environmental improvement schemes such as the Rochdale Improvement Area can tidy up the landscape areas for public enjoyment which otherwise may lie derelict and rubbish-strewn permanently. (Photograph: Architectural Press Ltd.)

Before. (Photograph: Architectural Press Ltd.)

174

The award-winning Rochdale Industrial Improvement area has reinstated and improved the canal, lock gates, bridges, wasteland and canal-side buildings. (Photograph: Architectural Press Ltd.)

After. (Photograph: Architectural Press Ltd.)

Before. The upgrading of land for public enjoyment can also enhance the landscape. From bomb-site to car park to public gardens in twenty years on the Southbank of the Thames, London. (Photograph: Civic Trust)

After. (Photograph: Civic Trust)

176

Before. The reinstatement of Parc Lead Mine in Aberconway, Wales, covered 18 acres of land and was totally grant-aided by the Welsh Development Agency in 1978 and undertaken by the Aberconway District Council. Engineers: Robinson Jones Partnership Ltd. (Photograph: A. J. Tollit Photography)

After. (Photograph: A. J. Tollit Photography)

Before. The Amey Roadstone Corporation has undertaken extensive reclamation of its mineral land throughout Britain. Extraction on land at Boxford Common near Newbury began in 1970 to provide sand and gravel primarily for the construction of the M4 motorway. Out of the 90 acres purchased for extraction, 40 acres were mined. The deposits were exhausted in 1973 and a three-month reclamation programme returned the land to agricultural grazing. The necessary earthmoving, grading and seeding were financed from a general reclamation fund operated by ARC on the basis of setting aside a special sum of money for every ton excavated. The example of ARC could well be followed by other mineral extractors. (Photograph: Amey Roadstone Corporation Ltd.)

During. (Photograph: Amey Roadstone Corporation)

After. (Photograph: Amey Roadstone Corporation)

178

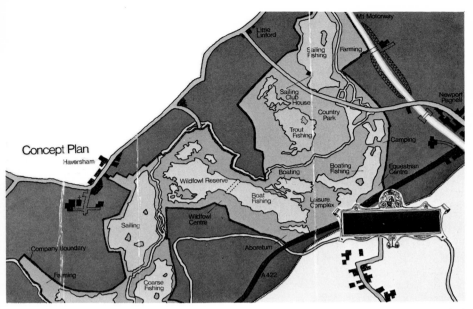

Concept Plan

Landscape plan. (Diagram: Based on material prepared by Amey Roadstone Corporation)

The restoration of the gravel pit at Great Linford, near Newport Pagnell, is also being undertaken by the Amey Roadstone Corporation. Extraction began in 1952 and Great Linford supplied general roadstone and concrete aggregate, using a barge and dredger system within flooded pits. The operation expanded at the end of the 1960s to supply aggregate for the building of Milton Keynes New Town and Great Linford now covers 700 acres of land. The restoration plan was drawn up at that time, to enable Great Linford to be gradually reclaimed for a mixture of uses including water-based leisure facilities, a wild-life reserve and cattle grazing. By 1980 over half of the land had been restored and the wild-life reserve had been completed. ARC will retain ownership when extraction of the land ceases, and will operate and maintain the new activities on a commercial basis.

179

Before. Great Linford gravel pit. (Photograph: Amey Roadstone Corporation)

After. (Photograph: Amey Roadstone Corporation)

180

Before (1919). The Forestry Commission was established in 1919 to replace the forests lost to the demand for munitions during the First World War. Aldewood (originally Rendlesham) in Suffolk was one of the first Forestry Commission plantations. As a result the Commission has reclaimed extensive areas of derelict heathland within the forest which covers 9,000 acres, 8,500 acres of which was under mature planting in 1980. Limited natural birch and oak cover (natural scrub) was retained as an integral part of the forest. Aldewood is a particularly good example of natural wasteland being made productive. However, the high initial capital costs and the long maturity period of forests has made such reclamation in lowland areas often better suited economically to agriculture. (Photograph: Forestry Commission)

Aldewood four years after planting. (Photograph: Forestry Commission)

Aldewood forty years after planting.
(Photograph: Forestry Commission)

Before (1936). Land covered by unstable sand dunes and a gravel pit has been reclaimed in the Culbin Forest near Nairn on the east coast of Scotland. Planting commenced in 1939 and the forest, covering 7,500 acres, includes original natural scrub and a small proportion of unplanted area used for fire-breaks, car parking and other operational and non-operational activities. By planting Corsican pine amid thatch weathering and natural Marram grass the sand has been stabilised as the forest and ground covering has matured. (Photograph: Forestry Commission)

182

Planting Corsican pine in thatch. (Photograph: Forestry Commission)

Culbin fifteen years after planting. (Photograph: Forestry Commission)

Before – Achray Forest. The Queen Elizabeth Forest Park, Aberfoyle in Scotland designated in 1953, is composed of a number of forests, including Loch Ard and Achray. Planting commenced in Loch Ard in 1929 and today covers 27,000 acres, of which 17,000 acres are under plantation, a further 2,500 acres remain to be planted and 500 are retained as natural scrub. Achray forest commenced in 1931 and covers over 12,000 acres of which nearly 10,000 acres are under plantation with 250 acres covered by natural scrub. The Park also contains land set aside for recreational and amenity activities. The uplands in Britain provide a natural reservoir of land suitable for a mixture of forestry, recreation and limited hill farming. (Photograph: Forestry Commission)

After – Loch Ard Forest. (Photograph: Forestry Commission)

Before. '. . . the bald unpalatable fact is emphasised that the Highlands and Islands are largely a devastated terrain. . . .' *Frank Fraser Darling, 1954. (Photograph: Reay Clarke)*

After. 'In the Highlands of Scotland the change from a peasant agriculture of cattle and transhumance to extensive sheep farming has destroyed the fertility of the land. Modern techniques of surface seeding with sound grazing practice can help to rebuild this countryside. The heather is first burnt off and lime, fertilisers and grass seeds are broadcast on the burnt surface. By autumn the seeds are well established. Skilful use of the grazing animal brings a tight-knit sward. The land, skill and techniques are available if the nation chooses to provide the political will and the financial resources.' Reay Clarke, 1979. (Photograph: Reay Clarke)*

CHAPTER 11

Can We Achieve a Better Understanding
of Land?

'There has been a marked increase in recent years in public concern about national environmental issues, and particularly the extension of urban development. This commonly leads to pressure for the Government to take relevant action, which is often supported by widely varying statistical guesses on the rate of land consumption for urban development. Reliable official statistics, specifically designed for this purpose, are required to provide a common basis for the consideration of these issues by Parliament, the public and the Department.'

Statistics of Land Use Change, Department of Environment, 1974

A dearth of information

The projects illustrated in the last chapter emerged from individual efforts by mineral extractors, developers, local authorities, community groups and individuals. In each case their actions, motivated by a strength of concern for land and the built environment, have produced inspiring results that stand as examples of what could be achieved elsewhere given equal enthusiasm. However, this degree of commitment is an exception rather than a rule and although individuals can readily see the results of their labours locally, we as a nation cannot see, as yet, the results of our collective actions, bad as well as good, upon Britain's landscape. While it is essential to continue to treat the effects of land misuse and despoilation, it is also essential for us to focus attention upon the causes at an early stage. But we do not have an information system that indicates where and why we should focus attention. Beyond the unofficial work of Stamp and Coleman, there is no official record of changing land uses available for each county of Britain. If unofficial information can be assembled and, in the case of the First Land Utilisation Survey, can be a major contributory factor towards establishing the 1947 Town and Country Planning Act, then why has the Second Land Utilisation Survey not been given official backing and finance to enable a more rapid and detailed survey process to be followed? Moreover if there is official criticism of this kind of survey why has the Government not established its own decennial land use survey? After all, the Ordnance Survey produces, in addition to its own national grid maps for Britain, geological, soil and historical maps all related to the national grid. In addition agricultural classification and farming type maps are produced for England and Wales by the Ministry of Agriculture, Fisheries and Food. Throughout this book many aspects of the argument over land have been weakened by inadequate facts and figures, with official statistics plagued by poor land use definitions, inconsistencies and sheer under-estimates.

186

(*Photograph: Architectural Press Ltd.*)

This kind of carelessness is quite unnecessary. It doesn't need understanding to maintain and care for the environment – only a sense of responsibility. (Photograph: Shelter)

188

Land holds an age-old mineral potential and soil capability, a varying quality and condition, a prodigous and flexible capacity for use, and a host of natural characteristics, physical forms, social and economic benefits and historic and cultural values. Land is also held under a multiplicity of ownerships. Knowledge of all these factors is essential to a better understanding of Britain's land. But apart from the difficulty of collecting and maintaining an up-to-date set of statistics, the work involved would be a mammoth task. There is also a strong body of official opinion that does not see any value in collecting such extensive information. It is arguable, however, that had we held at the very least a regularly updated and comparable set of official land capability and land use maps for Britain, then we would have been able to foresee the extensive waste and misuse of land that is the subject of this book.

There can be little doubt that at a local scale, knowledge of all the factors that I have mentioned is important if the most appropriate decisions are to be made. However, planning has been traditionally preoccupied more with the social and economic aspects of land, and the encouragement or control of development, and less with its biological and physical potential. As a result many thousands of acres are being used for purposes often least suited to their true potential; with a poor capacity to cope with their particular uses, or a damaging effect upon the condition of land. For example, highly productive and fertile agricultural land is being used for urban development around which existing roads and services do not have the capacity to cope without considerable investment and further loss of land, and where farmland and adjacent open space is, as a result, affected by a congestion of activities and people. Similarly the capacity of farmland is, in many cases, perhaps being pushed beyond its limits by a new agricultural technology that may be damaging to both soil and existing landscapes, or by concentrated recreational activities that erode the recreational land surface and damage adjacent farmland and livestock. By contrast urban wasteland, emerging from a developed state that deprived it of natural elements and sunlight for a century or more, is rarely able to revert to its natural state without considerable investment, or an extensive period of time necessary for natural processes to regenerate the soil.

Comprehensive planning can only begin on a foundation of careful study of the capability of land. Inevitably, some areas of land will continue to be used for activities that are better suited elsewhere, but this is one of the extreme difficulties of an inherited pattern of land ownership that is rarely inter-changeable with any rational pattern without impinging upon the freedom and rights of the landowner. Old cities, towns and villages standing on once rich valley farmland cannot be moved elsewhere, but with a better knowledge of land, we could ensure that the future loss of farmland is minimised while reducing misuse, under-use, waste and dereliction generally.

After-care of land

Land should be maintained not only during its use, but afterwards when the use has expired. There can be no excuse for land and buildings being abandoned or neglected by their owners, since limited maintenance can retain a tidy appearance. A well-husbanded farm for example produces a neat landscape of ever-changing field patterns and textures, keeping the land in 'good heart'. Where it is poorly farmed, particularly at the urban fringes, the mosaic looks unkempt and scruffy. Similarly

The dependence of society upon the biological potential of soil to produce food has not always been given sufficient consideration in land use planning. (Photograph: Joseph McKenzie)

with urban areas: well-maintained land and buildings enhance the townscape, while those poorly-maintained areas produce a derelict and unkempt atmosphere. If every acre of derelict land and buildings were to be maintained, then a self-perpetuating tidiness might bring a return of investment and people to inner-urban areas, producing a better living and working environment for existing residents. Land at the urban fringe would perhaps come to life, losing its disorderly pattern of conflicting land uses. The rural landscape could be rid of the many redundant tips and heaps, derelict workings and rubbish-strewn scars that characterise so much despoiled mineral land. The often needlessly scruffy buffer land lining roads and railways and surrounding industries could take on an altogether different appearance.

A high proportion of urban wasteland lies, as we have seen, in the ownership of local authorities or statutory bodies, who could, with a little effort, money and care, clean-up and landscape areas of wasteland and generally maintain a tidy appearance for their vacant buildings. This action would have an important effect upon the quality of urban environments throughout Britain. While environmental improvements of this kind would be unlikely to bring back immediate life to urban areas containing a high level of vacant and derelict land, existing local residents and businesses might be less inclined to move away. Similarly derelict or despoiled mineral land held in the ownership of statutory bodies and private organisations could, with a little effort, as the pictures in the previous chapter indicated, transform idle landscapes into working landscapes.

190

The ironies of planning

Official anxiety over aspects of the environment and land use has, in the past, all too often been preoccupied with political expediency, producing short-term palliatives rather than solutions that take a longer term view of the uses of land and the needs of people. Out of the political, if cynical, axiom 'a satisfied community means a satisfied electorate', there has emerged over the years a plethora of planning and development activity that has often produced less than satisfactory results. Towards the end of the 1970s an endless stream of ideas for action to stem inner-city decline was produced, each one larger in scale and more impossible than the previous one: a series of local villages or a waterside new town; a national arts centre or an international hotel complex; an expansive and fully landscaped river-side park; a duty free zone or a world trade centre; an Olympic village or world sports complex. This piecemeal and usually uncoordinated approach to problem solving has bred further untidy and fragmented land-use, not only within metropolitan areas, but elsewhere. In short, land use planning has been bedevilled by local politicians seeking to drive through instant solutions, often against the advice of their technical officers; by the pre-occupation of professional planners with plan-making for the sake of complying with statutes and political expectations; and by the unquestioning acceptance of a mediocre environment by the rest of us.

Planning procedures in the past have rarely been able to respond quickly to changing needs, because of the complexity of the legislation and the administrative processes involved. Equally, planning has rarely been able to foresee changing situations like urban or rural decline, because information is not usually comparable and therefore cannot provide a reliable assessment of land use changes either locally or nationally. Had we held detailed statistics of land use since 1947, we might have seen and perhaps even been able to lessen the decline of our cities and urban areas far sooner; the urban fringe might not have developed in such an untidy and fragmented way; and urban development might not have bitten into agricultural land at such a rate. As a result of poor information, planning processes have tended, in many cases, to work against the real needs of an area, and even the overall aims of planning policy. In the past this has been all too clear in the preparation of county structure plans and local plans, which is such a lengthy process that the basic principles of policy may have become out of date by the time the final plan has been approved — and yet it is still carried through. Equally, planning at district and local levels has in the past been over-prescriptive and inflexible, lacking discretionary powers and similarly unable to respond to rapidly changing needs. Towards the end of the 1970s, the need for discretionary planning was becoming increasingly evident, in certain declining areas where land use problems were at their worst — for example the dockland areas of inner-cities or the experimental land management areas in urban fringes or in the uplands. In the limited instances where planning has taken a positive lead, as for example in the award-winning Rochdale Industrial Improvement Scheme, the Swindon Railway Village Conservation Area, or the revival of Owen's Industrial Village in New Lanark in Scotland, the results have been extremely successful. Planning has responded more to need and less to assumed ideals, an approach that has been welcomed and rewarded by the enthusiasm of local people.

At national level, new legislation aimed at either changing or controlling planning or related laws, has since the 1960s in particular been dogged by paradox. Public

Even the most derelict and damaged soil, covered for decades by building, can, when exposed, be coaxed back to life and encouraged to sustain plant life once again. (Photograph: Civic Trust)

involvement in local planning, often much needed during the periods of high economic activity of the 1950s and 1960s, grew up instead during a period of severely limited development, when some of the worst environmental ravages had already occurred. Public inquiries concerning issues of national interest like oil, coal and nuclear development, have rarely been seen to take note of local opinion, while at a local level, participation has often taken the form of confrontation, with the odds piled high against local preference. Described as 'an albatross around the corporate neck of decision makers', public participation is seen as a time-wasting, expensive and often one-sided activity in an era when planning seeks fewer delays, democratic decision-making, and more economic stringency.[1] Local government reorganisation, initiated in 1972, arrived at a time when less and less finance was available for normal public spending. It was aimed at a larger and more comprehensive workforce, handling local affairs during a period of high economic activity, but by the time it came into effect that period had already passed. The Community Land Act, introduced in 1975 in response to massive land speculation by developers in the 1960s and early 1970s, emerged as law in a period of economic depression parallelled only by the 1930s. Together with Development Land Tax, both pieces of legislation began operating at a time when scores of developers were declared bankrupt, and during which many local authorities were only too thankful to see private development taking place. The final irony came when, in 1979, the Community Land Act was withdrawn, just as the very period of development activity for which it had been originally designed was returning.

Planning legislation and financial controls since 1947 have been introduced as a series of layers one over the other, each controlling a specific problem or closing a

192

Planning policy has in the past been more concerned with plan making and the arrangement of people and activities, and less concerned about land capability, land ownership, land use economics and environmental education. This approach has, all too frequently, led to unworkable strategic and local plans, badly located development, social unrest and inadequate concern for the upkeep of the local environment. (Photograph: Architectural Press Ltd.)

legal loophole. However, after the first oil crisis in 1972, the period of high economic activity which had produced the mass of recent planning and land taxation legislation had all but disappeared. In fact, in many areas like Glasgow, south and mid-Wales, Northumberland and Durham, economic prosperity has been declining since the War. The wide variety of social and economic conditions throughout Britain has brought into question the wisdom of 'blanket' legislation, financial and planning controls. One of the arguments used in Europe for regional economic planning is that the small region is a more appropriate area in which to operate local decisions and policy making which is specifically aimed at local problems. This devolution of power from central Government is seen by the European Parliament as an essential pre-requisite to dealing with population imbalance and the problems of inner-city and rural decline. By the end of the 1970s there was concern that current planning practices were not always appropriate to the needs of land use and human settlements and were themselves contributing in large measure to many of Britain's land use problems.

193

Understanding the relationship of people to land can bring well-tempered environments to town and country alike. Planning must become more responsive and less prescriptive in declining urban areas; while exerting stricter controls over the release of active farmland or potential farmland to urban development. In general planning needs to give greater guidance and more positive direction in the location of development and investment in land use. (Photograph: Architectural Press Ltd.)

194

(Photograph: Geoffrey Berry)

Official concern about land wastage

To find out the reaction of local authorities to Britain's land use problems, in particular to idle, vacant or derelict urban land and diminishing farmland, I undertook a brief survey in 1979 of all county and metropolitan authorities in England and Wales and all regional and district authorities in Scotland.[2] The main findings of the survey were that:

Few metropolitan authorities were operating regular and detailed surveys of vacant urban land

Few authorities held detailed and up-to-date information about land — those that did so were mainly authorities with urban fringe or inner-city land

Not all metropolitan authorities saw vacant derelict land as a problem — but more a consequence of natural change in population levels and industrial needs

A number of authorities emphasised the need to hold an adequate area of vacant land in the best interests of planning, to be able to respond to changing needs. Some of these authorities suggested that Government might provide an indication of the extent of such land that should be held, and give guidance upon the temporary uses to which land could be put, whilst being held in readiness for more permanent use

A number of authorities containing urban fringe land considered that the

Vacant and Despoiled Land Survey definitions prepared by the Department of Environment were inadequate and that in their experience the extent of such wasteland or potential wasteland was well in excess of the 1974 figures. Totals of between two and three times the official 1974 area, for example, were considered to be a more accurate statement

Few local authorities held or were concerned about holding information on agricultural land, and referred to information that was kept almost exclusively by the Ministry of Agriculture, Fisheries and Food in England and Wales and by the Department of Agriculture in Scotland. A number of authorities emphasised that planning policy already contained adequate safeguards against unnecessary use of agricultural land for non-agricultural purposes

Several authorities expressed concern over the level of information held about rural land uses and their problems, and the inadequacy of county structure plans in taking account of the many varying local conditions and changing uses of rural land.

In general the survey revealed concern among planners not only about the question of vacant, derelict or under-used land, but also about their inability to improve the level of information, due either to a shortage of staff and finance available to undertake land surveys, or to the belief that more comprehensive information would be unlikely to serve any useful purpose, or contribute towards better land use planning. The survey also revealed that those authorities holding accurate and regularly up-dated information about derelict or vacant urban land appeared to be those better equipped administratively to take a positive approach to their area. Industrial development officers and community officers, vacant land survey teams and community shops invariably appeared within the boundaries of such authorities. Many local authorities in non-metropolitan areas tended not to regard vacant land in their area as a problem, and were wholly satisfied that their policies towards agricultural land were not wasteful. However, it was stressed that it was not necessarily the concern of local authorities to take notice of national trends towards vacant land or diminishing farmland. One inner-city authority, for example, known to contain a high level of vacant and derelict land, did not acknowledge such land as a problem, but more as a natural consequence of change that should be left to work itself out. For this reason the local authority held few details relating specifically to vacant or derelict land.

The survey also indicated a strong preoccupation among authorities with plan-making and implementation. Many suggested that their statutory plan-making duties did not leave enough time or staff available to get to grips with more than 'a handful of local problems'. Others were concerned at the increasing difficulties of implementing plans and policies. A number of county authorities expressed impatience over preparation of the latest structure plans and the often 'pedantic attitude' of the Department of Environment, to whom the plans were submitted for approval. Several authorities, particularly those in metropolitan areas, admitted to setting policies that emerged from a strong preference among local councillors, rather than from a proven need identified through a specific local survey or from existing information. In these cases few details supporting local land policies had been gathered, and in the case of one such local plan it was emphasised that it had been fully debated and agreed both in public and by the Department of the Environment.

Organic change

There were clear indications from the survey that the general level of information contributing towards planning policies was insufficient and that there may be a certain unreality or idealism built into a number of planning policies, which have proved incapable of implementation despite rigid adherence to the principles. If this is true,, then the question of how much the planning process has contributed to the general land use crisis needs to be asked. To what extent have rigid land use policies stopped natural processes of land reuse and economic growth for the sake of complying with plans? To what extent have these plans therefore contributed to idle or derelict land?

We know that a major amount of land acquired by local authorities for comprehensive redevelopment is today lying derelict, having fallen victim to changing economic or social climates that have made development schemes redundant. For a number of

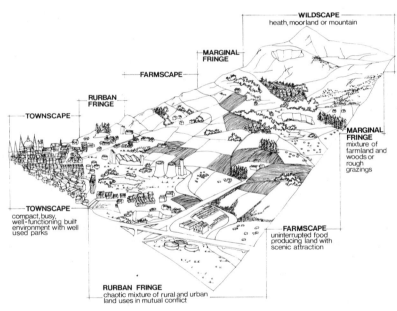

The unofficial Second Land Utilisation Survey has for many years used a land classification system and survey technique that has led to a better understanding and possible use of land in Britain. Land is divided into the five categories shown on the diagram: townscape, farmscape, wildscape, urban fringe and marginal fringe. If adopted officially on a national and local basis, this type of land classification system would allow the pattern of changing land uses to be reviewed. Planning would be able to encourage the increase of scape areas and the decrease of fringe areas, while at the same time, providing early warnings of rapid land-use changes and areas increasingly at risk from misuse or dereliction. (Drawing: Graham Moss Associates after Alice Coleman)

197

years now, concern has been expressed among professionals over the difficulty of planning for an ever-changing situation. Forecasting has only rarely been successful and is considered in many instances to have hindered policy making. Population change, varying educational and welfare needs, housing, roads and communications all present a dynamic situation that cannot easily be fixed. Local plans in particular need to be so regularly reviewed and brought up to date that contemporary planning must inevitably become a more responsive mechanism, and less the prescriptive system which it has been traditionally. Concern over this inflexibility led to a suggestion by the Department of Environment in 1979 that 'organic change' should form the basis of future planning. This suggestion received severe criticism from county and greater metropolitan authorities, who foresaw that their strategic powers could be eroded. District authorities generally could find little difference between a plan that changed 'organically' and a return to the pre-1947 days of a free land market. Whatever the criticism of organic change, it has not gone unnoticed that the recommendation came from a dying Labour Government whose experiences had indicated an inadequacy in the planning system which it had originally introduced in 1947.

In 1979 the Labour Government followed up its organic change idea by suggesting that planning powers should be localised and that district authorities should assume a greater proportion of the decision-making powers currently held by county councils in England and Wales and regional authorities in Scotland. Not surprisingly the Association of County Councils was outraged. However, pressures for change in the administration and operation of land use planning were emerging strongly. Critics of the existing planning system, like Alice Coleman, Director of the Second Land Utilisation Survey, saw planning as a failure and were critical of the expense involved in running the 'planning establishment, when free enterprise would do the same job free'. David Eversley, one of Britain's leading strategic planners, suggested in 1979, that 'people would go where they wanted, not where the planners directed'. The question being asked was how necessary was planning. By the end of the 1970s a number of the problems inherent in the existing planning system were being actively considered:

The difficulty of forecasting items such as population change and housing need (even on a short-term basis) and the difficulty of introducing such questionable results into planning policies

The difficulty of preparing an up-to-date policy or local plan under the present time-lag between evolution of policy and its implementation

The difficulties of implementing policies at county and district levels which take into account a continuously changing situation

The problems of delays caused by public participation processes based on confrontation rather than consultation

The problems posed by decision-making based upon inadequate or inaccurate information

The inherent difficulties of holding vacant land in a well-maintained state in readiness for use by planning authorities (particularly in inner-urban areas)

The problems of controlling the development of farmland at the urban fringe and elsewhere and of reducing the extent of despoiled and derelict mineral land.

Many of these issues were taken into account in the Local Government, Planning and Land Bill in 1980, not only by the introduction of legislation that would encourage the re-use of urban wasteland, but by procedures that would speed up the planning process by the introduction of less vigorous planning controls and decision-making powers. However many professionals feared that by exposing land to weaker controls, a rash of even more mediocre developments would emerge, worse than those bequeathed to us from the Macmillan era and after.

How far could the new breed of developer be trusted to produce a humane environment? Could professionals be relied upon to create open spaces that were appropriate to their location, and buildings that were carefully designed? How could we be sure that the new developments, however attractive architecturally and economically, would be occupied? The answers to the first two questions could only be tested by experience, but in response to the third question, it was the task of the Urban Development Corporations to manage the redevelopment of urban wasteland, as would a commercial developer, ensuring as far as possible that the development would be occupied.

Approaches to land use and planning generally at the end of the 1970s were moving, if only slowly, towards a better knowledge of land, awareness of the problems of its use and a greater scrutiny by the public of land use and development in both town and country. Environmental groups were everywhere active and there was a growing belief that the care of land and the environment was too important to be left only to planners and politicians. Society generally needed to be educated from an early age in concern and care in the use of land. Man and land, it was argued, could only work to each other's mutual benefit if society shared a common caring for land — a caring that would emerge from an attitude of respect for the environment and a better knowledge and understanding of the impact of man's actions upon land.

Notes

1. Graham Moss, 'Planning for the Planner or Society?', *Built Environment*, January 1975, p.25
2. The survey questionnaire was distributed in late 1978 and early 1979 to all county and district authorities in England and Wales and all regional and district authorities in Scotland. An average of 70 per cent of questionnaires were returned. All respondents answered the questions carefully and many volunteered additional information and opinions. In addition the main statutory undertakers such as the Gas Board, Electricity Board, Coal Board, British Rail, etc, received similar questionnaires. Although every organisation responded, several were not prepared to release certain statistics relating to derelict land or to give opinions regarding the official definitions of derelict and despoiled land.

CHAPTER 12

The Ethic of Responsibility

'The pre-eminence of prudence means that realisation of the good pre-supposes knowledge of reality. He alone can do good who knows what things are like and what the situation is. The pre-eminence of prudence means that so-called "good intentions" and so-called "meaning well" by no means suffice.'

Joseph Pieper, 1960

Landscapes of mediocrity

The absence of a strong guiding ethic in the use of land has meant that society, in particular, has been bred upon mediocrity and nurtured by a lifestyle that has accepted built-in obsolescence and wastefulness, ugliness and disappearing pride. This pride was for a brief period so much a part of the ethos of immediate post-war administrators and environmentalists as they set about the rebuilding of Britain: demonstrating their confidence in a flurry of enthusiasm, brashness and architectural adventure so well exemplified by the 1951 Festival of Britain. However, this enthusiasm slowly evaporated as architectural confidence had begun to wane. By the end of the 1970s the flame of modernism was kept alive by only a handful of designers. Large scale redevelopment schemes and tower-block living proved more unpopular than the declining quality of existing living environments. Graffiti and vandalism became expressive and enduring features of objection towards both the old and new: the old, with its often vacant and derelict slums standing wearily upon untidy and rubbish-strewn land and often devoid of living greenery, is frequently overpowered or further degraded by the new, with its bulky building forms that deprive surrounding land of sunshine and create a mixture of windy and unwelcome open spaces that make their use either a feat of human endurance or an act of aggression. Spray-can art and obscene hieroglyphics stare out at us from walls and doors, temporary fencing and pavements, rooftops and chimney stacks and a host of other convenient surfaces that will carry a message. Elsewhere, old bicycles, tin cans, broken glass, rusty bedsteads, abandoned cars and yesterday's rubbish are dumped as testimonies to the careless attitudes that beget wasteland. Like the work of the spray-can artists, this kind of man-made dereliction has become a permanent and forceful reminder of our complacent attitude towards maintaining the urban environment. Instead society has been moving towards the countryside leaving behind increasing areas of urban dereliction that leaves gaps in the urban streetscapes much in the same way that derelict and exhausted mineral workings, refuse tips and fragmented land have for decades interrupted the working patterns of an otherwise

200

Lord Asa Briggs (chairman of the Civic Trusts Heritage Education Group) discusses environmental issues with school children. (Photograph: Civic Trust)

fluent farmscape. Discarded and unkempt areas of land lurk everywhere. Mediocrity lies ready to greet the eye around the next street corner or bend in a country lane. Journeys by train reveal an apparently endless array of derelict industrial backland, disused sidings and generally unkempt and overgrown land — as much a part of the countryside as the town.

Uncleared ponds, vacant and dilapidated farm structures, broken fences, decapitated trees and eroded and rubbish-strewn acres of tourist-invaded land all add to the pockets of mediocrity that are woven into the patchwork of the countryside. In other cases, poor location, design and landscaping of new farm buildings and equipment, badly landscaped motorways and their service stations, lines of electricity pylons and substations marching across the fields, and the many features of power stations and the lattice work outline of mining structures can be unnecessarily

201

A working life spent in caring for a landscape that has been allowed to fall derelict. (Photograph: Architectural Press Ltd.)

obtrusive blots upon the rural landscape. Coppicing, the traditional art of pruning and tidying.up the the growth of trees in small woodlands to enable sunlight to penetrate and green undergrowth and wild life to exist, has become uneconomic and has largely died out, leaving derelict and overgrown woodlands to punctuate the unworkable corners of farmland. Early commercial forestry has produced extensive areas of mature upland forests that clothe the landscape in an unnatural and regimented order of trees. Elsewhere the expansive and treeless landscapes of modern agriculture, depleted of hedgerows and wildlife, are considered by many to be not only a second-rate working landscape, but a landscape that is rapidly losing its amenity value. However, the most recent changes in forestry practice and modern agriculture have brought more natural afforestation and tree planting, with the reintroduction of small coppices and shelter belt woodlands to the more expansive agricultural landscapes. These trends may eventually bring a more integrated pattern of mixed land uses that benefit farming, forestry, wildlife and amenity. However the countryside, like the town, will for the time being retain its fair share of mediocrity.

The once-hailed post-war society has all too often accepted a staid and soulless mixture of badly maintained old buildings and land, handed down through successive generations. Characterless and aggressive new environments have been forged out of right-angled corners, flat roofs, repetitious building forms and uninterrupted surfaces. The art of decoration has been lost, apart from the work of a band of committed 'street' artists who have brought to life the blank ends of half-demolished buildings or the dismal acres of concrete walls and temporary hoardings. Needlessly expansive highways, pavements and intersections, dingy pedestrian tunnels and exposed and windy bridges are all interlaced with weedy open spaces. Overgrown corner plots, desolate traffic islands and land alongside roads and motorways are frequently clothed in ailing grass and plants and stunted trees. The built environment has been created largely by a barrage of health and safety regulations and design controls, which, since the last century, have progressively (and in some cases necessarily) limited the extent of human activity over land. But these restrictions have all too often meant a stultifying of the environment and an excessive use and often needless waste of land. Contemporary man has, as a result, also wasted his opportunities for creative and thoughtful use of land.

The need for a better understanding

These wasted opportunities are clearly evident in so many of the completed post-war housing estates and new towns that reappear regularly throughout Britain stamping the countryside with their uniform and staid aesthetics. In giving way to planning, spontaneity and interest have disappeared from so much of Britain's recent architecture. Town redevelopment has tended to replace diversity and character with a similar uniformity. Instead these environments could have been enhanced by a mixture of repair and renewal saving building materials and minerals while retaining the existing social cohesion. Instant mass building and rebuilding of towns is as difficult to achieve architecturally as it is socially. Tradition and the sense of the familiar are deeply ingrained in most of us.

It is this same tradition however that has not allowed our outdated images of industry to be broken and is bringing increasingly wasted opportunities. More careful siting and design could have produced something better than an extension of Britain's industrial backyard, which we have tacitly accepted for generations as being a dirty, undignified and cancerous growth upon land. 'Where there's muck there's brass' and 'where there's industry there's muck' are clichés that have perpetuated mediocrity. And yet there is another attitude of mind that not only views industry as a social and economic need, but an opportunity of contributing to the environment by paying attention to design and landscape — the attitude of mind which created the industrial villages of New Lanark, Port Sunlight and Bourneville. Rarely is this spirit evident today. We cannot continue to delude ourselves that we only need the kind of land uses that do not dirty the landscape, and that we can dispense with those that offend our senses. Modern society is bred on an industrial lifestyle, amid the dust and fumes of coal, iron and steel production and surrounded by their dross and debris. Today a multitude of industrial processes, manufacturing plant and smaller assembly processes are spread over the surface of Britain. Mineral excavations and processing industries, oil refineries and nuclear installations, power stations and electricity power lines, industrialised farming and commercial forestry, water storage areas, refuse tips and breakers' yards and many other activities all have a call upon land. Modern society has become reliant upon these activities for survival, and in most cases has to learn to live with them. But in so doing we must ensure that their environmental impact is kept to a minimum, and that when their working life is over, any damage to the land is repaired and the landscape reinstated in preparation for future use, whenever and whatever that may be.

Because activity on a piece of land has fallen redundant, the owner's responsibility towards that piece of land does not also cease. The extent of unkempt, damaged or derelict vacant land and buildings is witness to the uncaring and irresponsible attitude of many landowners. Planning has been unable to ease this situation. Compulsory purchase powers have been used in cases where land was required for

(*Photograph: Shelter*)

204

Many youngsters are growing up in mediocre old and new living environments. (Photograph: Architectural Press Ltd.)

public development and rarely because land was lying derelict. It is already established that public authorities themselves hold the most extensive tracts of vacant and derelict urban land and despoiled mineral land. Planning could assist by using enforcement notice procedures to ensure that landowners maintain their land, but where the owner cannot finance such maintenance, planning powers are negated. Government itself could assist by offering financial incentives in the form of tax relief, but such an approach to encouraging the upkeep of vacant land and buildings would appeal to the goodwill and attitude of mind of the more responsible land-owners only. Britain's wasting acres are therefore the result of an attitude of mind that cannot easily be coerced by outside controls. Are these kinds of controls and incentives really the long-term answers to the problems of wasteland, or are they not merely short-term palliatives? Has not much of Britain's land-owning democracy become so insensitive to the condition of its investment and the contribution that its investment makes to the local environment, that nothing short of a guilty conscience will produce action? If this is true, then many landowners are purposely shirking their environmental responsibilities.

Amenity groups are becoming increasingly involved in the reclamation, land-scaping and reuse of areas of public open space. Given extended access to other public and private land, these community activities could not only assist in the maintenance of the landscape more generally, but could also provide temporary and permanent facilities that serve the local community whilst engendering an attitude of responsibility in those using the facility. However just as planning has limitations, so too does the goodwill of society and it is now incumbent upon landowners to develop

205

a public conscience also. In order to reach a situation in which landowners have an inherent responsibility towards the environment, and in which planning is able to manage land and natural resources more effectively and with greater public support than was evident during the 1970s, a change in the traditional thinking of landowners and planners towards land and its use will be essential. Ideally each needs to share a common concern and care for the state of Britain's land, and to understand the effects of each of their own individual actions. To imbue society with this understanding and care will take a generation or more of commitment and effort towards the environment — beginning with the very young and following them through adulthood to old age. This commitment and effort has already begun among the growing numbers of environmental groups, but as yet they are a minority. This attitude of care and responsibility must permeate the remainder of society and should be based on three aims:

1 Greater public *responsibility* towards land

2 Greater public *knowledge* about land, and

3 Greater public *education* in the care of land.

Responsibility, knowledge and education combined make a powerful force, as Chapter 10 has illustrated. Only from knowledge and education can an ethic of responsibility emerge within future generations.

Responsibility towards land

When in 1969 Sir Frank Fraser Darling called for an ethic of responsibility towards land and its use, he was voicing the single aim upon which most environmentalists are agreed. However it was suggested that our ethic already existed in the form of planning and that our collective responsibility had been entrusted originally to the 1947 Town and Country Planning Act and the 1947 Agricultural Act and successive new Acts and amendments since. But society has remained divided over the issues of development and conservation. Private landowners are generally keen at best to improve the value of their investment and at worst to maintain its market value, but always to put it to its most economical and profitable use within the planning constraints operating at the time. Public landowners by comparison have tended to protect their landholdings for continued existing use or future use. Only rarely have they taken a commercial attitude towards improving the value of their holdings. As a result planning has found itself caught between development and conservation, against a backcloth of militant public involvement, new development, the demolition of existing buildings or the continued dereliction of public buildings and land. Since the introduction of public participation under the 1968 Town and Country Planning Act, planning has been accused of favouring the more powerful sections of society like landowners and developers, while ignoring the public view. Planning has also been seen to perpetuate the often derelict and untidy state of much of local authorities' own vacant landholdings.

As a result of this growing conflict, the ideals of planning and the ideals of society have diverged, bringing double standards. We wish to preserve the countryside and

New environments have often produced characterless building shapes, interspersed with waste and untended land. (Photograph: Aerofilms Ltd.)

yet we harm it; we mourn the disappearing wilderness and yet we assail nature with toxic chemicals, liquid waste and fumes; we demand more food and yet we give away farmland; we cherish our villages and yet we watch them being transformed into impersonal towns or declining communities; we scorn the worst inheritances of industrial housing and yet we build modern slums; and perhaps worst of all, we admonish those responsible for despoiling land and leaving dereliction and waste areas and yet we continue to live with an increasingly scarred and damaged landscape of redundant mineral excavations and spoil heaps, and inner-city slums, dereliction and wasteland. These problems of land use in Britain have been laid increasingly at the door of the planner, as if we, society, were not involved. Yet how can we not be? Planning as a regulator of land use can achieve only so much; land ownership, land values, community initiatives and the activities of individuals are so often the real arbiters of land use. Statutory authorities themselves appear to be confused — on the one hand they exert development controls and environmental standards, and on the other hand they hold some of the most extensive and unsightly areas of derelict and unkempt land. As an administrative system, planning in Britain has been outstanding, but as a public ethic of responsibility, it has clearly failed. All too often, as we have seen, planning has been part of our modern throw-away society, treating land as just another used commodity to be discarded — hence our spreading acres of waste and derelict land. In 1979 the Inaugural Land Decade 1980-90 Conference called 'Save or Squander' emphasised the need for a new conservation ethic to replace the existing throw-away ethic.

207

Decoration, masking mediocrity, is brought by a committed band of street artists. (Photograph: Architectural Press Ltd.)

Gradually popularised by environmentalists like Fraser-Darling and independent thinkers like Aldo Leopold, the conservation ethic has been growing. By 1979 more than 22 departments of Environmental Studies in British universities and many more in polytechnics and schools of higher education had been established. As we have seen, this conservation ethic has also given rise to an increasing number of environmental organisations, particularly during the last 20 years, and progressively articulate public opposition to land-use proposals whose impacts on the environment may not have been given thorough consideration. Underlying this environmental concern is the growing belief that we all depend upon the resources of the earth, and that we should not go on taking more than the planet can replace. If we are not to continue living at the expense of posterity, then our ethic of responsibility must include the following aims:

1 Care and maintenance of all land at all times: there can be no excuse for letting land fall into an unkempt or derelict condition

2 Protection of renewable land in rural areas and parks, allotments and gardens in urban areas: these are resources that can serve us in perpetuity and should be kept in good condition at all times

3 Conservation of the built environment: unnecessary demolition not only causes disturbance and dislocation to urban communities, but also involves the unnecessary use of productive farmland for the extraction of minerals such as gravel and other building materials. Where demolition is necessary, then land should be re-used as far as possible for new urban development

4 Safeguarding of ecological values: eco-systems are the stable outcome of evolution, and there are many examples, dating back to Aesop's fables, of the consequences of man's interference with nature. The conservation of wildlife habitats and the safeguarding of the appearance of the countryside would be instrumental in retaining an ecological balance

5 Minimising the environmental impact of extractive industries, particularly upon the landscape, and the immediate restoration and landscaping of all despoiled land, either during or after use.[1]

Each one of us holds responsibility towards land as its owner, its tenant or its user. Care and use of land determines the prosperity of a nation — a prosperity that itself brings conflict between short-term gain and long-term needs, as demonstrated so well by the long debate and inquiry in Leicestershire over the use of the rich and fertile farmlands of the Vale of Belvoir for coal mining. The decision facing local people and ultimately the nation was not so much a choice between maintaining food stocks or increasing energy supplies, but more an examination of the effects upon food production of the loss of several hundred acres of farmland; or alternatively the consequences for society of not extracting the extensive seams of coal below the Vale.

The answers to such questions lie in facts and figures about land and natural resources nationally. Before we can arrive at a decision we have to know, not only

For a whole society to be imbued with a better understanding and knowledge of land and an ethic of responsibility towards its use, education must begin in infancy and will take many generations to achieve its aim. (Photograph: Architectural Press Ltd.)

how much agricultural land we have, but how much we are likely to lose in the interests of energy in the coming years. We do not have this information. We need therefore to improve our knowledge of land and its use if we are to be able to take our responsibilities at all seriously.

Knowledge of land

Ask any county authority how much agricultural land has been transferred into urban use in its area since 1947, and the chances are that it will not know. Ask most urban fringe authorities how much green belt land has been developed, or how much proposed development land lies in agricultural areas, and they will be unlikely to have an answer. Ask most metropolitan authorities how much derelict land lies in their ownership, and how much there is generally within their area, and only a few will be able to provide statistics.

Ask Government how much agricultural land has been lost nationally to urban development and they will refer to the Ministry of Agriculture Fisheries and Food agricultural returns, which are 'based on information contained in the course of collecting data throughout the year, and is by no means complete — individual annual figures may therefore be unreliable.' [2]

Ask Government how much land in London's green belt has been developed for urban purposes and they are likely to refer to their 1976 report on 'The Improvement of London's Green Belt', which emphasises that the survey 'excluded isolated sites under 5 acres and some evidence from countries suggests that there could be double the amount of development in the green belt than recorded in our survey'.[3]

Ask the Department of the Environment how much derelict and despoiled mineral land there is in England and they will quote from their own derelict land returns, which because of their definitions of derelict land only shows half the potential picture. Finally, ask Government or any authority for the comparative changes in land use during any period since 1947 and they will either not be able to answer, or will be likely to refer to information provided by a comparison of the unofficial First and Second Land Utilisation Surveys for 1933 and 1963.

The simple conclusion is that *official* land use information is grossly inadequate or is absent altogether, and that where it does exist it cannot be compared over the years. It is not enough that we have good ideas — we need to implement them from the strength of accurate knowledge. There is no official national picture of changing land uses and this must be a serious criticism of successive governments since 1947. After all, we care about changes in our population — a decennial population census makes sure of that — so why not a decennial land use survey?

There are those who consider that we should allocate our resources more wisely. Effort and money, it is argued, should be invested in problem areas like the uplands, the urban fringe, and inner cities, and of course this is right. But how can we know the extent and location of the various problems without an overall national picture? How can we know when and where to allocate national resources and where priority problem areas lie? Without such a national survey we will merely continue to respond to the effects of the problems as they arise and where they have become too serious to ignore, rather than to identify their causes. Surely our inadequate knowledge of land is the reason why we have not been able to foresee the extent and severity of the land-use problems discussed in this book. Inadequate knowledge may also be one of the main reasons why we have not planted forests more extensively in upland areas; why we have continued to release extensive and often unnecessary tracts of agricultural land to urban development; why the confused and often uneconomic arrangement of activities blights land on the edges of towns and cities; why derelict and despoiled mineral land continues to multiply; and why the 1970s discovered the severe problems of urban wasteland. Had we possessed a full and accurate national land use survey, these trends would have revealed themselves upon the land use maps and from the comparative statistics far earlier than they did. Not only would such surveys plot the changing nature of land use, they would also be a vital part in measuring the national extent of any one of the main land use problems and the likely cost to the nation of corrective action.

Land use is not the only area of concern. Knowledge about land ownership and land values is equally weak and yet between them these two tend to dictate land use. Given a national land use survey, it would be possible to register the location, ownership and varying values of vacant or derelict urban and mineral land. This information would not only enable us to understand better the reasons for idle land generally, it would also enable a joint public and private investment programme of land reinstatement and re-use to be undertaken. A number of metropolitan authorities such as the London Borough of Southwark hold such registers of actual or potential wasteland, and as a result both public and private investment have been directed into the areas of more serious wasteland. In general, therefore, the benefits of an official land use survey would be to identify areas where:

211

the rate of land use change is rapid

the individual land uses tend to be small in area and predominantly fragmented

unused, vacant or derelict land covers substantial areas

pressures to release green field sites to development are strong.

This information could be held in two ways:

in map form — using Ordnance Survey base and grid

as statistical information stored within computer data banks.

In addition, the Agricultural Land Classification and Returns, the Derelict and Despoiled Mineral Land Returns and the various official and unofficial satellite pictures could be used for confirming specific large-scale changes in rural land uses, such as urban growth, afforestation and reservoirs, whilst aerial photographs could be used in conjunction with field surveys for gaining more detailed information on a site-by-site basis in both urban and rural areas. For the present there seems no alternative to using field survey teams to record accurate land-use information, but it is not inconceivable that the development of satellite pictures and aerial photography, using infra-red techniques, will enable an accurate national land-use survey to be developed from processed photographs.

The Ordnance Survey has prepared and holds detailed maps of Britain, providing a gridded map base upon which the land-use survey could be plotted. This was the system used by both the First and Second Land Utilisation Surveys, which because of lack of finance and staff proved to be slow. For such surveys to be at their most effective they should be completed within a year, with the results published as quickly as possible. Facts and figures could be held in computer databanks and early warning signs of potential problems or unusually rapid land-use changes could be identified almost as they happen. Such surveys could be undertaken to coincide with the decennial population survey, with similar reviews after five years. In 1979 a major review of the future role of the Ordnance Survey did not include the possibility of its becoming responsible for a national land use survey. This can only be regarded as a missed opportunity.[4]

There can be no substitute for holding accurate land-use records and identifying problem areas early. There should be a public Land Use Records Office in each county where reference to land use maps and information could be made. If this information were available to the public, it could, if it so wished, take a more active part in considering the problems created, in many cases by its own activities. In addition, planners would be likely to receive more public support in the often unpopular actions that they are seen to take. If society can be made more aware and responsible for the effects of its actions, and the resulting land use problems, it is arguable that a more widespread ethic would emerge which would ease the planners' job. Knowledge, therefore, is one of the foundations of developing a conservation ethic nationally — education is the other.

From the land of waste and aggression can emerge a land of creation and make-believe – this is the beginning of a better understanding. (Photograph: Architectural Press Ltd.)

Education in the care of land

Education of the young is probably the most important and valuable investment that society can make for its future well-being. Educationalists and psychiatrists tell us that what is learnt from an early age forms an integral part of an adult's attitude towards life. Education, therefore, is a powerful medium by which to instill an ethic of responsibility and care towards land and the environment in the next generation of adults. Although an increasing number of environmentalists, amenity groups and headteachers are committed to environmental education, there is still not an officially co-ordinated approach to this aspect of teaching. Emerging from the European Architectural Heritage Year 1975, the Heritage Education Group, led by Lord Asa Briggs, together with education authorities, has responded to the need for more formal environmental education in schools and centres of higher and adult education. At the end of European Architectural Heritage Year, Lord Briggs wrote:

'A year means little in the continuous history of education, however many energies may be unleashed and however exciting its events . . . If 1975 is to remain significant in the history of education . . . the educational work which was accomplished during the year – some of it based on previous initiatives – must continue. Education processes cannot allow for "stops" and "go's".[5]

The Heritage Education Group's Avon Schools Environmental Project in 1977 involved children of all ages, and was originally devised as a competition, but because of the country-wide support it became a major exhibition of school work at Bristol Polytechnic. The outstanding feature was the close co-operation between professional planners and schools and the way in which 'The Young Environmentalists'

The Merseyside Planning Education Project included school broadcasts about local projects and structure plan issues, scripted jointly by Liverpool Polytechnic and Radio Merseyside Education Unit, together with girls and boys. In 1980 Liverpool Polytechnic produced an excellent Merseyside Schools Pack including guidance notes for teachers, illustrated descriptions of planning processes, land use activities and BBC radio transcripts. Such projects will make a significant contribution towards an ethic of responsibility. (Photograph: BBC Radio Merseyside)

book reviewing the project has opened up national debate on the nature of environmental education and its place in the school curriculum. A growing number of other educational experiments have been undertaken or are underway. The Merseyside Planning Education Project, for example, involved secondary school children, the County Planning Department and Liverpool Polytechnic, and brought local planning issues to schools in the form of projects, a series of school broadcasts on Radio Merseyside linked to the projects, and a demonstration project for children involving a one-day exercise in planning, using drama and games. Hammersmith in London, Nottingham, Tyne and Wear and Hampshire have all established similar substantial environmental projects. The Peak District National Park developed an early interest in environmental education with its publication 'People and Countryside' in 1970. Its course at Losehill Hall was opened in 1972 and has grown into a fixed study centre providing information sheets about local land uses and selected topics. Educationalists are surprised by the interest shown by young people and the enthusiasm they display in their projects generally. I recall holding one seminar with secondary school children in Highland Scotland, where young people are noted for their reluctance to enter discussion. After a ten-minute general introduction, I mentioned a few local problems concerning housing, traffic, wasteland, industry and wildlife and the remainder of the hour was devoted to an increasing exchange of views and ideas between the children. Environmental education works in schools if it is related to local issues involving 'live' local projects with which the children can identify.

Greater understanding of land will emerge not only from formal education, but

Analysing urban wasteland is the basis of fieldwork undertaken by joint liaison between Hammersmith Planning Department and pupils from local schools. Classroom discussions and slide presentations on local land uses, and land use changes are complemented by fieldwork studies. (Photograph: Hammersmith and Fulham Council)

from publications such as Nan Fairbrother's *New Lives – New Landscapes*, Colin Ward's *The Child in the City* and the expanding range of children's books like *The Spoilt Earth* published in the 'How and Why Wonder' series. These books and many more are powerful commentaries on the way we live and the way we use land and natural resources. Research and live experiments undertaken by landowners, urban and rural agencies, local groups and individuals, aimed at 'Keeping Britain Tidy', or encouraged by 'Tree Planting Week' or 'European Urban Renaissance Year' all set an example; and example is the most effective way of creating an ethic. Television, radio and the press could be encouraged to increase the environmental debate by publicising major projects and local initiatives, experiments and research that either reduce land use conflicts or contribute towards an ethic of responsibility. They could follow and report upon the progress of national and local projects, from the reclamation of disused mineral excavations to the clearing of the village pond, or from agricultural activities that preserve wildlife habitats to the revival, restoration or development of derelict urban land. The opportunities for recognition are enormous. Those activities that contributed most to the land use ethic could be acclaimed. There is no more interesting an education than by example, and the increasing number of land use activities such as those selected for inclusion in

215

Our responsibilities are towards the landscapes of future generations. Although we still have time to make good some of the wasting acres, educating the young to take over and hold this responsibility must be given priority. (Photograph: Graham Moss)

Chapter 10, 'Waste not, want not', offer fine examples of the way in which society can act towards land, given responsibility, understanding and knowledge.

Our future — their inheritance

I began this book by recalling that land is not only a living entity, but that it is a most precious and irreplaceable natural resource. I make no apology for repeating those words. I would also like to re-emphasise that until we have a national ethic of responsibility towards land and natural resources, we are likely to continue, often unnecessarily, to misuse and harm land, and to deplete minerals wastefully. I do not share the complacent view that technology will always be there to provide for our needs; that as a part of Europe, we can relax our ideals and draw upon the land and mineral stocks of other European nations; or that Britain's wasting acres are the responsibility of future generations. These arguments seem to me to be selfish in the extreme and dangerous in their degree of persuasiveness. If we have learnt anything since the last War, it is that Britain is still an island and will remain so. Unless we improve our levels of self-sufficiency we will continue to grow increasingly vulnerable to changing world markets for energy, food and commodities. At the very basis of these markets lies land and natural resources, which in times of difficulty become *our* land and *our* natural resources.

This is reason enough for us to increase our knowledge of land, to chart the changing trends in its use and to set this knowledge out for all to see. The facts must be analysed and interpreted. Prejudices must be laid aside and the nation must bring to bear a common ethic of responsibility. Creating this awareness and sense of caring in a nation cannot be achieved overnight; a committed and rigorous programme of environmental education aimed at our children may prepare future generations more carefully for their environmental responsibilities. By tackling the present inheritance of waste and preparing for the future, we may go some way to making amends. Whilst we have no control over past errors we can correct our present actions, starting with a better knowledge of land and environmental matters. Our responsibilities are towards the landscapes of future generations; our children and their children will not be interested in our excuses, they will judge us only by the landscapes that we bequeath to them.

Notes

1. Extract taken from an address given by the author to the Land Council's inaugural conference 'Land Use in the 1980s — Save or Squander', held at the Royal Geographical Society, 25 October 1979. Summaries of all conference papers were included in *Decade of Decision*, published by the Land Decade Educational Council, 1980
2. Ministry of Agriculture, Fisheries and Food, *Agricultural Statistics for England and Wales*, HMSO, 1976, p.xiii
3. Standing Conference of London and the South East Regional Planning, *The Improvement of London's Green Belt*, 1976, p.50
4. *The Report of the Ordnance Survey Committee*, HMSO, 1979
5. Heritage Education Group, *The Young Environmentalists*, Avon Schools Environmental Project 1977, Civic Trust, 1977

Select Bibliography

1. Wasteland

Aldous, Tony. *Battle for the Environment*. Fontana, 1972. (*288 pages*)
An account of the management of Britain's environment and the factors that influence change and conservation, and a critique of the social and political machinery that shapes the environment.

Barr, John. *Derelict Britain*. Penguin, 1969. (*240 pages*)
A petulant analysis of Britain's industrial wastelands – although certain information is dated it is still relevant to the debate on land use. Recommended among other things a National Reclamation Agency for derelict land.

Oxenham, J.R. *Reclaiming Derelict Land*. Faber and Faber, 1976. (*205 pages*)
The original definitive work tracing the incidence and distribution of dereliction and its reclamation potential. Advice on the design and technical implementation of reclamation schemes is given. Particularly interesting section combining the technical problems associated with landscaping redundant industrial land.

Wallwork, Kenneth L. *Derelict Land. Origins and prospects of land use problems*. David and Charles, 1974. (*333 pages*)
A detailed analysis of the distribution, growth and economic and technical factors associated with changing industrial land uses. Offers suggestions for the reduction of newly created dereliction and environmental problems surrounding industry.

Derelict Land. Civic Trust, 1964. (*72 pages*)
A study of industrial dereliction and reclamation possibilities based upon a combined exercise between the Civic Trust, county planning officers and others with expert knowledge of derelict land.

New Life for Dead Lands – Derelict areas reclaimed. HMSO, 1963. (*30 pages*)
The first official publication acknowledging derelict land as a national problem and urging local authorities to follow regular programmes for the treatment of derelict land.

Reclamation and Clearance of Derelict Land. The Countryside in '70 Conference — Study Group No. 12. Royal Society of Arts, 1965. (*24 pages*)
A concise and informative report on the contribution that the reclamation of derelict land can make to the environment.

Reclamation of Derelict Land. Civic Trust, 1970.
  Report of a Civic Trust Conference which stressed the inadequacy of official definitions of dereliction.

'SLOAP — Space Left Over After Planning'. *Architectural Review*, No. 920, October 1973, pages 201-266
  Still a stimulating and well-illustrated debate on the waste of land created by planning controls and regulations that militate against sparing use of land in the creation of new environments.

Survey of Derelict and Despoiled Land in England and Wales. Prepared annually from local authority returns by the Department of the Environment under the Housing and Local Government Circular 55/64.

The Use of Unused Lands for Community Purposes. London Celebrations Committee for the Queen's Silver Jubilee, 1977. (*31 pages*)
  Useful guide to the community use of unused, vacant or derelict land with case studies of those community activities such as inner-city farms, ecological parks and small urban gardens.

2. Rural land

Agriculture and the Countryside. Advisory Council for Agriculture and Horticulture in England and Wales, 1978. (*65 pages*)
  An analysis of the role of the countryside and its major interests including agriculture, recreation, amenity and nature conservation.

Agriculture into the 80s – Land Use. National Economic Development Office, 1977. (*32 pages*)
  An introduction to agricultural land loss and farm productivity, and a discussion of the possibilities of planning controls and the need to minimise loss of agricultural land.

Agricultural Statistics – Scotland. HMSO. (*131 pages*)
  Similar in form to the statistical returns for England and Wales, but excludes information on the transfer of agricultural land to non-agricultural uses. Usually completed a little more rapidly than the statistics for England and Wales.

Agricultural Statistics – England and Wales. Agricultural Census and Production House. HMSO, 1977. (*183 pages*)
  Annual report of agricultural returns covering agricultural and horticultural produce and including a general table on the transfer of agriculture to non-agricultural uses.

Boddington, M. A. B. *The Classification of Agricultural Land in England and Wales – A Critique.* Rural Planning Services, 1978. (*48 pages*)
  A well-produced analysis of the existing agricultural land use classifications and the changes considered necessary by the author to produce a more comprehensive system.

Bracey, H. E. *People and the Countryside.* Routledge & Kegan Paul, 1972. (*310 pages*)
  A well-produced and informative book prepared to mark the end of 'Countryside in '70' and covering all the aspects of land use in the countryside.

219

Cherry, Gordon (ed.) *Rural Planning Problems*. Leonard Hill, 1976. (*286 pages*)
A valuable collection of essays that analyse various aspects of rural land use and administration. Simply written, this book is an ideal introduction to rural planning.

Countryside Review Committee. *Conservation and the Countryside Heritage*. HMSO, 1979. (*25 pages*)
' *A simple introduction to the use of conservation policies and amenity designations in Britain.*

Crowe, Sylvia. *Tomorrow's Landscape*. The Architectural Press, 1956. (*207 pages*)
An interesting analysis by a distinguished landscape planner of the changing landscape of the countryside, offering ways of minimising the impact of industry, hedgerow loss and expanding agricultural field patterns.

Davidson, Joan and Wibberley, Gerald. *Planning and the Rural Environment*. Pergamon Press, 1977. (*227 pages*)
General introduction to the changing countryside and the planning methods used to ease the conflict of interest between major land uses and groups.

Fairbrother, Nan. *New Lives, New Landscapes*. Penguin, 1972. (*383 pages*)
Still the most beautiful and evocative book about Britain's changing land uses and a countryside threatened by technology, urban growth and economic pressures.

Farming and the Nation. HMSO White Paper 7458, 1979. (*34 pages*)
An analysis of government policy for agricultural and food production in Britain.

A Future for Rural Communities. A report of the Conference at the Peak National Park Study Centre, 1979. (*53 pages*)
An interesting collection of papers that discuss the problems of rural settlement and land use.

The Future of Land Ownership and Occupation. Rural Institute of Chartered Surveyors, 1977. (*69 pages*)
A carefully prepared report on land use, ownership and occupation of agricultural land in the United Kingdom.

Gilg, Andrew. *Countryside Planning*. Methuen, 1978. (*255 pages*)
A concise analysis of countryside powers and techniques used in Britain to tackle the various conflicting land uses that have become increasingly evident between 1947 and 1978.

Harris, A., Tranter, R. B. and Gibbs, R. S. *Land ownership by public and semi-public institutions in the U.K.* Centre for Agricultural Strategy, 1977. (*69 pages*)
A detailed analysis of public land ownership with statistics and land uses.

Hawkes, Jacquetta. *A Land*. David & Charles, 1978 (reprint)
A delightful mixture of whimsy, fact and outrage, tracing the geological formation of the earth and man's relationship with land.

Land for Agriculture. Centre for Agricultural Strategy, 1976. (*101 pages*)
A detailed and comprehensive study of agricultural land use and forecast availability of agricultural and forestry land in the year 2000.

220

Land Management for Farming, Conservation and Recreation. Peak National Study Centre, 1977. (*29 pages*)
A comprehensive set of conference papers that explore the main aspects of land use conflict and management.

Moss, Graham. *Reviving Rural Europe*, European Regional Planning Study Series No. 29, Council of Europe, Strasbourg, 1980. (*59 pages*)
A detailed assessment of rural problems facing Europe and in particular the difficulty of administering rural areas. The recommendations call for a rural campaign in 1984-5.

Moss, Graham, Associates. *The Trent Study*. Ernest Cook Trust, 1980. (*80 pages*)
A comprehensive village study, with recommendations, paying particular attention to population, employment, essential services, land use and buildings.

Moss, Graham, Associates. *The Strath Grudie Upland Study. 1974.*
A land use study of Strath Grudie in highland Scotland, recommending a programme of integrated land uses covering agriculture, forestry, ecology, recreation and amenity.

New Agricultural Landscapes. Countryside Commission, 1974. (*98 pages*)
Report into deeply disturbing facts about the nature and scale of change taking place in the appearance of the English landscape.

The Ownership of Land by Agricultural Landlords in England and Wales. National Economic Development Office, 1977. (*26 pages*)
An official statistical background to agricultural land ownership based on a major survey of tenanted, owner-occupied land and forestry and woodland.

Report of the Committee of Inquiry into the Acquisition and Occupancy of Agricultural Land. HMSO, 1979. (*378 pages*)
A comprehensive analysis of the trends in agricultural land acquisition and occupancy and their effects upon the agricultural industry.

Report of the National Park Policies Review Committee. Department of the Environment, HMSO, 1976. (*130 pages*)
A thorough review by Lord Sandford's Committee into the degree to which National Parks have fulfilled the role for which they were originally established. Recommended reference document.

A Study of Exmoor. HMSO, 1977. (*93 pages*)
Report by Lord Porchester into the changes in land use, particularly moorland, with a recommendation for control over agricultural use of moorland – heralding the 1979 Countryside Bill.

A Study of Management Agreements. Countryside Commission, 1978. (*138 pages*)
Detailed analysis of the problems and opportunities offered by management agreements in the countryside as a means of reducing land use conflicts and encouraging multiple use of rural land.

221

3. Urban land

The Bollin Valley – A Study of Land Management in the Urban Fringe. Countryside Commission, 1976. *(47 pages)*
An outline of land management experiments being carried out by the Countryside Commission in a southern part of Manchester's rural urban fringe.

Burrows, John. 'How Much Vacant Land? *Architects' Journal,* May 1977, pages 923-926.
A brief report on the author's post-graduate research into the causes and effects of vacant land in urban areas.

Burrows, John. 'Vacant Urban Land — A Continuing Crisis', *The Planner* (Journal of the Royal Town Planning Institute), January, 1978, pages 7-9.
A summary of the author's post-graduate research on vacant land – supported by statistics and a compressed text.

Change or Decay. Final report of the Liverpool Inner Area Study. HMSO, 1977. *(240 pages)*
A detailed analysis of the social, economic and land use problems of Liverpool, including recommendations for the economic regeneration of the city.

Elsom, Martin. 'Research Review: land use and management in the urban fringe, *The Planner* (Journal of the Royal Town Planning Institute), Volume 65, No. 2, March 1979, pages 52-54
A brief review of the changing pattern of land use at the urban fringe and the loss of agricultural land to urban development and recreational pressures.

The Improvement of London's Green Belt. The Standing Conference of London and South East Regional Planning, 1976. *(36 pages)*
A general discussion of the issues that have led to conflicts and misuse of land in London's Green Belt and the urban fringe generally.

Inner Area Studies – Liverpool, Birmingham and Lambeth. HMSO, 1977. *(49 pages)*
Summaries of the inner-city consultants' final reports of studies undertaken in 1972 into the possibilities of developing a more comprehensive approach to the improvement of the inner-city environment.

Kirkby, Andrew. *The Inner-city.* RPA Direct Editions, 1978. *(136 pages)*
An interesting documentation of the causes and effects of inner-city decline and the social and economic changes that have brought vacant and derelict land.

Land Use Conflicts in the Urban Fringe – A case study of aggregate extraction in the London Borough of Havering. Countryside Commission, 1979
An interesting local study of land use at the urban fringe with emphasis upon mineral working.

Land Values and Planning in the Inner-city. Report of the Royal Town Planning Institute, 1978. *(55 pages)*
A concise consultation document covering the effects of land values and planning in inner-city. Recommended reading for all involved in the re-use of urban land.

Thomas, David. *London's Green Belt.* Faber & Faber, 1970. *(190 pages)*
Comprehensive analysis of the constraints and benefits of Green Belt policy.

Travis, A. S. and Veal, A. J. (ed.) *Recreation and the Urban Fringe.* Centre for Urban and Regional Studies, University of Birmingham, 1976. *(98 pages)*
A report of a conference on recreation at the urban fringe. A collection of informative and useful papers on the problems of land use management.

Young, Michael and Willmot, Peter. *Family and Kinship in East London.* Penguin, 1977. *(222 pages)*
Still the most comprehensive social study into the impact of land use policy, of urban redevelopment and new and expanded towns. Highly recommended.

4. Technology and land

Blake, R. N. E. *Disused Airfields as a Planning Resource.* Trent Papers in Planning No. 78/8, 1978
A useful review of the post-war history of airfields falling into disuse; stresses their great potential and variety of alternative uses.

Blunden, John. *The Mineral Resources of Britain – A Study in Exploitation and Planning.* Hutchinson, 1975. *(544 pages)*
A comprehensive review of Britain's mineral resources, changing extractive technologies, planning problems and legislation.

Bugler, Jeremy. *Polluting Britain.* Penguin, 1972
Discusses the viability of the planning system to enforce restoration of mineral working and on industrial and military encroachments into Britain's National Parks.

Disused Railways in the Countryside of England and Wales. HMSO, 1970
A report to the Committee by J. H. Appleton, examining the record of British Rail and local authorities in disposing and making good use of disused railway lines, and considering thoroughly the range of possible uses and attendant difficulties for such lines.

Energy Development and Land in the UK. Report No. 4, Watt Committee on Energy, 1979
An incomplete but useful survey of the likely land requirements associated with different energy options.

Hutcheson, A. and Hogg, A. *Scotland and Oil.* Oliver & Boyd, 1975
A detailed review of onshore oil and gas related developments.

'Offshore Oil — A Cause for Regret?' *Architects' Journal,* 26 June 1974, No. 26, Vol. 159
An excellent analysis of the development and effects of North Sea oil upon land and people in Scotland. Recommended reading.

'Power for People — Prospects for the Land'. *Architects' Journal,* 23 January 1980, No. 4, Vol. 171
A fascinating special edition analysing energy needs and changing technology upon land and settlement patterns.

Tandy, C.R.V. *The Landscape of Industry*. International Book Co. (London).
Extensive, illustrated summary of the impact on landscape of mineral working and large scale industry, covering landscape management and design.

5. Environmental Education

Williams-Ellis, Clough (ed.) *Britain and the Beast*. Dent, 1937. (*210 pages*)
One of the most stimulating collections of essays of the 1930s about the future of Britain's land and environment. It is interesting to see how accurate were many of the forecasts for Britain's environmental future.

Darling, Sir Frank Fraser. *Wilderness and Plenty*. Transcript of 1969 Reith Lectures. Ballantyne, 1970. (*110 pages*)
An outstanding Reith Lecture by the most famous land conservationist and ecologist of the post-war era. An eloquent statement of the dependence of all living things on one another. Highly recommended.

Heritage Education Group. *The Young Environmentalists – An account of the Avon Schools Environmental Project 1977*. Civic Trust, 1977. (*36 pages*)
Report of a countrywide schools project on environmental education.

Land, Air and Sea. The Natural Environmental Research Council, 1975. (*48 pages*)
A well-illustrated study of environmental matters with which the Council has been involved. A useful introduction for fifth-form students and others interested in the interaction of land, air and sea.

Nature at Work – Introducing Ecology. Cambridge University Press, 1978. (*84 pages*)
An excellently illustrated and written introduction to ecology and land use for primary school children onwards. Highly recommended also for adult reading.

Nature Conservation and Agriculture. Nature Conservancy Council, 1977. (*40 pages*)
An informative paper on the importance of wildlife and the effects of modern agriculture. Recommended introduction to nature conservation.

Schumacher, E.F. *Small is Beautiful – A study of economics as if people mattered*. Abacus/Sphere, 1977. (*255 pages*)
A powerful text on the problems of economic determinism and population growth – questioning the future of the 'big is better' lobby. Thought-provoking.

The Sleeping Beauty in the Wood. Avon Youth Association, 1978. (*16 pages*)
A short but fascinating account of the City Land Use project in Bristol. An excellent example of what can be achieved with care and responsibility.

The Spoilt Earth. How and Why Wonder Book, Transworld Publications, 1972. (*48 pages*)
Excellently simple and well-written introduction for young people from eight years upward of the effects of man's demands and technologies upon land and nature. One of a wide series of information and educational books for young people. Recommended.

Ward, Barbara and Dubos, René. *Only One Earth – The care and maintenance of a small planet*. Penguin, 1972. (*305 pages*)
An unofficial report for the United Nations, packed with statistics and information on

world resources. A timely warning about our misuse of land and minerals. Highly recommended.

'World Conservation Strategy — Living Resource Conservation for Sustainable Development', International Union for Conservation of Nature and Natural Resources, United Nations and World Wildlife Fund, 1980. (*100 pages*)
A world programme for conservation and rational development of the resources of the world. Land forms the basis of the strategy. Well illustrated.

6. General titles on land use, planning statistics and maps

Agricultural Advisory Council. *Modern Farming and the Soil.* HMSO, 1970. (*120 pages*)
A well detailed examination of the biological potential of soil and the problems of keeping it productive and in good heart.

Airport Strategy for Great Britain - Part 1 The London Area. A consultation document. HMSO, 1975. (*78 pages*)
A useful summary of the critical land issues involved in airport strategies and land use, comparing four main airports of Heathrow, Gatwick, Stanstead and Luton.

Best, Robin H. 'The Extent and Growth of Urban Land', *The Planner* (Journal of the Royal Town Planning Institute), Vol. 62, January 1976, pages 8-11
A brief but definitive report on the growth of urban land and loss of agricultural land, by an expert land use statistician.

Cadman, David and Austin-Crowe, Leslie. *Property Development.* E. & F. N. Span, 1978. (*245 pages*)
A useful and well-produced book on a strangely neglected subject.

Champion, A. G. *An Estimate of the Changing Extent and Distribution of Urban Land in England and Wales 1950-70.* Centre for Environmental Studies, 1974. (*123 pages*)
A thorough research document that examines the patterns of urban expansion and land use change and the difficulties of accurately measuring change and distribution of urban land.

Coleman, A., Weller, J. and Moss, G. *Land Use Perspectives.* Land Decade Educational Council, 1979. (*145 pages*)
A general introduction to land and settlement planning in Britain including discussion of land use mapping, conservation and urban and rural planning and villages.

Coppock, J. T. and Gebbett, L. F. *Land Use - Town and Country Planning.* Pergamon Press, 1978. (*219 pages*)
A valuable review of land use and town and country planning statistics relating to land, mapping and legislation. Contains a full bibliography.

Cullingworth, J. B. *Town and Country Planning in Britain.* Allen & Unwin, 1972. (*326 pages*)
An historical account of town and country planning until 1970. A valuable record of the emergence of planning and the background to the 1947 Act.

Developed Areas 1969 - A Survey of England and Wales from Air Photography. Department of the Environment, 1978. (*50 pages*)

The first results of the Department's national survey of 'developed areas' in 1969, using the latest air photography techniques.

The Editors of *The Ecologist. A Blueprint for Survival.* Penguin, 1972. *(139 pages)*
A controversial review by 34 distinguished environmentalists of the problems facing the world's supply of natural resources. This book drew international attention to many issues that have since emerged.

English House Condition Survey 1976 – Part 1, Report of the Physical Condition Survey. Department of the Environment, 1978. *(30 pages)*
A statistical report on the physical state of housing stock in Britain, relating to age, ownership, type, size, value, repair, costs and extent of problem.

Evans, Hazel (ed.) *New Towns – The British Experience.* Charles Knight, 1972. *(196 pages)*
A review of the progress of Britain's new town programme, compiled by a number of contributors involved in new town development since the 1946 New Towns Act.

Hoskins, W.G. *The Making of the English Landscape.* Penguin, 1955. *(326 pages)*
A definitive work on the historical evolution of land use and the landscape by a distinguished English historian.

House, J.W. (ed.) *The U.K. Space – Resources, Environment and Future.* Weidenfeld & Nicholson, 1977. *(528 pages)*
Comprehensive and detailed collection of studies on planning, administration, people, work, environment, landscape and transport.

Howard, Ebenezer. *Garden Cities of Tomorrow.* Faber & Faber, 1970. *(168 pages)*
Howard's original 1898 publication reprinted with contributions from F. J. Osborn and Lewis Munford outlining the background and theory of the garden city movement.

McEwan, John. *Who Owns Scotland? A Study on Land Ownership.* Edinburgh EUSPB, 1978. *(137 pages)*
A fascinating study of land ownership and land use in Scotland. Aggressively written; McEwan has not always endeared himself to Scotland's landowners.

McHarg, Ian. L. *Design with Nature.* Doubleday, 1971. *(198 pages)*
An evocative and well-detailed analysis of land use and the methods needed to plan comprehensively with nature. Highly recommended to all involved in land use and ecology.

Moss, Graham. 'A discussion paper on issues related to policies and administrative procedures dealing with distribution of population and allocation of resources.' Organisation for Economic Cooperation and Development, 1979. *(70 pages)*
A technical memorandum discussing the administrative practices dealing with the national distribution of population with particular emphasis on rural-urban imbalance.

Pearce, B.J., Curry, N.R. and Goodchild, R.N. *Land Planning and the Market.* University Library, Cambridge, 1978. *(96 pages)*
A short and well-produced occasional paper that sets out the reasons for Government intervention in the land market.

226

People and their Settlements – Aspects of housing, transport and strategic planning in the UK. Bedford Square Press, 1976. (*107 pages*)
A broad collection of papers covering housing, transport and strategic planning as a contribution to the Vancouver Conference on Human Settlement.

Planning Control over Mineral Working. Report of the Stevens Committee. HMSO, 1976. (*448 pages*)
A detailed analysis of the operation and land requirements of mineral operators. Highlights the need to reinstate land that has planning permission for mineral working but no conditions requiring the land, when exhausted, to be reclaimed.

Report of the Defence Lands Committee 1971-73. HMSO, 1973. (*432 pages*)
A report by Lord Nugent's Committee into the land use needs of defence and military strategies indicating changing needs, distribution and use throughout the United Kingdom.

Rogers, Alan and Rowley, Trevor (ed.) *Landscapes and Documents.* Bedford Square Press, 1974. (*85 pages*)
A worthy historical guide to changing landscapes, mapping and aerial photography.

Rogers, Alan W. (ed.) *Urban Growth, Farmland Losses and Planning.* Rural Geography Study Group, Institute of British Geographers, 1978. (*64 pages*)
An interesting debate on the loss of agricultural land to urban development and the difficulty of collecting and maintaining comprehensive land use statistics.

Stamp, L. Dudley. *The Land of Britain.* Longmans, 1962. (*546 pages*)
The land use masterpiece that summarised the state of Britain's land for the first time and recorded the lifelong work of Stamp's First Land Utilisation Survey. A catalogue of misuse and waste of land and natural resources.

Stamp, L. Dudley. *Man and the Land.* Collins, 1955. (*272 pages*)
A gentle study of the way in which Britain's land has been able to withstand exploitation from far back in time. The author was director of the First Land Utilisation Survey.

Technology in Conservation. The Countryside in '70 Second Conference, Study Group No. 3, Royal Society of Arts, 1965. (*156 pages*)
An analysis of the impact of modern technology upon land use and its relationship with nature conservation and ecological policies. A particularly useful summary of the sources and types of pollution. Highly recommended despite its age.

Trueman, A. B. *Ecology and Scenery in England and Wales.* Penguin, 1970. (*312 pages*)
A definitive work by a distinguished geologist, dealing with the geological formations that have produced the landscape of Britain.

Whitten, D. G. A. and Brooks, J. R. W. *The Penguin Book of Ecology.* Penguin, 1978. (*517 pages*)
Invaluable reference book on the origins and history of rock formations, with a ready reference table of minerals and their characteristics. Highly recommended for those interested in ecology or land use.

Index

229

230